Praise for *Sangharakshita: the boy, the monk, the man*

Nagabodhi gets us close to what made Sangharakshita so remarkable and so complex. Consistently subtle, perceptive, and engaging, this book is a vivid description of what it was like to be around Sangharakshita, a nuanced evocation of the emotional forces beneath his outward activities (including the controversial bits), and, above all, a perceptive account of Sangharakshita's growing understanding of what it means to live an authentic Buddhist life. No one but Nagabodhi could have written this wonderful book. – **Vishvapani Blomfield**, author of *Gautama Buddha: The Life and Teachings of the Awakened One*

Nagabodhi writes with great warmth and candour, and as one of the early members of Triratna he is perfectly placed to tell this tale. Living and working closely with Sangharakshita for many years, he provides a textured and nuanced account of the many conversations, experiences, growing pains, complexities, triumphs, and deep reflections that arose along the way. I feel very moved and grateful that Nagabodhi has given us this book, so that the story of Sangharakshita and Triratna has a personal, deeply human quality from which future generations can benefit. – **Vidyamala Burch** OBE, co-founder of The Breathworks Foundation and author of *Living Well with Pain and Illness*, *Mindfulness for Health*, and *Mindfulness for Women*

For anyone wanting to know more about Sangharakshita – the man and his teachings – this is an essential guide from an informed and engaging writer. With wit and panache, Nagabodhi compresses a huge amount of detail covering all aspects of the life of this unique and enigmatic man. We come away with a greater appreciation of Sangharakshita's spiritual genius and a clearer sense of how his history shaped his approach to life and the Dharma. – **Michael Chaskalson**, author of *Mindfulness in Eight Weeks*

Nagabodhi's beautifully written story of the life of Sangharakshita is a gripping read. Sangharakshita was clearly a great man, with tremendous courage of his convictions and a life totally dedicated to the path of Awakening both for himself and others. He led the way in the West in creating a viable model of how a non-monastic sangha community could work, as well as among the Dalits in India. That alone was a tremendous achievement requiring great vision, self-sacrifice, and determination, not to mention hard work, courage, patience, and perhaps a certain degree of audacity. We all have much to be grateful for to him. This is a balanced and fair account of what were sometimes tumultuous years, as the Dharma first started taking hold in the modern-day West. – **Lama Shenpen Hookham**, founder and principal teacher of the Awakened Heart Sangha, and author of *The Buddha Within, There's More to Dying than Death, Keeping the Dalai Lama Waiting*, and *The Guru Principle*

'With loyalty to my teacher…' How is it possible to say this about someone you haven't met and will never meet? This book will help. Nagabodhi has a warm, authoritative voice that gives an account, first hand, of Urgyen Sangharakshita. It is a nuanced and subtle portrait of a brilliant and complex personality; it handles Triratna's history with care but doesn't brush over the controversies. This is a must-read for anyone involved in Triratna – for those who will never know Bhante, and for those who knew him at a distance; this will fill in the gaps. For those who knew Bhante first-hand, the observational nature of the storytelling creates perspective and possibly new insights. This book fleshes out the detail on an extraordinary man and does so with love. – **Dharmacharini Kamalagita**, Chair of Cardiff Buddhist Centre

This is a wonderfully engaging account of the life and work of a remarkable man. Sangharakshita will be remembered as one of the great teachers of Buddhism, especially as it interacts with the modern world. And yet he is still comparatively unknown. Nagabodhi's sympathetic, engaging, and searching account is an excellent introduction to the boy, the monk, and the man. Written on the basis of many years of friendship, Nagabodhi's portrait tells the story of Sangharakshita with panache and imagination. For anyone seeking to understand this brilliant and complex man, this is a great place to start. – **Maitreyabandhu**, author of *Life with Full Attention* and founder of PoetryEast

Nagabodhi lived, travelled, and studied with Sangharakshita for nearly fifty years. His vivid portrait of his teacher and friend reveals a remarkable life – brilliant, visionary, and controversial. Most of all, drawing extensively from Sangharakshita's words and writing, we see clearly the roots and branches of Buddhism come to the West as a living and continuing spiritual experiment that has touched the lives of thousands around the world. Bows of gratitude to Sangharakshita and to Nagabodhi. – **Hozan Alan Senauke**, Abbot, Berkeley Zen Center, Berkeley, California

This is Sangharakshita more or less as I knew him. More or less, because no man as many-sided and creative, so utterly unique, can be caught in a few pages. We can know him through the facts of his life, through what he says of himself, but perhaps best through the eyes of those who were his disciples, friends, and colleagues – and no doubt others will need to share their story of him.

However, it will be hard to better this. In Nagabodhi's skilful telling, in well-crafted, clear prose that Sangharakshita himself would have enjoyed, we see him from all three perspectives, so that even Sangharakshita's failings are revealed as part of the whole man. This is a very fine achievement and we all owe Nagabodhi a great debt of gratitude. Future generations of disciples will be able to form a relationship with the founder of their tradition through this account, and perhaps it will help those who are confused or conflicted now by what they hear of him to understand better this remarkable human being in all his brilliant light and sometimes uncomfortable shadow. *Sadhu!* – **Dharmachari Subhuti**, Secretary to Urgyen Sangharakshita 1979–90, Former Chair of Preceptors' College, President of the London Buddhist Centre and Adhisthana

This is the Venerable Sangharakshita seen through the eyes of a disciple and friend in an intimate testament of an Englishman who contributed to the spread of Buddhism in the Western world during the 20th and 21st centuries. *Boy, Monk, Man* is a jewel of a book that weaves together anecdotes, Buddhist history, and Awakening insights, while also shining the light onto a multifaceted and nuanced human being. Nagabodhi has written a must-read for those who want to get to know the authentic Sangharakshita. – **Vimalasara**, author of *Eight Step Recovery*

As a non-member of Triratna I found Nagabodhi's wonderful book fascinating, informative, and deeply compassionate in equal parts. The controversial figure of Sangharakshita becomes multi-dimensional as we meet a complex and nuanced person who took advantage of a unique historical moment to realize his vision of a new Buddhist movement. – **Nigel Wellings**, author of *Present with Suffering: Being with the Things that Hurt*

NAGABODHI

SANGHARAKSHITA

THE **BOY**, THE **MONK**, THE **MAN**

Windhorse Publications
38 Newmarket Road
Cambridge CB5 8DT
info@windhorsepublications.com
windhorsepublications.com

Cover design by Dhammarati
Typesetting and layout Tarajyoti

British Library Cataloguing in Publication Data:
A catalogue record for this book is available from the British Library.

ISBN 978-1-911407-97-3

Contents

Contents

About the Author

Born in June 1948, Nagabodhi made contact with Sangharakshita and the FWBO (now the Triratna Buddhist Order and Community) in November 1970. He has been a member of the Order since January 1974.

Leaving his job with the BBC in September 1974, he set up Windhorse Publications and directed its growth for the next twenty-five years, while also editing the FWBO's in-house magazines.

He has also been involved as a teacher, trustee, chair, and president of several FWBO/Triratna projects and public centres in the UK and abroad. He was a founding trustee – and one-time chair – of the Karuna Trust, a project that raises funds for social and Dharma projects in India and elsewhere.

Nagabodhi lived with Sangharakshita for some years, and travelled with him throughout an extended 'lecture tour' in India in 1982 – an experience Nagabodhi chronicled in his book *Jai Bhim! Dispatches from a Peaceful Revolution*.

Nagabodhi and Sangharakshita, summer 1976

Author's Acknowledgements

A day or two into my first retreat with Sangharakshita, a berobed friend from his Eastern past paid him a visit. Before leaving, he shared a word with a fellow retreatant: 'If you've read Sangharakshita's *Survey of Buddhism* you hold the key to the entire Sūtra treasure.' I was a newbie, so those words meant almost nothing to me, but they alerted me to something I should know: there was more to Sangharakshita than I'd realized.

Since then, countless conversations or reported remarks have added to my knowledge and understanding of the man – too many to calculate and too many to acknowledge here. But if you've ever talked to me about Sangharakshita, or discussed him in my hearing, or written about him on Facebook or in *Shabda* (the Order's monthly circular), then you have probably added something to this portrait. All the same, some more recent conversations have carried extra weight and deserve mention: many thanks to Dhammarati, Dhammadinna, Kulananda, Saddhanandi, Sanghadevi, Siddhiratna, Vajrapushpa, Vidyasri, and Vishvapani.

As drafts emerged, I called on a number of friends – of mine, of Sangharakshita – to read, comment, and fact-check. I'd especially like to thank Abhaya, Ananda, Kalyanaprabha, Mahamati, Paramartha, Suvajra, Vidyadevi, Chris McKenna,

Dario Travaini, Kim Richardson, and Nigel Wellings. Finally, Subhuti deserves special mention. During breaks on a retreat he was leading in the dusty air of Ladakh's 'cold desert', he coughed and sneezed his way through a series of WhatsApp voice messages, reminiscing, sharing his perspectives, and giving valuable feedback.

The editorial board of Windhorse Publications – Dhamma-megha, Dhiramuni, Dhivan, and Sagaraghosha – handed me this challenge, read the first draft, and gave enough encouragement and guidance to keep me going (extra thanks, though, to Dhiramuni, who cast his expert eye and mind over three generations of the draft). Vidyadevi, Michelle Bernard, and Claire Taylor-Jay have made it possible for the reader to locate all the passages I've quoted from Sangharakshita's writings in the twenty-six volumes of his *Complete Works*. Along with wrangling a flock of errant commas, Dhatvisvari has performed the copy-editor's magic of saving me from myself and the reader from having to ponder the meaning of some well-intentioned but bewildering passages.

In composing this account of Sangharakshita's life, I've tried to let him speak for himself as much as possible. I would never have been able to do this were it not for the many hours given by innumerable people over the years, recording, transcribing, editing, and publishing his words in books, magazines, or online via Free Buddhist Audio. There are too many of you to mention here by name, but you know who you are. I hope you realize how much you've given us.

If, as he once confessed, Sangharakshita was 'a mystery [even] to myself', then it would be a foolish writer who'd claim to have caught him for all time in such a short book. So, if you stumble on a misunderstanding or false assumption, then know that it was my decision to put it there, nobody else's.

Nagabodhi
Stroud, July 2022

Publisher's Acknowledgements

Windhorse Publications wishes to gratefully acknowledge a grant from the Future Dharma Fund and the Triratna European Chairs' Assembly Fund towards the production of this book.

We also wish to acknowledge and thank the individual donors who gave to the book's production via our 'Sponsor-a-book' campaign.

Introduction

The cars and coaches were gone. The open-sided barn where we'd performed rituals, listened to eulogies, and said goodbye was a barn once again. Already thousands of people around the world would be streaming a replay of the day's events over the internet.

Those of us left at Adhisthana[1] ended up in the library building's atrium, becalmed in a complicated afterglow of memories – of the day, of a life. There had been grief and warm reunions, continuity and finality. In the eccentric way these things happen, a visitor from Spain treated us to a run of flamenco-jazz fusions on the guitar.

Beyond the glazed doorway at the back of the room, a straight path led to the earthen mound. Set at the heart of a mandala of walkways and flower beds, this was where Urgyen Sangharakshita's ninety-three-year journey had come to its end. This place, this grave, was the still point at the end of a busy day, a remarkable life, the last full stop.

From my place in the gallery I took in the room, the guitarist, my friends, and the statue of Manjusri that commands the space. Randomly, my eyes strayed to a small framed photograph placed at Manjusri's base, one of thousands taken over the years, onto glass plates, onto celluloid, and in pixels. But this one was special: it was the first time I'd seen a photograph of Sangharakshita since that would be the only way I *would* see him again.

Browsing in Adhisthana's bookshop the next day, I was struck by a row of photo-cards. The majority showed an aged Sangharakshita looking feeble but reflective in his wheelchair as he inhaled the scent of a delicate red flower. For sure, in his last years he'd been touchingly frail in body and voice, and almost blind. Although managing to meet a couple of visitors most days, he'd required constant, detailed care from attentive friends. But sitting with him laid out in death a few days before the funeral, I'd been reminded of how tall he was until age bent and reduced him. So why weren't there pictures of a young, vigorous Sangharakshita on display? Back in the day, in Maharashtra, he would stride from one Buddhist locality to another at such a clip that his friends couldn't keep up, and after a day of 'village programmes' he'd lie down in the stubble to sleep under the stars. Maybe the person running the bookshop, having lived around him through his final years, wasn't ready to shake off the memory of an old man.

The image of a friend or loved one in their last days can take a while to fade. But that's just one of the ways we fix people in our minds, see only what we're able to see or want to see. The Buddha's parable of the blind men and the elephant applies to more than just his teachings. It applies to everything and everyone we think we know.

Sangharakshita was aware of the ways people fixed him at different times in his life:

According to who it was that did the seeing, I was 'the English monk', 'a rabid Mahāyānist', 'a narrow-minded Hīnayānist', 'the Enemy of the Church', 'a Russian spy', 'an American agent', 'the Editor of the *Maha Bodhi*', 'an impractical young idealist', 'a good speaker', 'the invader of Suez', 'the guru of the Untouchables', and so on. More recently, here in England, I have been 'a good monk', 'a bad monk', 'the Buddhist counterpart of the Vicar of Hampstead', 'the author of the *Survey*', 'a crypto-Vajrayānist', 'a lecturer at Yale', 'the hippie guru', 'a first-class organizer', 'a traditionalist', 'a maverick', 'a misogynist', 'a sexist', 'a controversial figure', and 'an Enlightened Englishman'.[2]

Some of those characterizations were even true. He did live a remarkably rich life, and manifested in a number of ways. The introverted London child who'd been moored to a bed for two years with nothing but books for company died as the founder of a worldwide Buddhist movement. Along the way he'd lived among Hindu swamis and saints, Theravādin bhikkhus[3] and incarnate lamas; he'd worn the shaven head and robes of a monk, the shoulder-length hair of a sixties hippy, and the sports jacket of an English country gentleman. On balmy Indian nights he'd addressed thousands of 'ex-untouchable' converts seeking dignity and freedom in their new life as Buddhists, and in a small London basement he'd inspired and galvanized a couple of dozen English twenty-somethings in search of answers.

If a palm reader ever stole a glance at his life line, maybe they'd have noticed a zigzag somewhere halfway along, representing the point in time when he left India to start teaching the Dharma in the West. The next fifty-two years would be dedicated to nurturing a new Buddhist order and movement into being, the Friends of the Western Buddhist Order (FWBO), more recently known as the Triratna Buddhist Order and Community.

Sangharakshita once described that movement as his chef-d'œuvre. It is what he will be known for. But you'd be wrong to think the shift from East to West marked the beginning of that masterwork. It was a transition, a shift of location, not direction. Triratna's embrace of the total Buddhist tradition, its prioritization of commitment over lifestyle, its outward-going vitality, and its pervasive atmosphere of friendship emerged from a lifetime's experience and reflection. It was the outer-life actualization of inner-life processes that animated Sangharakshita's life even from childhood.

Triratna was a project that drew on all his resources and gave him room to exercise every aspect of his being. But what follows isn't intended as a history of Triratna.[4] Rather, it is an attempt at a glimpse of the man who almost accidentally founded it, and then, as he interacted with the people who responded to him, devoted the rest of his life to it.

One day someone will write the comprehensive, 'official' biography. They'll not lack for data. There are his books, including four volumes of memoirs that cover the first forty-five years of his life. These offer a direct line into the process by which he turned the raw material of inner and outer experience into insight and character. There are thousands of hours of audio and video recordings, of talks, interviews, and study seminars. There are book reviews, essays, and poetry, as well as boxes full of diaries, correspondence, and notebooks, signs of a life thoroughly lived, a mission set in motion, the undeniable evidence of a rather contained man's driving wish to share himself in as many ways and on as many levels as time, his genius, and craft would allow.

This is not that comprehensive biography. In fact I was initially approached by Windhorse Publications with an invitation to write 'a short life of Sangharakshita, aimed at newcomers to Triratna, about 20,000 words. One important feature would need to be an account [...] that presents Bhante[5] as a whole in the way we now understand him.' During the follow-up conversation we agreed that such a treatment should embrace what people currently tend to term the 'controversial' aspects of his behaviour. After agreeing that some anecdotes would add interest and colour, we accepted that I'd probably need a more generous word count.

I first met Sangharakshita at the end of 1970, and joined his Order in January 1974. I was his publisher for a number of years and have been closely involved in a wide range of FWBO/Triratna projects. I practised and studied with him and lived alongside him in a couple of residential communities. In 1982 I travelled with him and his 'support crew' on a three-month tour of Buddhist communities in India, and wrote a book about it afterwards.[6] I knew him as my teacher, and I am honoured to say I knew him as a friend. Being a disciple and a friend, and having spent so much of my life in his orbit, it has felt natural to shapeshift as I've chronicled his life – especially once the story moves him back to England – writing sometimes as your narrator and sometimes as a participant. I hope the shifts will feel as natural to you as they did to me.

In the coming pages I've tried to tell Sangharakshita's story. I've done my best to give a balanced and textured view of the man appropriate to an introduction of this sort. I'm assuming you're sufficiently involved or interested in Triratna to be wondering where we came from and who Sangharakshita was. You've maybe read or studied some of his writings, heard a few of his talks (maybe warming to his rhetorical idiosyncrasies, maybe not). More than likely you'll have heard of allegations, controversies, and criticisms surrounding anything from the way his sexual activity and opinions on gender and family life might have affected the early days of his community to the sheer nerve of establishing a new kind of Buddhist order in the modern world. It has been a considerable challenge to compress such a fully lived life and such an exceptional but complex mind into a book of this size. I hope I have done the task – and Sangharakshita himself – some justice at least.

A few writers, notably Subhuti, have published books, tracking key elements in Sangharakshita's thinking.[7] Vidyadevi has assembled some invaluable 'compilation volumes' that grant easy and stimulating access to key aspects of his Dharma teaching[8] and cultural reach. More books will follow, no doubt, some I hope from people who worked with, related to, and understood Sangharakshita in ways or on levels I've had space only to touch on.

So who are you? *When* are you? If you're sufficiently motivated to be reading this, say, thirty, forty, or fifty years since Sangharakshita died, then the defining elements of Triratna's presentation must have survived. Things change, but Sangharakshita's invitation to a life of intensity, the emphases, pillars, and lineages of Triratna, and the essential spiritual principles he articulated over the years must have remained fit for use.

Here in 2022 it is obvious that the world, society, even the way people experience and identify themselves as humans, is in a state of flux that will dwarf the technological and social revolutions of the 1960s when Triratna was born. It is clear too that there are a host of serious, even existential threats around. It is easy to catastrophize, but who knows what will happen, what solutions might be found?

The Buddha discovered, 'rediscovered' as he put it, something quite simple. No matter how easy or tough things are, whether in our personal lives or out in the world, we each have the uniquely human capacity to recognize and take responsibility for our states of mind. With intelligence, commitment, and support we can even transform them. We may not know it, but we really are free to react or create, to hate or to love. We can live in a dream, following the tramlines of biological and cultural conditioning, or we can wake up and break free. There are dimensions of clarity, imagination, and empathy that could be our natural home, and there are sources of inspiration, energy, and creativity waiting to be accessed, tapped, and shared. Will we be happier if we make the effort to realize that potential? Yes. Will it save the world? Who knows? But does the world need it? Yes it does.

Like pioneer Buddhist missionaries before him, Sangharakshita mined his own genius and tapped his own mysterious sources of energy to bring the Buddha's message into the modern world. He did it his way, by talking and teaching meditation, of course, but above all by being himself, being a friend. Whatever his limitations or complexity, he trusted himself as an authentic 'carrier' of the Buddha's compassionate spirit, and so made it his focus to connect with people and form community. In doing so he managed to remind enough of them, enough of us, of the journey we could be making, alone and together, within and without.

If these pages put you in touch with Sangharakshita and capture something of his initiating spirit, if they introduce you to that journey or inspire you along its way, I will feel I have done my job. And if this evocation of Sangharakshita supports your efforts to carry the Three Jewels[9] out into the world, then I think he would be delighted.

He said many times that his last few years were the happiest of his life. He could hardly walk or see, but met visitors from every corner of the movement each day. And if his body was no longer fit for any more adventures, his mind certainly was.

Not long before Sangharakshita died, Paramartha, his close friend and companion, found him seated in an armchair, quite still, deep in thought. He'd just finished listening to an audiobook of Carlo Rovelli's *Reality Isn't What It Seems: The*

Journey to Quantum Gravity for the second time. He'd already listened to Stephen Hawking's *A Brief History of Time*, also a couple of times, and would go on to hear Carlo Rovelli's *The Order of Time*. He was fascinated, even moved, to discover the depths that scientific thought was touching on, what wonders, what further mysteries it was revealing. He had never been particularly drawn to science before and had, if anything, maintained a rather Blakean suspicion of it as a by-product of alienated reason. But he was always willing to learn, and for him nothing was ever too late.

While he was being got ready for the journey to hospital the day before he died, he heard that someone was waiting outside his apartment, hoping for a chance to talk something over with him. His carers tried to persuade him to relax and avoid exhausting himself. Paramartha put it to him calmly but squarely: 'Bhante, the doctor says things are looking very serious.' 'Yes,' said Sangharakshita, 'but *life* is serious!'

All he could say at the end – if he spoke in such terms at all – was that he had done his best to honour his deepest understanding of what a human life is for. He had done it on a number of levels, and done it the only way he knew how, drawing on all the resources and energies he had at his disposal, heights and depths, boots and all.

Early Days

I had a very happy childhood, especially early childhood, despite the fact that for two years I was confined to bed. I always remember my parents with gratitude. I think I can say that I remember them every day, and I'm grateful to them for giving me that happy and secure childhood.[10]

It was one of those stop-start motorway jams, first one lane nudging forward then another. I tried not to stare, but it passed the time to take in my neighbours as they drifted in and out of position alongside. And then I saw him. At the wheel of an ordinary family car, perspiring slightly in the summer heat, the sleeves of his white shirt neatly rolled, a wife beside him and two kids in the back, it was Sangharakshita!

Okay, a doppelganger. Not an exact carbon copy, but close enough to have sent me into a spin. '*Could* it be him? A secret life? A twin brother he's never mentioned?' I looked more closely and, okay, it wasn't him. There were subtle physical differences, but more to the point there was something about the man that didn't set him apart from the crowd in the way something about Sangharakshita would have done, even in a traffic jam at the wheel of a Ford Mondeo.

All the same, the double take had left me wondering as I sat there. *Could* it have been him? Might Dennis Lingwood of Tooting, South London, have turned out differently and lived the sort of life that would have found him, a family man in late middle age, driving along a motorway to who knows where?

It's tempting to begin a shortish book about Sangharakshita with the often repeated line that, on reading Madame Blavatsky's *Isis Unveiled* at the age of sixteen, he realized he was not a Christian 'and never had been', and, on reading the *Platform Sūtra of Wei Lang* (or *Huineng*) and *The Diamond Sūtra* shortly afterwards, he realized he was a Buddhist 'and always had been'. Wasn't that when things really got going? Weren't they the experiences that defined him and set the course of his life and mission? Why not start the story there?

But whose life? Who was the young man in whose mind those insights dawned? What was the raw material, and how might it have influenced the way the insights landed and played out over the next seventy-seven years?

Let's just consider a few life events that a young Dennis Lingwood had to deal with. Born in 1925 into a comfortable and happy working-class family he was (mis)diagnosed at the age of eight with a heart condition. Ordered to keep his movements to an absolute minimum, he was confined to bed for such a long period that, by the time the diagnosis and treatment came to be challenged, he'd lost the use of his legs and had to learn to walk again.

He returned to school, where it became obvious that the reading with which he'd occupied himself for those two years[11] had put him on a different plane from his peers, and his parents were advised to move him to a better school. But when the Second World War broke out he was evacuated to Devon. Not only was he dumped, unwanted, in an austere household and under the care of a woman with little time for evacuee children, but his formal education came to an end. A year or two later, back in London with the war still raging and his parents' marriage falling apart (and some extraordinary visions and insights arising in his mind), he worked for the London County Council until he was conscripted into the army and sent to India. It's worth adding that one day, while still in the UK training for duty as a signals operator, he returned home for Sunday lunch to find his father sitting on the pavement beside the rubble of their home, which had just been destroyed by a flying bomb.

By any standards that's a fair amount for anyone to deal with – enough, surely, to mould a few character traits. But what part might such a childhood have played in forming the Sangharakshita who created the Triratna Buddhist Order and Community? Maybe we should go back, slow things down, and fill in some details.

◆

As a very young child, Dennis had a happy life with two loving parents, a playful sister, and a dog. In a part of London virtually devoid of traffic, he and his sister, along with their friends Robbie, Frances, and Gerald and all the children of the neighbourhood, would treat the streets as their playground.

But one of his favourite adventures as a toddler was to visit his paternal grandmother. Her home was packed with relics of her second husband's time in the Far East as a merchant seaman. In this little world of ornate vases, dragons, and chopstick sets, Dennis would beg to be lifted up so he could gaze at a Chinese painting of the Buddha on the wall, or the statuette of Guanyin on the mantlepiece.

These visits woke the nascent collector in him. Later, when he was old enough to wander the shops with a bit of pocket money, he'd keep one eye open for a tempting second-hand book and the other for an affordable curio, the more exotic the better. Chief among his finds was a small reproduction of the Kamakura Buddha in front of which, back home, he'd light sticks of incense without knowing why... But what about those second-hand books?

Try to imagine the plight of his parents, confronted by an eight-year-old boy condemned to extreme immobility. It wasn't long before he'd had enough of comics. Next came his father's library, an eclectic mix that included *An Outline of English Church History*, a pocket *Johnson's Dictionary*, E.W. Hornung's *Raffles*, Kingsley's *Hypatia*, and Charlotte Brontë's *Jane Eyre*. He devoured them all.

A kindly neighbour donated a complete set of periodicals that made up *Harmsworth's Children's Encyclopedia*. Here was a universe of knowledge, of stories, of possibilities as limitless and transcendent as a young boy freed from the everyday world could project himself into:

Thanks to Mr. Harmsworth I was no longer alone in my little room with the nasturtium-patterned wallpaper, the owl clock, the model yacht, and my one dozen oft-read volumes. I could now speak with the good and wise of all ages; I could follow Nature into her innermost recesses and explore all her secrets, from the constitution of the heavens to the structure of a crystal. The pageant of history from its first dawnings in Egypt, China, and Babylonia, passed with all its kings and princes, its priests and nobles and common people, before my eyes. The buskined and unbuskined heroes of ancient and modern tragedy trod my bedside rug for their stage. Perseus slew Medusa the Gorgon, Hercules performed his Twelve Labours, and Jason went in search of the Golden Fleece, in my sight. Shining presences of marble and bronze rose as though to music and stood before me in the naked glory of their perfectly proportioned Hellenic manhood; pensive Italian madonnas smiled. The cross on which Christ was crucified, the tree beneath which the Buddha attained Enlightenment, had their roots in the floor of my room, wherein, as into a garner, the harvest of the ages was gathered unto me for the making of the bread that would keep my soul alive. The body was forgotten, and my imagination, now possessed of 'infinite riches in a little room', rejoiced in the freedom of all the heavens of the spirit.[12]

Those sixty-one magazines offered more than a distraction from Dennis' bed-bound existence. They gave the boy a way to live on another, richer plane accessible through an imagination illumined by history, art, and literature. He became an avid and prodigiously fast reader.

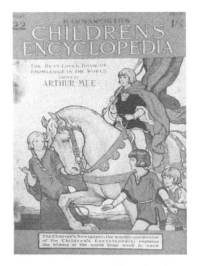

When he returned to school at the age of ten, life in the classroom seemed strange and colourless. By then, as he once put it, he was living in two worlds, one that he shared with others, and one 'that was all my own'. The world of school was starkly inadequate to his developing interests and educational needs. But there were always libraries and second-hand bookshops, and the lifelong adventure of self-education beckoned. After that flying bomb had destroyed the greater part of his home when he was seventeen, ignoring all warnings, he clambered over the smoking wreckage, anxious to know how many of his 1,000 books he could salvage.

So many books to read, but he was also drawn to music, the visual arts, and painting. Little of his childhood oeuvre remains, but he showed enough commitment and talent to spark family conversations about the possibility of art college.

However, such talk came to an abrupt end, first when his mother discovered the amount of nudity he would be exposed to and then by a significant gift.

Heading his wish list for Christmas 1938 was *Paradise Lost*. The effect of Milton's epic on this thirteen-year-old was dramatic:

> That morning I had the greatest poetic experience of my
> life. If it was the reading of Spencer that made a poet of
> Keats, it was the apocalypse of Miltonic sublimity that made
> of me, from that day onwards, if not a poet yet at least a
> modest practitioner of the art of verse. Thereafter I knew no
> rest until I had planned an epic of my own.[13]

He records that he wrote 'only' 900 lines of his Milton-inspired epic, before moving on to other themes, other poetic forms, and then on to prose, with extended accounts of the reign of Queen Elizabeth, life in ancient Egypt, and 'The Life of Siddhartha Gautama the Buddha', 'which when I finished I copied out in purple ink on my best notepaper'.[14]

His relationship with writing, as a medium for intellectual precision, self-expression, and communication, was at least as significant as his appetite for reading. From then on the practice of writing was melded into his sense of who he was and what life was for. He would admit one day in the far-off future that he couldn't say whether he was a Buddhist who writes or a writer who is a Buddhist.

Missing school altogether for two years and then being shifted to another school after a year or so must have played havoc with Dennis' social life and the natural processes of socialisation. Even after being moved on to that better school, he was shunted forward a couple of academic years so that, 'except for my best friend Clement, who was six months older than I was, all the other boys in the class were senior to me by two years'.[15] Although his confinement had meant losing contact with his early friends, he would write of new friendships he formed with boys at the new school as well as a long-standing friendship with Frances, the girl next door, to whom he would one day show his first poems.

There were playground games and playground fights. On one occasion, he intervened when he saw a bully beating another child. On another occasion it was he who hit another boy simply because he didn't like the jumper the other child was wearing – an act that led him to realize, with upsetting clarity, how much one's actions can hurt other people. He also made friends with the boys in his ward during a short stay in hospital, and saw the Boys' Brigade, a Christian version of the Boy Scouts, as satisfying 'my gregarious instincts' and 'my natural human craving to belong to a group'. Despite all the time confined to his bedroom, he seems to have emerged as a sociable boy.

Someone else he chose to write about was Sid, an older member of the Boys' Brigade, but he was in another category:

Among the members was a friendly, affable, good-looking boy about two years senior to me, and for him I at once developed an ardent affection. This early love, to which I

remained faithful throughout the whole of my BB career,
as well as for some time afterwards, was one of those dumb
adolescent attachments which nobody seems to notice, least
of all its object.[16]

Schoolboy and schoolgirl crushes are commonplace, and
Sangharakshita never suggested any connection between his
inarticulate feelings for Sid and what was to come. For, as he
moved towards adolescence, something else was stirring:

I became aware that I was physically and emotionally
attracted to members of my own sex. [Some pictures in
a magazine] of well-built young men, naked except for
a posing pouch [...] reminded me of sculptures of the
Greek gods – Apollo, Hermes, and the rest. [...] That I
was attracted to older boys, and to young men, in this way,
did not make me feel guilty; nor did I feel guilt when the
attraction started to assume a definitely sexual character, as
it did a year or two later. It was a feeling that had arisen in
me quite naturally; it was part of me, and I did not question
its rightness. At the same time I instinctively knew, even
at that early age, that it was something of which society
disapproved and that I should not talk about it to anyone.[17]

All the same, maybe for Dennis to add the moral solitude
of a homosexual in 1940s England to a somewhat attenuated
relationship with a world beyond his own interests and
imagination caused hardly a ripple. 'Whereas most people lived
much more in the outer world of sights and sounds than in the

inner world of ideas and the imagination, with me it was the precise opposite.'[18] Even when war broke out he could write, 'Living as I did as much in imagination as reality, I was at that time no less concerned with a war that had been fought 3,000 years earlier than the one in which I was personally involved.'[19]

However, once the 'phoney war' of 1939 was over and aerial bombing began, the war did impinge on life and Dennis was evacuated to the Devon town of Barnstaple where he was billeted, along with his friend Clement, first with the warm and busy family of a local vicar, and then with a cold-hearted woman who took an over-keen interest in the burgeoning masculinity of sixteen-year-old Clement, but an immediate dislike to Dennis: 'She disliked my preoccupation with books, which she thought unnatural, my manner of speaking, which she jeeringly said was more like that of a man of forty than a boy of fourteen, and my habit of not spending money – except on books, which to her way of thinking was no better than not spending it at all.'[20]

He moved on to Torquay to stay with his mother, sister, and uncle Charles. This was where he'd pass his final days as a schoolboy and get his first real job, with a coal merchant. The work was not demanding, but it did take up a lot of time. All the same:

I continued to read in a week more than the average boy
of my age read in a year. Some of the books I consumed at
this time exercised a decisive influence on my whole life and
thought. Among my discoveries was Schopenhauer, in whom

I at once recognized a kindred spirit. Classical authors
included Plato (in the complete Bohn translation), Aristotle,
Theocritus, Longinus, Demetrius, Tyrtaeus, and Lucian, but
my most ardent admiration was for Seneca and the Emperor
Julian. The ethical sublimity of the Roman moralist struck
for the first time a chord which has vibrated in me ever since.
Strange to relate, it was not from the Bible or *The Holy War*,
but from the *De Beneficia* and *De Consolatione*, that I learned
not only to love the good life but to strive after it.[21]

Given the books he lists here and elsewhere, the landlady's
comment that he seemed more like a man of forty, and his
own account of himself, living more in his imagination than
in the real world, one might make the mistake of assuming
him to have been a rather dull, unsociable boy. But when we
take into account the curiosity and fascination with ideas and
stories that powered his appetite for books, we realize there
was something very much alive behind those reader's eyes.
Then, if we read his accounts of the people around him and
incidents of the time, set down on paper decades later, we
can only marvel, not just at his powers of recall, but at the
close detail, perception, and empathy with which he was so
obviously taking people in. This was no bookworm.

Returning to London, and not yet old enough to receive
his call-up papers, he got a job with the London County
Council. This is where fascinating, good-natured Sonia, 'with
the clearest and most musical voice I'd ever heard', came on
the scene, and revealed that he was not entirely immune to the

allure of feminine charms. One lunch hour, needing to consult some files, he walked into a neighbouring room:

> The red-headed girl was alone in the office, reading a book. My heart thumped painfully. 'What are you reading?' I asked, to make conversation.
>
> Instead of replying she blushed deeply and covered the open pages of the book with her two hands.
>
> 'Let me see', I insisted, approaching her desk. Blushing more furiously still, she took away her hands and looked up at me in smiling confusion as I examined the book. It was Santayana's *Egotism in German Philosophy*. Her conquest of me was complete.[22]

They did go out together a little but in truth the connection didn't stray far beyond cosy chats beside the filing cabinets. That didn't stop Dennis from spending his summer holiday composing 'the first and last love letters I ever wrote', comparing his love for Sonia with the love of Dante for Beatrice. From his account we get the impression that Sonia, two years older than he, materially aspirational and equipped to recognize the difference between real and imaginary life, liked him and was fascinated by him, but that was all.

The end came when Sonia was drafted into the Auxiliary Territorial Service. At the time, his parents' break-up had reached its most painful pitch, so after work on the day of their final goodbye he didn't go straight home but went 'with a grief more acute than I had yet known clutching at my heart [...] like some stricken beast returning to its hole to die in the familiar premises of the second-hand bookshop'.[23] He spent two hours among the bookshelves, noticing with some shock afterwards that while in their comforting embrace he hadn't given Sonia a single thought.

'A genius, but quite mad' was how Sonia had once described him. Maybe she hadn't put much thought into her words, or maybe she had. 'As stubborn as your father' was how his mother saw him, and a bit self-centred to boot as he repeatedly commandeered the wireless so he could listen to his classical-music programmes while she knitted and he read.

One can only wonder what he was really like, how he came across to others, and what it was like to be him, still so young, with such a set of childhood experiences behind him. Sensitive yet highly self-possessed, idealistic, romantic, tirelessly driven by so many passions that it is tempting to wonder how this native of an intense inner world, nourished more by the great artists and thinkers of the past than by the living world around him, planned to negotiate the serious business of getting though life.

3

Something Happened

Just as on a dark and cloudy night
A flash of lightning for a moment illuminates all...[24]

So what happened? How did a sixteen-year-old boy living in South London before the Second World War, with no exposure to Buddhism except a few Asian ornaments, become a Buddhist and in time founder of a pioneering Buddhist order and movement?

For that matter, why did those Buddhist artefacts in his grandmother's home exert such a fascination? What made him not only buy the little Kamakura Buddha from a curio shop but light incense in front of it? What induced him to make a 'Life of the Buddha' one of his first attempts at extended prose? And why, as a toddler playing at 'dressing up', did he feel happiest when, draping himself in a flag, 'I achieved a toga-like effect which, though not exactly right, was to some extent what I desired. Gravely holding grandfather's silver-mounted amber cane, I would then stand gazing at my reflection with solemn pleasure.'[25]

It can't have had much to do with his parents. His father briefly and quaintly belonged to 'The Ancient and Mystical

Order of Druids', while his mother allowed herself a brief
flirtation with the Rechabites, a tiny teetotal Christian sect,
before dabbling in spiritualism. Dennis had been baptized in
the ordinary way, and attended weekly Christian study groups
with the Boys' Brigade. He'd read a number of books about
Christianity as well as substantial portions of the Bible, which
he appreciated as literature and myth while being repelled
by stories of bloodshed and crucifixion. The *Harmsworth's
Children's Encyclopedia* had opened his mind to the fact that
Christianity was just one among several world religions. But
at that time in his life it was to the visual arts, literature, and
music that he turned for inspiration and a gateway to higher
orders of experience.

Should we consider rebirth? Sangharakshita believed in it,
and said on several occasions that you can't call yourself a
Buddhist if you absolutely deny the possibility. But he never
spoke of it or discussed it in dogmatic terms. And even if he
did sometimes wonder about himself in that regard, he never
spoke on any platform about the possibility of a connection
between the rebirth doctrine and his childhood attraction to
Buddhism, or the overwhelming way the Dharma took hold of
him. Even his close friend and teacher in Kalimpong, Dhardo
Rimpoche, himself recognized as an 'incarnate lama', spoke
lightly about his own rebirths. Apart from anything else, such
talk came dangerously close to 'making claims', something
frowned upon even in the Buddha's time.

Sangharakshita did record in his memoirs some experiences
that opened his mind to a sense that there could be more to

reality than meets the eye. But how exceptional that made him isn't clear. His precocious immersion in literature, music, and the realm of imagination had introduced him to refined states of consciousness, but had also left him, as he put it, living in two worlds, the imbalance between them being 'far greater than it generally is in the case of those who are labelled introverts'. Still very young, and in the prosaic setting of Tooting Broadway, he would be visited by what he called 'mystical experiences':

> As I crossed from one side of the street to the other I
> suddenly awoke to the complete absurdity of the mind being
> tied down to a single physical body. Why could I not look
> at the world through the eyes of the man standing on the
> opposite pavement? Why could I not know his thoughts as
> easily as I knew my own? As these questions flashed upon me
> I felt my consciousness desperately struggling to free itself
> from the body and project itself into all the bodies [nearby].[26]

On other occasions,

> It suddenly seemed as though I was moving in a world of
> ghosts. The whole street with its houses, shops, and people
> suddenly receded into the infinitely remote distance. The
> roar of the traffic faded into an intense silence. My own
> body felt light, airy, insubstantial, and it seemed I no longer
> walked on the solid pavement but floated, clearly conscious,
> through an immense void. This void was simultaneously
> coterminous with my own consciousness, so that it also

seemed that I was floating through myself. [...] For upwards
of an hour the objective world, though again visible, seemed
strangely unreal, as if it had no business to be there and
might disappear at any second.[27]

Perhaps these experiences suggest that young Dennis was
special in some way, 'an old soul', primed to meet and grasp
his true destiny the moment it presented itself. Or perhaps they
weren't particularly exceptional; any sensitive child might have
had them. But years later he would remember and honour
them. They'd added to the mix, played their part in shaping
his outlook and his mind.

It is possible to imagine Dennis, by the time he was sixteen,
as a young man with a striking quality of physical and mental
self-possession, a highly developed capacity to enter sustained
periods of reflection as well as to immerse himself completely
in realms of beauty and imagination. Out in the world, a
war was going on. That, and the dawning realization of his
homosexuality – and its implications – could have dominated
anyone's mind. But, so long as there was a book in his hands
or a poem on his mind, he could have been living on another
planet.

It was into this particular mind that fate would introduce
three books: *Isis Unveiled*, *The Diamond Sūtra*, and *The Platform
Sūtra of Wei Lang* (now better known as *The Sūtra of Huineng*).
Between them they would spark a series of life-changing,
life-defining insights of a different order from anything he'd
experienced before.

First came *Isis Unveiled*, and Madame Blavatsky's critique of Christianity. He'd never felt drawn to Christianity as a source of spiritual support, nor particularly oppressed by it. And yet he would credit his reading of that book as the essential prelude to his Buddhist epiphany. Maybe back in the world of kind-hearted Christian adults running activities for the Boys' Brigade, the absolute and final realization that he was 'not a Christian and never had been' loosened an unthinking and limiting mental configuration, and cleared the way for something new. Here's how he described the experience:

The realization which dawned most clearly upon me, and which by the time I had finished stood out with blinding obviousness in the very forefront of my consciousness, was the fact that I was not a Christian — that I never had been, and never would be — and that the whole structure of Christian doctrine was from beginning to end thoroughly repugnant to me. This realization gave me a sense of relief, of liberation as from some oppressive burden, which was so great that I wanted to sing and dance for joy. What I was, what I believed, I knew not, but what I was not and what I did not believe, that I knew with utter certainty, and this knowledge, merely negative though it was as yet, gave me a foretaste of that freedom which comes when all obstacles are removed, all barriers broken down, all limitations transcended.[28]

Writing for *The Middle Way* a couple of years later, he'd declare, 'I believe that Christianity is dead, that its life is only a movement as it were of worms in a dead body. [...] But I mourn it, for I owe much to it.'[29] Despite the conviction with which he rejected Christianity as a spiritual path, he never lost his respect for the genius with which poets and artists throughout the centuries had engaged with the Bible, winnowing its stories to reveal universal myths of the spiritual life.

It was just a few months later that he happened upon *The Diamond Sūtra* and *The Platform Sūtra of Wei Lang*:

> Though [*The Diamond Sūtra*] epitomizes a teaching of such rarefied sublimity that even arahants, saints who have attained individual Nirvāṇa, are said to become confused and afraid when they hear it for the first time, I at once joyfully embraced it with an unqualified acceptance and assent. To me *The Diamond Sūtra* was not new. I had known it and believed it and realized it ages before and the reading of the *Sūtra* as it were awoke me to the existence of something I had forgotten.[30]

To say that *The Diamond Sūtra* is a difficult text would be an understatement. It chronicles a dialogue about the ultimate nature of things between the Buddha and his sharp-minded disciple Subhuti. Although the setting is homely, the words they exchange form a tumbling torrent of mind-bending non sequiturs, negations, and paradoxes. The *Sūtra* does, however, conclude with some accessible lines:

> As stars, a fault of vision, as a lamp
> A mock show, dew drops, or a bubble,

A dream, a lightning flash, or cloud,

So should one view what is conditioned.[31]

Sangharakshita never spoke in detail, if at all, about what it was he experienced, what *The Diamond Sūtra* actually revealed to him. Paramartha, his closest friend through the last thirty years of his life, commented on their conversations: 'If he ever suggested anything about the nature of the experience, it was about something quite direct, intuitive, a sudden flash of understanding. One thinks of that line from the *Bodhicaryāvatāra* – that reference to a sudden flash of lightning – when suddenly you see the entire landscape. Everything is revealed. You get it all at once.'

But, really, the experience was beyond words, not because Sangharakshita couldn't find the right words to describe it, but because the very nature of the experience, and the dimension it revealed, transcended the human mind's conditioned mechanisms for forming everyday perceptions, concepts, and, therefore, words to capture it. But he instinctively knew that he'd caught a lightning-bright glimpse of what the *Sūtra* was saying. He'd touched the core truth out of which the Buddhist tradition had evolved, and knew, immediately and for sure, that he was a Buddhist and, as he'd invariably put it, always had been.

Seemingly more accessible than *The Diamond Sūtra* as a work of literature, but no less sublime in parts, *The Platform Sūtra of Wei Lang* enabled him to maintain a connection with that initial experience, and throw himself into 'a kind of ecstasy' whenever he read it. Perhaps too he allowed himself to identify with its author, for Wei Lang had experienced a life-changing insight into the nature of things when he overheard a monk reciting *The Diamond Sūtra* in a busy marketplace.

Blissful though it was to recollect, even revisit, that experience, he knew already that it was asking more from him than that. As he once put it, 'Beyond this point lies a realm belonging solely to the *yogacarin* – the man yoked to spiritual practice [...] The important thing is to practise, to practise hard and continually – advice so simple that a child can understand it, but so difficult that even an old man cannot practise it.'[32] If we really want to know what happened to him back then, we could do worse than to look at what he did with the rest of his life.

If *The Diamond Sūtra* confronted Dennis with a transcendent reality underlying things, then his visit to a performance of a ballet called *Everyman* initiated the process of grounding it on the human plane:

> Perhaps for the first time in my life I realized that Friends and Kin, Wealth and Possessions, must all be left behind, and that only our Good Deeds can go with us when Death summons us to make our last journey. So deeply was I impressed that when I tried to write an appreciation of '*Everyman*' I found my feelings too strong for expression.[33]

As he sought to make sense of his experience, and perhaps to frame it intellectually, he immersed himself in as much Buddhist scripture, history, and philosophy as he could find. He also basked in the literature of Confucianism, Hinduism, Islam, Sufism, and Christian mysticism, and for a while felt strongly drawn to the 'wonderful distillation of concentrated spiritual wisdom' he found in the sayings of Laozi, recorded in the *Dao De Jing* – which he read in seven translations.

It's as if he was involved in a love affair with the truth he'd glimpsed, a Truth with a capital T. He'd forever be drawn to the words with which people had tried to snare it – like a lover finding excuses to hear or mention the name of the beloved. As he read, he once admitted, it was as if he disappeared into the mind of their author. He *became* the writer for a while, and it would be some time later that his critical or synthesizing mind would get involved. The words he read granted him an experience of kinship at the highest level, one that his outer life would not provide for a long time.

When you have received an overwhelming glimpse into the truth that lies at the heart of things, the question isn't just 'How do I talk about this with others?', but 'How do I talk about it even with myself?' 'How do I live and act from now on in a way that best expresses this realization?' Because his insight had been triggered by *The Diamond Sūtra* and *The Sūtra of Huineng*, Dennis knew that the Buddhist teachings would be his primary medium, the framework around which he could fashion an articulation and a life expressive of the experience – and in time share its fruits with others. But, paradoxically, implicit in the experience was the realization that, at their best, words can only inspire the journey towards a direct, lived apprehension of truth. At their worst, words can enshrine and sanctify delusion. This of course applied equally to the Buddhist teachings. Something he wrote a short while after the experience, possibly influenced by his reading of the

Laṅkāvatāra Sūtra, offers an insight into young Dennis' state of mind:

> I believe that it is a weakness to believe anything. For a belief implies its opposite; it is the fruit of discrimination. To believe in nothing is equally foolish; for belief in something is again as easily opposed to it. I believe that the only solution is a 'letting go' which is no letting go, a 'turning about in the deepest seat of consciousness', which is no turning about.
>
> At the root of things there is an unfathomable mystery – perhaps I believe this. At any rate I know that any attempt to 'know' or 'cognize' this mystery is to play – with concepts, ideas, etc. – a game of chess whose conclusion is inevitably and always stalemate....
>
> I believe in an infinity of relatives, and I believe that these constitute the One Absolute which is beyond all – even itself.'[34]

The honesty and wisdom with which Buddhism recognized, even played with, the limitations of words and concepts were precisely what bonded Dennis to it. Securely moored in his sense of a relationship with the Buddha's Enlightenment, albeit new and partial, his belief at that time in 'an infinity of relatives' probably explains the freedom he gave himself to explore the breadth and depth of *all* Buddhist teachings, and for that matter to seek inspiration wherever he could find it.

◆

Dennis was not just an avid reader, but also an avid writer –
not simply because he enjoyed the craft of writing, but because
he had things to say. Before long he even had things to say
about the way Buddhism was being transmitted to the West.
In his view the Buddha's message was being distorted by a
combination of narrow scholarship and a religious culture of
unrevised, post-Christian assumptions. This was the theme
of his first published essay, 'The unity of Buddhism', which
he submitted to *The Middle Way*, the journal of the London
Buddhist Society:

> [T]hose doctrines which an Occidental mentality found
> difficult of comprehension were precisely those which in the
> Pali canon are only mentioned, or touched upon very lightly
> without the profound investigation, the thorough grasp, of
> the later protagonists in the history of Buddhist thought,
> such as Nāgārjuna, Vasubandhu, Asaṅga, etc. Thus were we
> given only that which we could assimilate without having to
> reorganize the processes of our cognition, while the equally
> valuable doctrines which were in later ages developed, or
> logically expatiated, from primitive Buddhism by the lucid
> and profound minds above mentioned, we either did not
> know, or knowing, did not appreciate.[35]

At the time the article was published, he'd not yet visited
the Society's London establishment. But a while afterwards he
made his way there and was browsing in its library when Clare
Cameron, editor of *The Middle Way*, came upon him and was

astonished to see a boy instead of the middle-aged man she had imagined. Christmas Humphreys, the Society's president, was equally surprised. Whether it was the breadth of his knowledge, his literary style, or the unassailable confidence with which the young army conscript had arrived on the Buddhist stage, we don't know. Probably all three. But it was by any standards a remarkable calling card.

The personality behind 'I believe', the essay from which those earlier lines were drawn, showed a very different side of Dennis from the one revealed in 'The unity of Buddhism'. 'I believe' was also published in *The Middle Way*, but not until a year or so later. If any of the magazine's readers had troubled to notice that the two articles were written by the same author, they might have scratched their heads and wondered what this young man would do next. Maybe someone with imagination could have foreseen the books, essays, and lectures, the Triyana Vardhana Vihara in the foothills of the Himalayas, and in time a new kind of Buddhist order and movement.

Forty years later, over a quiet cup of cocoa in Ahmedabad, Sangharakshita would confide to me, 'None of my practice as a Buddhist, none of my scholarship, none of my encounters with other Buddhists have ever led me to question the validity of that original insight I had when I was sixteen.' After a pause he smiled and added, 'I do realize that is quite a claim to make.'

4

The Signalman
and the Swamis

I have sometimes wondered how my life would have
developed if I had not been conscripted at eighteen, had
not experienced life in the army, had not been posted to
India, had not become a Buddhist monk, had not written
A Survey of Buddhism, and had not become the disciple of
Tibetan lamas, all of which had followed from the simple
fact of having been found fit for military service.[36]

This was no gap-year adventure. But nor was this a normal
nineteen-year-old. As the troopship nosed its way through the
muddy water towards the cranes and godowns of Bombay
docks, Signalman Dennis Lingwood, his kitbag weighed down
with some Hegel, *The Penguin Book of English Verse*, and *The Light
of Asia* among other volumes, took in his first sight of India. He
could hardly believe his luck. Rather than dragging him away
from his preoccupation with Buddhism and Eastern religion,
the war had transported him, *gratis*, to the land of the Buddha.

There had been nothing magical about the cramped
conditions on the ship, but the onward journey to Delhi
gave him his first glimpse of 'tree-lined streets, bullock

carts and thin dark figures in flapping off-white garments'. However,

> Ghastly poverty whined around us whenever the train stopped. Emaciated women in filthy rags pushed rusty tins through the windows and pleaded with gentle insistence for alms. Spindly-limbed children with enormous protruding bellies clamoured for coins and scraps of food. [...] Even more dreadful than the poverty was the apathy, the patient, hopeless resignation, apparent on the faces of the beggars.[37]

The company's quarters in Delhi were ordered and relatively calm. Squirrels and geckos scampered among margosa trees that grew in the lanes between thatched buildings, while crows and kites circled the hot air-currents. Dennis' duties as a Morse-code operator, scanning the airwaves for 'suspicious transmissions', filled just a few hours of his day. This left plenty of time to read Buddhist texts, immerse himself in Indian literature and philosophy, and search the local bazaar for curios and eatables. He would also make his first acquaintance with the marvels of Indian architecture. His *Children's Encyclopedia* would surely have introduced him to the Taj Mahal; now he could wander among lesser, though no less remarkable, examples of the county's heritage. Of his first visit to the Red Fort he would write:

> The contrast between the red sandstone walls of the Lal Khila, or Red Fort, massive enough to enclose a town, and the row of white marble palace buildings that overlooked

the River Jumna from the rear battlements, struck me as tremendously effective. Is not this wedding of strength and grace, of the stupendous and the delicate, one of the greatest charms of Mogul architecture? [...] As I stood in the multi-columned Diwan-i-Khas, or Hall of Private Audience, where at the feet of emperors a shallow stream had once flowed over a gem-studded silver bed – flowed the length of the building and out under the pierced marble screens into the private apartments – I felt the truth of the Persian couplet inscribed in flawless calligraphy above the windows overlooking the tree-tops and the slow, sad river: 'If there is Paradise upon the face of the earth, it is here, it is here, it is here.'[38]

Before long he'd be sending back to England precociously erudite essays, about Indian music, poetry, and philosophy:

I have always been animated by the profound conviction that whatever work of art or system of religion or philosophy that has ever been produced anywhere in the world is capable of becoming a guiding and sustaining force not only to the people and the age by which it was produced and which it helped to produce (or at least to perfect), but to all peoples and to all ages as well. Provided it contains within itself a spark of the fire divine it will not die, but remain coeval with our common humanity.[39]

That early prose style has convinced numberless readers that their author must have been a dusty, surely long-dead, savant. But they've got him wrong. Actually, the very earnestness and floridity of his prose, although already out of date, was this young man's attempt to articulate an almost prodigious capacity for wonder and aesthetic appreciation. To help us imagine him as he would have been at the time, we have another snapshot, of a journey back to base in the 'liberty wagon' after a day's sightseeing: 'As we rushed through the blackness of the night along the deserted highway, with the wind fresh in our faces and the sky thick with brilliant stars, it seemed, after the heat and dazzle of the day, that life had no purer enjoyment to offer.'[40] Here we get a glimpse of the young man behind the crafted prose, of an insatiably curious intelligence revelling in the adventure of being in a new and exciting world and a tantalizing hair's breadth away, or so he thought, from the possibility of a living connection with the Buddha and his teaching.

How young he was! Just nineteen when the ship docked. Next time you pick up one of his books or come across an early poem, bear in mind those childhood years spent in bed communing with the greats from earlier days. He'd effectively grown up in their world. Little wonder then that he wrote with their voice, in their language, and (almost to the end of his life) with their unthinking devotion to the masculine pronoun. But the passion, curiosity, aesthetic and intellectual energy with which he threw himself into things were all his own.

The final year of the war saw him posted from Delhi to Sri Lanka (Ceylon in those days), then to Calcutta and Singapore. Wherever he went he explored temples, met and talked with thinkers and holy men of every stripe. But in India he met very few, if any, Buddhists who met his expectations.

It was during his time in Colombo that he discovered a community that would play an important part in his life through the next couple of years. It began in a bookshop, of course, when he picked up a couple of biographies, of Ramakrishna and of his disciple Vivekananda. He was immediately and instinctively drawn to them: 'Perhaps it was because they demonstrated that the spiritual life could be and had been lived in modern times. Their influence encouraged me not merely to study but actually to practise the teaching to which I was already committed, the teaching of the Buddha.'[41]

He'd hardly finished reading about Ramakrishna when he stumbled on a branch of the Ramakrishna Mission at an ashram close to his barracks. Soon he was spending his evenings there. Charmed by his youthful seriousness and curiosity, its incumbents inducted him into Indian ways of life, teaching him to sit on the floor cross-legged and to discover the delights of Indian food while eating with one hand (stabbing at his food 'with the sharp, jerky movements of a crow pecking with a beak'). They talked about poetry, the intricacies of Indian philosophy and religion, and took him to musical performances. Through them he met a succession of exotic and eccentric holy men, and gained access to a network of contacts that would stand him in good stead over the coming years.

For a while he was so taken by Ramakrishna that he was moved to write, admittedly in one of the Mission's own journals, that his birth was one of the 'outstanding events' of the nineteenth century. 'We cannot calculate beforehand what will be his influence upon the future of East and West, and upon the whole world. But certainly he is the herald of the dawn of a New Age.'[42]

Ramakrishna, an Advaita Vedantist, was the universalist's universalist, and so, it would seem, was Dennis:

> How many men have ever seen God? Only a very few. Who
> has been able to go to Him through all gates? Fewer still.
> But Sri Ramakrishna went through them all not once only
> but many times. He said: 'I have practised all religions,
> Hinduism, Islam, Christianity, and I have also followed the
> paths of the different Hindu sects. I have found that it is
> the same God towards Whom all are directing their steps,
> though along different paths.'[43]

In later years Sangharakshita would dismiss the idea that a person could traverse a series of distinct spiritual paths from their beginning to a (common) end as if starting out afresh each time. If one has truly seen things as they really are, he said, it is simply not possible to unsee them and so start the journey again as a spiritual innocent. But at the age of twenty he had been deeply moved by the man.

Ramakrishna's position was rooted in his direct experience of a fundamental Oneness behind not just the world's religions but *everything and everyone*. It was a visionary stance that captivated the romantic in Dennis: 'For the essence of religion is to recognize the Divine everywhere in the universe', he wrote in an inspired mood. 'If you recognize it in every [stick] and stone, shall you not recognize it in the highest aspirations of your fellow men, even though they are different in expression from your own?'[44]

For all his admiration of Ramakrishna, he remained instinctively clear that his loyalty to the Buddha's teaching was non-negotiable. He resonated with Ramakrishna's reference to a common divinity at the heart of every path, perhaps because it echoed, at least poetically, his own initiatory insight that had revealed a transcendental principle underlying the many branches of the Buddhist tradition.

It would be a while before he would clarify his thinking around the philosophical, moral, and above all practical distinctions between his Buddhist position and Ramakrishna's, but his spiritual intuition was already alert to the differences. The defining impact of *The Diamond Sūtra* lay in its uncompromising rejection of any attempt to tie things down with words or concepts. The insight triggered by that text had revealed a unifying singularity, but not in the form of a thing, a divine force, a 'Oneness', and certainly not a God.

The Buddha avoided such talk. If he approached the subject at all, he tended to talk about what ultimate reality is *not*. Such positive statements as he made would point not to some static unchanging 'thing', no matter how refined, but to a *principle*, *paṭiccasamuppāda*, 'conditionality' or 'dependent origination'. This was his attempt to evoke a vision of reality as a vast, timeless process of becoming in which nothing whatsoever has a fixed, independent 'selfhood', be it a galaxy, a state of mind or oneself. Once you reduce the truth at the heart of things to, but no further than, a divinity, or a supreme force, no matter how vaguely or ethereally proposed, you've opened the way for some less than ethereal real-world outcomes.

Here, for example, is how the head of the Ramakrishna Mission's Calcutta branch justified hiring thugs to evict tenants from one of its properties: 'The ātman, the Spirit, was one and indestructible in all men: who then could hurt another, who be hurt? Had not Sri Krishna himself exhorted Arjuna to fight and slay? One who performed his duty, whatever that might be, with mind fixed on God, committed no sin.' 'This sermon', wrote Dennis some time later, 'opened my eyes to the sinister implications of Hindu philosophy [...] And I recoiled from the Mission like one who, when a lamp is lit, sees that he had been about to step on a snake in the dark.'[45]

Despite these concerns, Dennis' connection with the Mission's swamis enriched and supported his aspirations at a time when and in a place where it was virtually impossible to meet any living Buddhists. They had demonstrated the possibility of living a spiritual life. One in particular, Swami Pavitrananda, impressed him deeply when speaking of

> the necessity for renunciation, and of the happiness of a monk's life, compared with which worldly happiness was as dross. As I listened my heart burned within me. Whether he asked me if I wanted to be a monk, or whether I asked him if he thought it possible for me to take up monastic life, I do not remember, but from that time onwards I was resolved upon a life of renunciation.[46]

Twenty or so years later, the Beatles would sit at the feet of the Maharishi Mahesh Yogi and spread the word about 'Transcendental Meditation'. But back in the 1940s meditation, whether Transcendental, sacred, or secular, wasn't easy to come across in the West. It was seen as something people did in the East, just as miracles were something that had happened in the past. Where were the meditation teachers, the sanghas, the books even? In 1940s England there was just one shop in the country, the marvellous Watkins Books (still a presence at the heart of London). Dennis had tried meditating a little at the Buddhist Society, but perhaps his experience with *The Diamond Sūtra* was, in itself, sufficiently significant to have shaped his thinking, his interests, and his ideals. But now, having met the Ramakrishna swamis, he started to see the possibility of taking up a thoroughgoing 'spiritual *life*' – in which meditation would have a part to play. In a Delhi bookshop he came upon a book that included a description of an ancient meditation technique. It involved 'dissociating oneself successively from the body, the mind, and the empirical ego'. Back at the barracks, he gave it a try:

> At night, seated cross-legged inside the mosquito curtain while the other inmates of the room slept, I practised according to the instructions given in the book. 'I am not the body, I am not the mind,' I reflected, 'I am the non-dual Reality, the Brahman; I am the Absolute Existence-Knowledge-Bliss.' As I practised, body-consciousness faded away and my whole being was permeated by a great peaceful joy.[47]

Interestingly, and perhaps unaccountably, it seems that one try was enough, and, although Dennis practised hatha yoga, so far as we know he never practised that meditation again. Some time later, though, still in his barracks dormitory, he experimented with *prāṇāyāma*, a meditation technique based on breath control:

> After a few days various abnormal experiences started occurring. Generally it was as though tremendous forces descended into me from an infinite height with a terribly disintegrating effect upon my whole being. Sometimes I felt I was being slowly lifted up into the air, then dashed violently to the ground. Since these experiences did not lead to peace of mind, happiness, or illumination, I soon gave up practising *prāṇāyāma*. But the experiences continued. For about three more weeks they disturbed me, sometimes interrupting my sleep seven or eight times in the course of a single night. It seemed that I was getting shocks of tremendously high voltage from a great dynamo of spiritual electricity the assaults of which I was powerless to resist. So violent were these shocks, and so extraordinary the experiences which accompanied them, that I sometimes prayed, to whom I knew not, 'O Lord, take them away and let me rest!'[48]

Whatever the effect, for better or worse, it seems that Dennis had something of a natural aptitude for meditation practice. Maybe this was hardly surprising given his powers of absorption honed through years of undistracted reading and writing. Or more probably it had something to do with a refined capacity to access psychic states relatively easily. But it would be a year or more before he'd take up meditation as a regular practice.

Throughout this time the pull towards a life of renunciation was gaining strength, but for the time being he was a soldier and member of a family. When he was posted to Calcutta it was natural that he'd spend time with his Uncle Dick, a clarinettist in the governor of Bengal's band. These visits maintained a thread of connection with family life, but also exposed Dennis to the crude humour and racist double standards of the imperial expat community.

Out of politeness and a sense of obligation he accepted an invitation to join his relatives at the annual Government House Ball. Watching the proceedings from the sidelines, he suddenly entered an altered state of consciousness: 'The dancers became ghosts, the ballroom vanished, the music faded into the distance, and I was left alone in a great void with a strong feeling of disgust and revulsion. Unreal though it appeared, it was not the phenomenal world itself that disgusted me, so much as the spectacle of an existence so entirely devoid of meaning.'[49]

In Search of the Buddhist East

Whatever duty I had to my country I had done, and my life
was now my own to do with as I wished.[50]

He was in Delhi, still new to the sights, sounds, and smells of
India, exploring the precincts of a Hindu temple complex,
when he came across a side temple, 'of modest dimensions
and distinctive architectural style. [...] Removing my shoes,
I ascended the two or three white marble steps and for the
first time in my life found myself in a Buddhist temple.'[51] We
are not told what a Buddhist temple was doing within the
extensive grounds of a major Hindu establishment. Possibly
it had something to do with the fact that many Hindus regard
the Buddha as an incarnation of Vishnu.[52]

> Facing me from the far end was a life-size image of the
> Buddha. Before it, on the white marble altar, candles burned
> among offerings of flowers. Incense hung in the air. The
> stillness was intense [...] On a patch of lawn outside the tiny
> bungalow next door two or three bright yellow robes had
> been spread to dry in the sun. To my romantic imagination
> it was as if the golden petals of some gigantic celestial flower

46

had fallen on the grass. In the hope of being able to meet a Buddhist monk I tried the door. It was locked from within. The windows were shuttered. There seemed to be no sign of life in the place at all.[53]

Later, when the army took him to Sri Lanka, Dennis expected to feel at home in a nation with such an assured place in Buddhist history. Buddhism had effectively died out in India centuries earlier, but Sri Lanka saw itself as a Buddhist country. Its monks and nuns had kept the flame alive and preserved the texts for centuries. Sadly, his experience was disillusioning: lifeless temples, Buddhist teachings confused with non-Buddhist or even party-political, nationalistic elements, and apathetic monks with little or no interest in sharing their spiritual riches with lay people. In Colombo he was surprised to see an orange-robed *monk* directing traffic. One bhikkhu could do the job better than a dozen policemen, he was told: 'No one will dare to disobey a bhikkhu.' Soon afterwards he was surprised to see a little shrine just inside the gateway of a famous Buddhist monastic college: 'To my astonishment it contained, not an image of the Buddha, as I had expected, but figures of various Hindu gods. "These are just for the lay people," explained the *bhikkhu* who had received us, with a superior smile. "We never worship them."'[54]

In Kandy, though, Dennis managed a memorable visit to the Temple of the Tooth, in the hands of a local guide:

On the way we met a little wizened monk of about ninety bowling along in a rickshaw. My guide at once dropped on to one knee and joined his hands in salutation. The rickshaw stopped. A brief conversation ensued, of which I understood not a word, but the monk looked at me with a friendly smile and nodded. 'He High Priest,' said my guide, when the rickshaw had passed on. 'He say we go side door ten o'clock open.'[55]

This advice allowed Dennis to enter the temple before the crowds, even to spend time alone in the holy of holies, close to the reliquary that reputedly contains one of the Buddha's teeth. Whether the high priest granted this privilege because he intuited something special in the English visitor, or because he knew the guide would extract an appropriate gift from him, is unclear.

Later, during his travels in the south of India, Dennis would hear the story of a Sinhalese bhikkhu who'd been invited to cross the water and teach the Dharma to a small, beleaguered community of Buddhists. Sadly, it soon became clear that he'd shown

more concern for his own creature comforts than enthusiasm for his pastoral duties, and his demands eventually became so unreasonable that he had to be sent back to Ceylon. [...] So many variations on this theme did I afterwards hear, in different parts of the country, that I eventually concluded that bhikkhus from South-east Asia often did more harm than good to the cause of Buddhism in India.[56]

In a letter he wrote to the editor of *The Middle Way* back in London, Dennis summed up his impression of Buddhism in that island nation: 'if Ceylon is Buddhist, cannibals are Christian'.

The bombing of Hiroshima and Nagasaki brought the war with Japan to its end, and soon afterwards Dennis was posted to Singapore. Still finding its feet after years of harsh occupation, the newly liberated city was a melting pot of allied soldiers and Chinese, Malay, and Indian residents, while Japanese war prisoners were helping to get the city cleared and restored. It was a bustling world of colour, sounds, food, rich and poor, as well as new kinds of music to discover and new forms of entertainment.

Dennis' occasional visits to a Sinhalese temple on the outskirts of town did little to change his opinion of Buddhism in Sri Lanka. 'Perhaps because of my Western preconceptions, life at the temple seemed not tranquil but merely stagnant.'[57] He did, however, seize an opportunity to ask a senior monk for his views on the *ānāpānasati* meditation – the mindfulness of breathing. He'd come across a booklet on the practice in a Colombo bookshop, but hadn't yet felt ready to give it a try. Established on a foundation of close attention to the sensations of in-out breathing, this revered Buddhist practice sets the meditator on a journey from bare sense-awareness and grounding concentration to an encounter with the subtlest regions of the mind and mental activity. The monk's enthusiastic response to his question gave him the assurance he needed, and, 'This time success was immediate. My mind became at first buoyant, then filled with peace and purity, and finally penetrated by a quintessential, keen, ethereal bliss that was so intense I had to break off the practice.'[58]

As well as being familiar with meditation practice – something not to be taken for granted among the Buddhist monks Dennis had met so far – this bhikkhu was even cautiously sympathetic to the Mahāyāna developments within Buddhist tradition, something truly rare among Theravādin monks anywhere, let alone among Sri Lankans. Meanwhile, Dennis' meetings with some of Singapore's senior Chinese Buddhists gave him a chance to talk with living practitioners of the Mahāyāna, and he was impressed by their warm-hearted and altruistic spirit. One, a successful businessman and devoted lay supporter, had founded an 'International Buddhist Union' in an attempt to bring the heterodox mix of Singapore's Buddhists into communication with each other. One Chinese monk he met was so friendly, so engaged, and so humble that he brought to life Dennis' vision of the 'Bodhisattva monk', someone who practised the Buddha's teaching as much for the sake of others as for himself. This monk also gave him his first close-up encounter with a striking feature of the Chinese monastic world: 'Whenever he bowed, which was often, one saw on top of his shaven head the scars left by the candles which, in accordance with Chinese Mahāyāna tradition, had been burned there at the time of his ordination. These scars signified his readiness to suffer for the sake of all sentient beings.'[59]

Dennis' months in Singapore were a kind of watershed. As well as getting to meet Theravāda and Mahāyāna monks and laypeople, he also made a connection with the local branch of the Theosophical Society. Despite the definitive blow dealt to his Christian conditioning by Madame Blavatsky's *Isis Unveiled*, he'd never felt drawn to the movement she co-founded. But, getting to know some of its members in Singapore he was especially struck by the way they embodied the Society's ideal of Brotherhood: 'Never before had I seen the members of so many different races, nations, and religions associating on terms of perfect equality and friendship, and the sight impressed me profoundly.'[60] He attended their meetings and made some lifelong friendships among its members. With their prompting, he also discovered a talent for public speaking, and he honed his craft at the Theosophists' Lodge and in the town's temples, often confronted by 'rows of devout old Chinese ladies in black silk jackets and trousers sitting on little wooden stools'.[61]

It was in Singapore too that Dennis would meet Rabindra Kumar Bannerji, an irascible, idealistic Bengali Brahmin, a keen supporter of the Congress party as well as the more extreme Hindu Mahasabha. His path was one of passionate political activism rather than religion, but the two of them became fast friends from their first meeting and would come to play an important part in each other's lives.

With the war over, the drills and routines of army life felt more than ever like a waste of time. But there was more to it than that. Dennis' conversations with Theosophist friends had helped him to see that he wasn't really living in the light of his spiritual ideals as fully as he could. After a particularly telling conversation he became a vegetarian overnight, and never looked back. More similar conversations led him to recognize a contradiction between being a Buddhist and being a soldier. His discovery of Evans-Wentz's *Tibet's Great Yogi Milarepa* in the Lodge library took things further:

> As I read it my hair stood on end and tears came into my
> eyes. If I had any doubts about the nature of my vocation
> they were now dispelled, and from that time onwards I lived
> only for the day when I would be free to follow to its end the
> path that, as it seemed, had been in reality mine from the
> beginning.[62]

The arrival of a new commanding officer in the spring of 1946 brought stricter conditions and an absurd regime of pointless exercises. It was enough to take a conflicted young man past his tipping point. Dennis applied for leave to visit his uncle in Calcutta from where, he'd decided, he would quietly disappear:

> Technically of course I would be deserting. But about this
> I had no qualms. [...] Whatever duty I had to my country
> I had done, and my life was now my own to do with as I
> wished. [...] The nearer the day of liberation drew, the more
> violent became my desire to escape from the pettiness and
> futility of army life. But at last, one morning, as in a dream,
> I found myself in the QM's store handing in my rifle, my
> webbing, and the rest of the much-hated equipment that
> had never been of the slightest use.[63]

He headed back to Calcutta and paid what would be his last visit to his uncle's family. He would also renew his connection with his friend Rabindra, or 'Bannerji', as he is always referred to in the memoirs, who was now living there. Perhaps as a result of reading the books Dennis had given him back in Singapore, he'd now come to believe that culture and religious activities could act as crucial catalysts in the struggle for India's uplift. He was therefore happy to accompany Dennis on his still regular visits to the Ramakrishna Mission's headquarters. The two of them even moved into the Mission's premises and did what they could to help with its administration. The moral ugliness of those forced evictions from the Mission's property, however, finally disgusted and disillusioned them both. They moved on.

Alternative accommodation, and even work, was available nearby. Nominally at least, the work would take Dennis a step closer towards the more Buddhist life he yearned for. The Maha Bodhi Society, established in Bodh Gaya in 1891 by the Buddhist missionary Anagārika Dharmapāla, had its headquarters in Calcutta. Dennis had visited the place when he'd been posted there, but, despite the passionate zeal of the Society's campaigning founder, the place seemed to be 'in the grip of a strange inertia'.[64] Even so, he'd made a connection with its incumbents, and now that he was back in town started helping out in the office and even editing its international magazine, the *Maha Bodhi Journal*. Before long he and Bannerji were invited, first to work full-time in the office, and then to run a Society-funded orphanage.

These were desperate times. With independence and the prospect of partition around the corner, inter-religious violence and even killings were a feature of Calcutta life. The orphanage was in a vulnerable area and, when Mohammed Ali Jinnah called for 'direct action', murder was in the air. Responsible for thirty boys and Miss Albers, an elderly German lady who lived on the premises, Dennis and Bannerji experienced days and nights of genuine danger, not knowing if or when one of the gangs careening around the locality would break into the building and wreak havoc.

On the second morning of the riots, Dennis looked out of a window

> to see three men knocking on the door of the Hindu house opposite. From their demeanour they seemed to be friends come to enquire after the safety of the occupants. Slowly, cautiously, the door opened and a middle-aged man in a white shirt and dhoti appeared. A few words were exchanged, a knife flashed in the air, and before I could realize what had happened the visitors had vanished and a dead body lay bleeding in the street. This time we were completely unnerved. There was not a moment to be lost.[65]

As a young Westerner in civilian clothes, Dennis was deputed to seek help. After a nervous walk through streets dotted with corpses, he arrived at the Society's headquarters from where the police were contacted. Eventually, and under police escort, the boys, Dennis, Bannerji, and Miss Albers were evacuated to safety.

Sadly, Miss Albers, a deeply devotional eighty-year-old, was treated with astonishing harshness, even cruelty, by 'His Holiness', as the leading figure at the Society's headquarters was called. He was not happy with the expense of supporting her. His treatment of the innocent lady shocked Dennis, and amplified a nagging sense of the place that had always troubled him: 'Apart from the shrine, which, though unused was kept reasonably clean, the whole place exhaled an atmosphere of dirt and decay that was somehow not only physical but moral.'[66] Before long he and Bannerji would move on, if not altogether from their connection with the Maha Bodhi Society, then at least from their involvement with its Calcutta branch.

It was on the Society's behalf that Dennis attended the first post-Independence 'All-India Religions Conference'. To his surprise he found himself, a young, English ex-soldier, to be the sole Buddhist present at this vast event. This was despite the presence of an impressively plausible gentleman who, although he was a Hindu, announced himself as the leading representative of Buddhism. This man, always referred to as 'Pandit-ji', was something of a rogue and charlatan. Nevertheless, he will play an important part in our story for a few crucial months.

Another visitor to the conference was the Shankaracharya of Puri, the highest-ranking figure present and a major hierarch in the Hindu world. Fascinated by the man, who'd sit motionless on a tiger-skin-draped throne throughout the proceedings, Dennis sent a message to his staff, asking whether it might be possible to meet the man. The Shankaracharya and his retinue stayed in a sort of encampment a little way off of the main campus, and it was to one of its private rooms, illumined by just a single flickering oil lamp, that Dennis was led. Even here the Shankaracharya sat on his tiger-throne holding a crystal rosary and his silver staff of office. Nothing earth-shaking seems to have been shared during their meeting. They talked easily about their lives and backgrounds. Handing Dennis a visiting card at the end of the audience, the Shankaracharya suggested they correspond.

It's worth pausing to wonder how this twenty-one-year-old lad from London found himself in such a situation. Given the kind of access he seems to have been granted, and the seriousness with which he was taken in these contexts, we can suppose he was someone you'd notice. To most of his fellow soldiers back in the army, he probably came across as a bit of an eccentric (even if he was, apparently, a Morse-code prodigy). And his habit of burning incense in the dormitory couldn't have won him many friends. But here, among the devotees of all and any religious persuasion, he was in his element, mixing easily and spontaneously, and consistently respected even at this early stage in his life.

At the other end of the spectrum, rogue or not, there was something about Pandit-ji that fascinated and attracted Dennis. His enthusiasm, his capacity to spin dreams and schemes, was infectious, and, when he mobilised his formidable eloquence in the service of a scheme, he was hard to resist. So when he mentioned his devotion to the female yogi-saint Anandamayi-

Ma, Dennis' interest was piqued. And when it turned out that the venerable lady would soon be spending time at Dehra Dun, and that Pandit-ji was planning to head her way, Dennis and Bannerji decided to go with him.

6

The 'Going Forth'

Above me broods
A world of mysteries and magnitudes.
I see, I hear,
More than what strikes the eye or meets the ear.

Within me sleep
Potencies deep, unfathomably deep,
Which, when awake,
The bonds of life, death, time and space will break.

Infinity
Above me like the blue sky do I see.
Below, in me,
Lies the reflection of infinity.[67]

Anyone who's read *A Survey of Buddhism* or *The Eternal Legacy*, or listened to Sangharakshita's recorded lectures, will know how well versed he was in Buddhist doctrine and the many byways of the Buddhist tradition. It came as a surprise, though, when he once observed that he possibly knew even more about Hinduism. Through those early years in India he read and reflected constantly on the Buddha's teachings, and did not allow his failure to find many Buddhists who impressed him dampen his resolve to seek ordination as a Buddhist monk. But it would be a while yet before he'd be practising in anything like a positive Buddhist context. In the meantime, what could he do but follow intuition and nourish his spiritual appetite in whatever ways presented themselves?

So it was that he decided not to return to Calcutta and the Maha Bodhi Society's HQ, but to travel with Pandit-ji and spend time around Anandamayi-Ma. It was a decision that represented another stage in his 'going forth'. He'd walked out of the army and more or less cut off family ties. Now, although the decision to follow Pandit-ji meant he'd be spending more time in a Hindu environment, his intuition told him this was the right thing to do.

Born in 1896 and once described as 'the most perfect flower the soil of India has produced', Anandamayi-Ma was considered a yogi and a saint.[68] Her followers believed her to be blessed with healing powers, precognition, and the ability to perform miracles. For most of them it was enough to spend time in her radiant presence, but she did speak and offer teachings in a quiet conversational voice. Her utterances – such as 'The supreme calling of every human being is to aspire to self-realization; all other obligations are secondary' or 'Only actions that kindle man's divine nature are worthy of the name of actions' – might have appealed to Dennis at that point in his quest.

But life in Anandamayi's circle quickly demonstrated that these things are never straightforward. The atmosphere of devotion that surrounded her was tainted by sycophancy, competitiveness, and a pervasive rumble of internal politics. Perhaps this was especially obvious to Dennis' outsider's eye as she played with her disciples, mothering, flirting, whimsically preferring first one then another as she offered someone a particularly warm glance or a titbid of *prasad* from her plate. She was the adored centre of her own universe, and, to Dennis' mind, rather knowing in the way she toyed with the adulation she received and kept followers in her thrall. And yet, and yet, there *was* something special about her. He never doubted that:

> Either because of the way in which she wore her hair in a topknot, or because of her simple dignity of demeanour, her poise, and the smile that played faintly about her lips, despite her femininity she at once struck me as being strangely Buddha-like in appearance. At the same time I became aware that an intense peace, purity, and coolness, of a quality such as I had never before experienced, was not only pervading the room but as it were blowing from her like a delicate fresh breeze.[69]

Palpably in touch with refined states of consciousness though she might have been, Dennis never believed her to be enlightened, and saw no evidence of the kind of wisdom he associated with an enlightened mind. He came to find many of her utterances commonplace, even banal. And in her little world, as he would discover in many similar communities, traditional Hindu conventions around caste were strictly observed. In fact, Anandamayi's community was so highly stratified along caste lines that even Brahmins were divided into three grades, only the highest of which enjoyed the privilege of dining with their goddess. As a foreigner, Dennis was considered beneath caste altogether, so he and Bannerji (who, albeit high caste, was considered tainted by association) received low-class treatment in many areas of daily life. They were expected to eat apart from others, often getting their food after everyone else. Of the subtly pervasive way those social conventions insinuated themselves into the atmosphere, he would write: 'So much was it possible even for one not believing them to be influenced by the atmosphere of the place where such restrictions were observed that when, once, I was allowed to remain – either because I was not sitting too near Anandamayi or because my unclean presence had gone unnoticed – I actually felt quite elated.'[70]

Ashram evenings would be given over to devotional chanting directed of course towards Anandamayi herself:

One of the bhajans consisted of the single word 'Ma' repeated a dozen times: Ma, Ma-a, Maaa; Ma, Ma-a, Maaa; Ma, Ma-a, Maaa; Ma, Ma-a, MAAA! This was a great favourite among the 'inner circle' of disciples. The crane-necked youth, who at the same time officiated at the harmonium, would sing it with passionate abandon, head flung back, body swaying and jerking violently, eyes either tightly closed or fixed beseechingly on Anandamayi, and Adam's apple bobbing vigorously up and down. To me the spectacle of grown men and women singing Ma, Ma-a,

> Maaa like so many kittens crying for their mother was a
> gross caricature of religious devotion.[71]

Although doing nothing to reform or critique her caste-ridden community, Anandamayi was shocked to discover how Dennis and Bannerji were being treated. She made this clear in ways that upset her more conventional followers by arranging for the two of them to be fed well, and by granting them a rare personal interview. Dennis took advantage of the opportunity to explain the *ānāpānasati* meditation practice to her, and in return received her blessing to take it up as a regular practice. She also gave Bannerji a new name, Satyapriya, and affirmed the name that Dennis had given himself a while before: Dharmapriya. For the next two years they would go by those names, and throughout their travels together the two friends would meditate at least twice every day.

Years later, Sangharakshita would explain that for the first ten years of his Buddhist 'career' the *ānāpānasati* meditation, a general practice of mindfulness, and reflecting on the Buddha's life and teaching were his sole working grounds. 'During those years,' he said, 'the Buddha, or some aspect of his teaching, would be on my mind all the time.' He made the statement so baldly that I asked him whether he meant it literally. There was a reflective pause before he said, 'Well, perhaps there were a few lapses for just a few minutes at a time.' Had anyone else made such a claim I would have found it easy to take it as an exaggeration. In Sangharakshita's case, I couldn't be so sure.

Everything about his life and character at the time, including his self-admitted stubbornness, makes it possible to believe that his mind, whether the front or back of it, was constantly engaged, constantly chewing over something he'd come across in a scripture or commentary.

Now, for the first time, his reading and reflection were being supplemented by regular meditation practice. It's tempting to wonder how the effects of regular meditation would have mingled with his book learning and the resonating impact of his original insight experience. For he still had a lot to work out on a personal level. Looking back on that time in his life, he would write with characteristic precision:

> Whether the distinction between the exalted, but still
> mundane, states of superconsciousness that can be attained
> through continuous practice of the proper spiritual exercise,
> on the one hand, and the transcendental faculty of Wisdom
> (prajñā), in its distinctively Buddhist sense of an awakening
> to the true absolute nature of existence, through which alone
> Freedom and Enlightenment can be attained, on the other,
> was as clear to us then as it became subsequently, I would
> hesitate to affirm.[72]

Over the coming months, the little company of Dharmapriya, Satyapriya (as I must call them now), and Pandit-ji migrated from one of Anandamayi's ashrams to another, from Dehra Dun to Kishengunj, to Raipur and then to Kasauli, a lot of miles and a range of climates. Wherever they stayed, Dharmapriya and Satyapriya would have some contact with Anandamayi and her disciples, as well as with Pandit-ji, but they usually lived as quietly as they could, at some distance from the noise and fuss, devoting themselves to meditation, to study, and, in Dharmapriya's case, to writing essays and composing poems.

A time came when Pandit-ji and Satyapriya both had business to deal with in Delhi, which meant that Dharmapriya would be left on his own for a couple of weeks. A couple of nights after they'd left, however, he woke to see Satyapriya, clear as day, sitting across the room meditating. The vision was so real that it only vanished when Dharmapriya reached out a hand to touch it. A few days later he received a letter from Satyapriya explaining that he had tried to visualize Dharmapriya while meditating late into the night, and wondered whether his friend had noticed anything. This was not the first or last time Dharmapriya (or Sangharakshita) would have experiences of this kind. He never seems to have made much of them, but they're worth mentioning since they give us a sense of the mental plane on which the two friends were living at the time, and the strength of their friendship.

While they were staying in Raipur, one of Anandamayi's followers took Dharmapriya to visit a remote hermitage in the wilds. The place was sacred to the locals because a holy man had once lived there observing a vow of silence:

As we stood there thinking of the occupant of the
hermitage, about whom were related many strange tales, I
became aware that there existed between the old recluse and
me a bond of profound sympathy, an occult understanding,

and that there were wings fluttering within me yearning to spread themselves in the same infinite sky as that wherein, scorning all earthly ties, he had made his ascent.[73]

Learned and intelligent, affable and generous though Pandit-ji was for much of the time, there was an ever-present, nagging sense that he wasn't all he seemed. The end came when a friendly official took Dharmapriya aside to let him know just how immoral Pandit-ji's 'fund-raising' schemes were. He was, it turned out, little more than a serial con man, promoting and then collecting funds for some grand philanthropic plan in one town before moving to another, with never a backward glance and no intention of redeeming any of the promises he'd made.

It was time to bring the fellowship to an end and move on. Despite his faults, Pandit-ji had been a friend, a companion, a guide, and a philosophical sparring partner. He'd opened doors for his young friends, just as, with their transparent sincerity, their youthful energy, and Dharmapriya's status as an Englishman, they'd opened doors for him. It was, sadly, a rather bitter parting, which came just a few days after India's Independence Day.

Disillusionment with Pandit-ji was just one example in a string of similar experiences that convinced Dharmapriya that religious societies, organizations, and groups had 'a natural tendency to degenerate, in the hands of selfish human beings'. Arriving in Kasauli, he knew it was time to follow the Buddha's example and 'sever at one stroke our connection with an incorrigible world and go forth as homeless wanderers in search of truth'.[74]

Dyeing their shirts and sarongs in the time-honoured way with a muddy mixture of earth and water, selling their watches, giving away their clothes, and – significantly in view of later developments – burning their identification papers, Dharmapriya and Satyapriya said goodbye to a sullen Pandit-ji and to the friends they'd accumulated during their travels in Anandamayi's orbit. As they set off, walking barefoot along a rough track that would lead them to the plains, a sudden rainstorm filled the sky with a succession of double, even triple, rainbows.

Of all the defining moments in his life, Sangharakshita celebrated and referred back to this one most warmly. This radical 'going forth' echoed in his mind the great Going Forth, when Siddhartha Gautama left his wife and child, and all the pleasure and conveniences of his father's palace, in search of truth and liberation. Years later, Sangharakshita would still speak of that day in Kasauli as the most significant moment in his life. It was the day he seized his personal myth to the full, and inhabited it with complete commitment. It was 18 August 1947. He was just twenty-two years old and had been in India for a few days less than three years. But what changes those years had seen in him!

7

The Two Wanderers

Here in the villages
Which ploughed, sowed, reaped and threshed
The ricefields and wheatfields
I have found you, India,
At last, and embrace you
And feel on my shoulder
Your cool flowing tresses.[75]

What were they thinking? What possessed them to think they could step off a boat and stroll into Ceylon without any papers?

In his memoirs Sangharakshita devotes just half a page to an account of how the pair's plan to get ordained as Buddhist monks in Ceylon fell at the first hurdle. They arrived without passports and refused to reveal their nationalities, arguing that as Buddhist wanderers they had no nation or worldly identity. They were met with astonishment and told to get straight back on the boat to India.

Writing about the episode years later, Sangharakshita reflected on their decision to render themselves stateless:

> Though we eventually found it impracticable to maintain in
> all its uncompromisingness the attitude we had adopted, I still

consider it logical and right, and though, owing to the exigencies of the modern state, accommodations have had to be made, I cannot even now feel that I owe an exclusive loyalty to any nation or race. A bhikṣu, a member of the Buddhist monastic order, is, or should be, a citizen of the world, and his sole allegiance is to the Buddha, the Dharma, and the Sangha.[76]

This was a significant moment. He sometimes wondered how things might have turned out had they been let into the country. It would have been reasonably easy to get themselves ordained as monks. Then they would have settled down in a monastery somewhere to study, write, and maybe teach while following the prescribed monastic lifestyle. And that could have been that. Actually, it's hard to imagine the future Sangharakshita settling down for life within any one branch of the traditional Buddhist world, but, in an authentic spiritual community, with a quiet room, a simple life, a library full of books, and a supply of ink for his pen, who knows? For now, though, for this idealistic twenty-three-year-old, keeping the initiative in his life and refusing to compromise his understanding of the Dharma life trumped other considerations.

Back in India, undaunted, the pair formed a plan. It would be an odyssey, a mythic journey from Cape Comorin, the southernmost point of the Indian peninsula, to the Himalayas. Two thousand miles. They would travel on foot. For food and lodging they'd rely on the generosity of people they met along the way. And they would maintain a regular meditation practice throughout the journey, whatever the conditions.

Clad in their simple mud-dyed clothes, the two of them would have been immediately recognizable as *sadhus*, wandering holy men, and would receive a measure of hospitality wherever they went. The food and company was generally crude, but there were exceptions. Early in their journey, an educated Tamil Brahmin provided an excellent meal of rice and curries. Squatting before them while they ate, fanning away the flies, he was eager to talk. His two guests intrigued him. The combination of a seemingly high-caste Indian and a young Englishman was surprising enough, but their refusal to discuss their background or nationality was highly irregular. There followed an increasingly heated exchange between their host and Satyapriya about the legitimacy of their chosen lifestyle. They weren't both Brahmins, nor were they conventional *saṃnyāsin*s. So what were they?

Their travels exposed them to a dazzling kaleidoscope of landscapes, people, temples, and religious processions. Along the way, wherever they went they'd hear of a local self-realized saint who lived on a hill, in a cave, or in a deserted temple. One, they heard, lived beneath a tree and had never been seen to eat. As he wasn't far off they made a point of visiting him:

> Utterly indifferent to heat and cold, summer and winter he wore only a *langoti* or jock-strap. [...] But a disappointment awaited us. The *jīvanmukta* was sitting beneath his tree, smoking a cigarette. Body and hair were covered with dust, so that it was difficult to judge his age; but he might have

been fifty – or thirty-five or sixty. His features were coarse, his expression dull and bestial. He took no notice of us whatever. After gazing at him for a few minutes, as at an animal in a zoo, we returned to the library. He was, perhaps, a hatha yogi who, by means of certain psycho-physical exercises, had developed the power of living without food; but having made the acquisition of this power an end in itself had sunk to the level of a brute.[77]

In Trivandrum they came into contact with the Eazhavas, a sizeable community of people considered to be 'untouchable' within the Hindu world. Making up at the time about 17 per cent of India's population, and listed by the former British rulers as 'Scheduled Castes', the so-called 'untouchables' were seen as impure and treated as the lowest of the low. Spending some days with the Eazhavas and getting to know them a little, the pair came to hear of their plan to shrug off the stigma of untouchability by converting to Buddhism. It was not unknown for 'untouchable' or Dalit ('oppressed') communities to convert to Islam or Christianity, but this was the first time Dharmapriya came to hear of such a community seeking refuge in Buddhism. It would certainly not be the last. Before long a movement of mass conversion to Buddhism would gather pace and play an important part in his life.

Through a dreamlike landscape of beaches, coconut groves, temples, rivers, and sleepy villages they walked, pausing sometimes for a night or sometimes a few days in a village ashram. After covering 250 miles this way, feeling footsore and in no hurry, they decided to take a pause and concentrate on meditation for a while. But where?

This was when Dharmapriya's connection with the Ramakrishna Mission proved helpful. A swami they met told them of a town called Muvattupuzha, just a little way off their northerly route. The Mission owned an ashram there, which hadn't been occupied for while. It was haunted, he said, but they'd be welcome to spend some time there and give it a bit of life.

◆

Here perpetual incense burns;
The heart to meditation turns,
And all delights and passions spurns.

A thousand brilliant hues arise,
More lovely than the evening skies,
And pictures paint before our eyes.

All the spirit's storm and stress
Is stilled into a nothingness,
And healing powers descend and bless.[78]

The ashram stood on a rocky hill beside a river. Although only twenty-five years old, it already looked 'so dilapidated as to seem ancient'.[79] But it was remote, set on its own patch of land on the edge of town and surrounded by coconut groves and paddy fields. Peaceful, spacious, and quiet, it offered the two friends everything they wanted. They didn't know it at the time, but they would be spending a year and a half there.

They followed a routine of meditation practice, hatha yoga, periods of silence, periods of fasting. For Dharmapriya this was an opportunity to get down to some literary work, while Satyapriya experimented with *prāṇāyāma* (yogic breathing exercises), which had a dramatic and disturbing effect on his mental states. They kept the shrine tidy, refreshing the flower offerings each day and honouring the ashram's inspirational figures by placing dots of sandalwood paste in the traditional Hindu way on the foreheads of their photographed images. For Satyapriya, still hovering in a sometimes highly polarized way between Buddhism and Hinduism, this was an expression of religious devotion. For Dharmapriya, holding no belief in gods of any kind, it was a meditative, aesthetic experience, giving him an opportunity to nourish a natural capacity for reverence.

The ashram had a small library, well stocked with Hindu classics. Dharmapriya mentions reading the *Yoga-Vāsiṣṭha*, but he mainly used this time to absorb some Buddhist classics – Śāntarakṣita's encyclopedic *Tattvasaṃgraha* and sections of the Pali *Majjima-Nikāya* – and generally push deeper into the most foundational Buddhist teachings. Pacing the ashram's lengthy veranda, he would reflect on the four noble truths, the doctrine of *paṭiccasamuppāda* ('conditioned co-production'), and the three *lakkhaṇa*s, or 'characteristics of conditioned existence' (impermanence, insubstantiality, and unsatisfactoriness).

'Though [these teachings] were all well known to me, I had given them very little systematic attention. Now they occupied my mind virtually to the exclusion of everything else.'[80] He would come to speak of this interlude as the time when his 'falling in love' with the spiritual ideal, his intuitive bond with the Buddha's teaching, was clarified and balanced by a deeper intellectual grasp of its principles, which in turn led to an even deeper bond, which took him to places far beyond the merely intellectual. 'Besides reflecting on them during the day I meditated on them at night. Or rather, as I meditated, flashes of insight into the transcendental truths of which they were the expressions in conceptual terms would sometimes spontaneously arise.'[81]

A poem he wrote around this time offers a tantalizing glimpse of a young man caught between the intimation of a transcendental dimension and the ego's deep fear of what it might demand:

> I listened all day for the knock of the Stranger,
> And I often looked out from the door.
> The table was scrubbed, the brass shining,
> And well swept the floor.
>
> The shadows grew longer and longer,
> In the grate the fire flickered and died.
> 'It's too late. He never will come now'
> I said, and sighed.
>
> I sat there musing and musing,
> The spinning-wheel still at my side.
> The moonlight came in through the window
> White like a bride.

As the clock struck twelve I heard nothing
But felt He had come and stayed
Waiting outside. And I listened –
And I was afraid.[82]

Despite Dharmapriya and Satyapriya's wish for a quiet life in seclusion, people were getting to hear of them, and before long they were interacting with the local population more than they'd planned. This was driven in part by Satyapriya's gregarious nature. But they also wanted to repay the Ramakrishna Mission for this gift of time at the ashram by contacting its local members and collecting subscriptions. Their trips into town led to conversations, the conversations led to friendships, discussion groups, public talks, and even a degree of fame throughout the region.

Although styling themselves *anagārika*s, a Buddhist category of homeless wanderer, with their shaven heads, mud-dyed clothes, and reclusive way of life, they appeared in that Hindu world as *sadhu*s or *saṃnyāsin*s. Once again people wondered what two young men were doing living that kind of life. A few people resented the implicit criticism, as if the two young men were taking their religious duties seriously while others were not.

In one form or another, often with chaotic detours through a tangled maze of Hindu metaphysics, the theme would come up again and again. What part does renunciation play in a holy life? Is it essential, is it the ideal for everyone? Can one not live a spiritual life within an ordinary everyday life so long as one performs one's religious duties? Aren't ethics and compassionate action just as important as the cultivation of wisdom through practices like austerity and meditation? In a culture where religious *duty* (which is the general meaning of the word *dharma* in Hindu India) is so central, these questions were important.

In some of the essays he submitted to an Indian Buddhist magazine at the time, Dharmapriya allowed himself to explore these questions. This journey had a definite goal: ordination as a Buddhist monk. But these conversations with Hindus were feeding his passionate exploration of the spiritual life, as well as his capacity to empathize with others and appreciate the lives and minds of religious people wherever he met them.

But one thing remained constant. Despite – or to some extent because of – his immersion in Hindu literature and the Hindu world, his loyalty to Buddhism remained absolute:

> Indeed, so firmly was I convinced of the truth of Buddhism, that even had I never met another Buddhist whom I could respect, or had I been the only Buddhist in the world, it would have been quite impossible for me to follow any other path. My present isolation in the midst of a completely Hindu environment served only to intensify my awareness of Buddhism.[83]

That immersion in a Hindu environment also confronted him with the everyday evils of caste. India was newly independent, change was in the air, but millennia of cultural and religious conditioning couldn't be spirited away. Just as the two friends were arriving in Muvattupuzha, they'd been given a shocking reminder. A little way along the road ahead, they'd seen a couple of people,

> whether male or female we could not tell, who had been coming towards us from the opposite direction. Suddenly they flung themselves into the ditch and remained cowering there with their hands over their heads until we had passed. They were outcastes who, since there was no place for them in the Hindu social system, were treated by members of the higher castes not only as Untouchables but as 'Unseeables'. [...] It would not be uncommon to hear a far off cry of 'Hooooooooo-in! Hooooooooo-in!' as these folk warned caste Hindus of their approach.[84]

Caste was an essential and ubiquitous aspect of Hindu life. The observance of caste and caste duty were defining features not only of a Hindu life but of Hinduism itself. Even those who were intellectually, even morally, against caste still observed it in various ways, great and small, even down to the kind of poppadoms they'd eat. Dharmapriya came to like and respect many of the people he met in town, but it was impossible to ignore the extent to which caste and the accompanying observance of untouchability were lodged in the heart of their society. By virtue of his volatile nature, it was Satyapriya who threw himself into most of the arguments, but Dharmapriya was no less shocked and no less minded to challenge the practice in his own way whenever he encountered it.

Satyapriya's excitable nature was becoming something of an issue, even a problem. Being a man of extremes, he was taking his practice of austerity to alarming levels, while also practising *prāṇāyāma* without the support of an experienced guide. Not only did he start to fill the ashram with activity and noise as he set about building an 'industrial school' on the ashram's land – a project he dropped as suddenly as he'd started it when his mood changed – but he was also prone to disturbing, even violent, mood swings.

Satyapriya's absorption in the school project meant that Dharmapriya would often go into town on his own. No longer seeing him as 'the quiet one' who sat in the background while Satyapriya did all the talking, people began to discover how much Dharmapriya had to say for himself and how quickly he grasped the issues they were dealing with. Before long they'd look forward to his visits and turned to him for advice. This was painful for Satyapriya, not least when on one occasion his attempt to participate in the conversation was met with a rebuff: 'Be quiet, Swami-ji is going to say something.'[85]

The tensions were coming to head:

Talking in the semi-darkness of the veranda one night after dinner, we happened to find ourselves disagreeing over something. Knowing how sensitive Satyapriya was, and how impatient of contradiction, I at once saw the danger and stopped pressing my point, but it was too late. Despite all my efforts to pacify him, my friend insisted on enlarging the difference as much as possible and working himself up into one of his usual terrible rages. It was as though he wanted to be angry. This time, however, pausing in his tirade, he suddenly struck me a tremendous blow in the face with his fist.[86]

As soon as the blow was struck, Satyapriya's mood evaporated and he was stricken with remorse. But clearly something wasn't working. For an impatient, impulsive man of action like Satyapriya, it couldn't always have been easy to spend his time around such a dauntingly mindful, reflective, and focused man as Dharmapriya. His experiments with *prāṇāyāma* must have been playing their part too. Something had to be done; it was time for a quantum shift.

There was a book in the ashram's library they'd both read, the biography of a self-realized saint called Ramdas. He sounded like the perfect man to share their problems with. But the books were so old and worn, the two young men assumed he must be long dead. When somebody told them that he was actually still alive and lived in an ashram not too far away, in Kanhangad, they set off for an exploratory visit.

The visit went well and convinced them they could only gain by spending time around the holy man. So, after eighteen months, and after handing over the ashram's accounts, along with a healthy financial balance from the subscriptions they'd collected, they made their way to Kanhangad and Swami Ramdas.

8

Two Saints, a Bell, a Cave, and a Vision

One night I found myself as it were out of the body and in the Presence of Amitābha, the Buddha of Infinite Light, who presides over the western quarter of the universe....[87]

As the rickety old bus took them away from Muvattupuzha on the 200-mile journey north to Anandashram in the tropical greenery of upper Kerala, it was taking them just a few steps closer to ordination as Buddhist monks. That isn't to say that Hindu India was done with them. In the coming months she would put on a spectacle, distinctly her own, if not to divert them from their goal, at least to embellish it in a distinctively Hindu setting.

There were more temples to visit, ashrams to pass their nights in, people to meet, and inevitably a succession of eccentric holy men, each a local legend in his lifetime: the one-eyed yogi, the 600-year-old swami, the aged ascetic who lived in the cleft in a hillside without ever speaking, and the self-realized boy wonder who'd burned out early and gone half-mad. Some were outrageous fakes, some displayed remarkable knowledge and depth. One boasted of beautiful princesses who took turns to bathe him, while others sat around doing nothing in a cloud of ganja smoke. Towering above all of them, however, were three figures of unquestioned spiritual power and global fame: Swami Ramdas, Ramana Maharshi, and Sri Aurobindo. Our two wanderers would meet two of them, and it was with Ramdas that their odyssey continued.

Although very old, he acted more like a playful, affectionate child than a hoary sage or frigid ascetic. Sitting comfortably in an armchair with slippers on his feet, a pince-nez perched on his nose, and distractingly long earlobes, he communicated exceptional warmth and an unshakeable commitment to the holy life. The trials he'd put himself through as he made his way towards the light were the stuff of legend, but he spoke about himself in a light, inviting way. His efforts had been rewarded when, waking up one morning in a remote mountain cave, he discovered that his ego had completely disappeared. Speaking of himself in the third person, he said he 'searched high and low [...] but he couldn't find the fellow anywhere – and he hasn't been able to find him since!'[88]

On leaving Muvattupuzha, the two friends had been handed a gift of cash – not a vast amount, but enough to sustain life for a while. On their arrival at Anandashram they handed it to Ramdas, saying they'd remain with him for as long the money met their support.

To their minds Anandashram really was the 'abode of bliss' its name suggested. Entirely free of caste-consciousness, the twenty or so people staying there at any one time lived in perfect harmony. In its lush tropical environment it offered ideal conditions for meditation and time to work with the *Oṃ maṇi padme hūṃ* mantra that Ramdas had given them during their trial visit. Now they lived and practised in their own way while spending as much time in Ramdas' orbit as they wished. Dharmapriya wrote essays, committed Buddhist sūtras to memory, and lovingly copied some of his favourite texts into a notebook by hand, among them Aśvaghoṣa's *Awakening of Faith in the Mahayana* and William Blake's *Marriage of Heaven and Hell*.

Whether in informal talks or formal discourses, Ramdas would urge his disciples to maintain at all times a strong sense of their goal and a clear understanding of what it would take to achieve it. Given the serious person Dharmapriya was, this could hardly have been new to him, but years later he would record how deeply the words had affected him, as if there was something about the way Ramdas spoke that turned a simple homily into an initiation.

The pair's final months at Muvattupuzha had been coloured by serious, even violent tensions, but they still valued each other's company and hoped to carry on travelling together. They asked 'Papa', as the ashramites called Ramdas, for advice. The old man listened while Satyapriya gave a thorough account of their time together, their travels and the practices they'd taken up:

> Eventually, when Satyapriya had finished, [Ramdas] hastened to point out to us the error of our ways. Austerities which endangered one's health were sheer madness, he

declared emphatically. On no account should we commit the mistake of thinking that they could facilitate the process of spiritual development. The one thing needful was wholehearted love and devotion towards the spiritual ideal. From that everything would follow. Health and strength were to be preserved by all reasonable means. Without them, spiritual practice was difficult, if not impossible.[89]

Ramdas was very concerned about the effects of *prāṇāyāma* on Satyapriya's mental states, and advised him to stop doing it. He also spoke extensively and warmly of the benefits of brotherly love. But mainly he just listened, and, by virtue of the attention he gave them, the sadness he displayed as they spoke of their difficulties, and the respect he showed each of them for the path they'd chosen, he seemed to calm the turbulent waters of their partnership. They came away feeling as if he had reactivated all that was positive in their friendship.

Their idyllic time at Anandashram would last just a few weeks. It was Ramdas' way never to let anyone settle for long. Kind to the last, he surprised them with a couple of train tickets for the next stage of their journey.

Bhagavan Sri Ramana Maharshi, to give him his full title, lived in Tiruvannamalai, Tamil Nadu, close to the sacred mountain Arunachala. He had been drawn there at the age of sixteen in the wake of a profound spiritual experience, and lived in a cave on the mountainside. His sense of a personal self, he suddenly saw, was a mere echo of its true nature, which was a force, an impersonal, all-inclusive awareness that for him could only be thought of in terms of God, and characterized by Śiva. As his fame grew, a community formed around him.

Although he communicated almost entirely through silence, the atmosphere of his ashram was more conventionally Hindu than anything the pair had witnessed at Anandashram. Caste was observed, especially the distinction between the Brahmin followers and others. A partition divided the dining hall, with Brahmins on one side and everyone else on the other. The Maharshi, wearing nothing but a loincloth, would sit somewhere beyond the end of the partition from where he could see and be seen by everyone, and silently transmit his influence even as his devotees ate their lunch. He would sometimes speak, and transcripts of his question-and-answer sessions were published and well received even in the West. But silence was his characteristic way of teaching. Perhaps it reminded his devotees that the holy life is a matter of experience, not of words and arguments.

People flocked to sit at his feet and 'take *darshan*', to gaze at him as he sat in silence. At other times they would jostle and compete to touch something he'd touched or eat a morsel of his meal, for such treats were considered *prasad*, consecrated by his touch. Over time, the crowds and their demands had become so exhausting that he would try to escape from the ashram, but his retainers would find him and bring him back. He would weep when his mind took him back to the blissful years he'd spent alone in his cave on the side of that sacred mountain.

It was in that very cave, a short distance from the ashram, that Dharmapriya and Satyapriya, with the Maharshi's blessing, spent most of their time. They'd return to the ashram for sessions of *darshan*, but devoted most of their time to meditation, strolling in the natural surroundings, or just sitting in silence. At the base of the mountain, a way below their cave, was a lively Hindu temple. It could be a source of considerable noise when people gathered, sang, and chanted, but it was the temple bell that made the deepest impression on Dharmapriya's mind:

> Long before dawn, as well as at intervals throughout
> the day and night, we heard the temple bell. [...] The
> bell sounded louder than any of the instruments that
> accompanied the evening worship, louder than all of them
> combined. It was so loud that it penetrated rock as easily
> as air, so loud that it made no difference whether we were
> inside the cave or outside it. When we were inside the
> cave, indeed, it was as though the great bell swung not
> somewhere inside the temple but up in the air, directly
> outside the cave. Sometimes I heard it in my dreams.
> Hour after hour it seemed to toll, incessant and insistent,
> wave after wave of brazen sound breaking upon me like
> the repeated thunder of surf on the sea shore. Sometimes
> it was as though the bell, swinging outside, was striking
> against the hill, and that the hill was the bell and the bell
> itself the hammer that struck the bell. Again, the hill was
> not bell but anvil, and the bell the hammer that, stroke
> after sonorous stroke, smote upon the anvil. The point
> of impact, the point where the hill and bell met, where

hammer smote anvil, was the cave, was me. Between the hill and the bell, between the anvil and the hammer, I was being reshaped, was being beaten into something, I knew not what. I was being changed.[90]

And then came a climax, not just to this time of retreat but to the journey he and Satyapriya were on, even to the journey Dennis/Dharmapriya had been on since the age of sixteen. It came in the form of a vision:

One night I found myself as it were out of the body and in the presence of Amitābha, the Buddha of Infinite Light, who presides over the western quarter of the universe. The colour of the Buddha was a deep, rich, luminous red, like that of rubies, though at the same time soft and glowing, like the light of the setting sun. While his left hand rested on his lap, the fingers of his right hand held up by the stalk a single red lotus in full bloom and he sat, in the usual cross-legged posture, on an enormous red lotus that floated on the surface of the sea. To the left, immediately beneath the raised right arm of the Buddha, was the red hemisphere of the setting sun, its reflection glittering golden across the waters.

How long the experience lasted I do not know, for I seemed to be out of time as well as out of the body, but I saw the Buddha as clearly as I had ever seen anything under the ordinary circumstances of my life, indeed far more clearly and vividly. The rich red colour of Amitābha himself, as well as of the two lotuses, and the setting sun, made a

particularly deep impression on me. It was more wonderful,
more appealing, than any earthly red: it was like red light,
but so soft and, at the same time, so vivid, as to be altogether
without parallel.[91]

A vision of that sort might tempt some people to stay
where they were and hope for more. But it had the opposite
effect on Dharmapriya, who took it as a message that their
apprenticeship was over. It was time to move on, time to follow
his aspiration to become a Buddhist monk.

Their destination was Sarnath, a village just a few miles
from Benares (Varanasi). This was where the Buddha had
made his first attempt to communicate his discovery, his
Enlightenment, to a few of his friends. There was now a
significant Buddhist vihara there and a sizeable community
of monks. Surely one of them would ordain them.

Given the Indian context – and their enthusiasm for
discovering temples, sacred caves, and fascinating people –
the journey was not without incident, but they kept moving.
Unfortunately, Satyapriya's mental states were turning volatile
again, if anything more extreme than ever. One day, a minor
disagreement precipitated an escalating spiral of rage during
which he swore with complete conviction that he was going to
drown Dharmapriya in a nearby pool.

For the first time in my life I was actually face to face with
death. Strange to say, though I was frightened, I had no
intention whatever of withdrawing the offending remark.
On the contrary, I became aware of the existence within me

86

of a rock bottom of obstinacy that made it utterly impossible for me to retract or disown any opinion which I genuinely believed to be true even to save my life.[92]

After a while Satyapriya's mood evaporated, almost as suddenly as it had arisen, and the pair moved on, arriving at last in Benares. They spent a few days there, resting and taking in the riotous Hindu excesses of that Ganges-side holy city, and then continued on foot to Sarnath.

This was Dharmapriya's first visit to a Buddhist pilgrimage place. To walk paths the Buddha had once walked, to see sights he'd seen, even to breathe the air he'd breathed, was a profound and joyous experience. Here was where the 'Blessed One' had set rolling the 'wheel of the Dharma'. This was where Siddhartha, now the Awakened One, had met five of his old friends and found words to convey what had happened to him beneath the bodhi tree. After weeks of discussion, the Buddha could tell that one of the five, Kondañña, had 'got it'. He knew it could be done. 'Kondañña knows! Kondañña knows!' he exclaimed.

Now, as the two friends walked among the ruins and circumambulated the commemorative stupa, the significance of that moment in the Buddha's life and the significance of the step they were about to take must have been mingling in their minds. Soon they would be joining the community the Buddha had initiated in this very place. Soon they would be Buddhist monks.

◆

But the pair's attempts to communicate their wish to be ordained fell on distrustful, even contemptuous ears. Barefoot and probably travel-worn with no identification papers and hardly a rupee between them, the new arrivals appeared to the resident monks as a couple of chancers seeking ordination in order to be housed and fed. There was no question of ordination. They weren't even offered a meal.

The two young men were astounded. Surely the choices they'd made and the way they'd been living for more than two years demonstrated their commitment to the Buddhist life. So, just as the monks feared they were being exploited by a couple of beggars, Dharmapriya thought that here, in the very birthplace of the Buddhist tradition, the resident monks were only interested in money. 'No amount of spiritual whitewashing', thought Dharmapriya, 'could disguise the fact that the monks at Sarnath were a worldly-minded lot, without the faintest spark of enthusiasm for spiritual things, and that in refusing our request for ordination they had been activated by mean and unworthy motives [...] I was mortified as a Buddhist, and disgusted as a human being.'[93]

His mood was softened when one of the monks explained how they'd been mistaken for beggars. In that world, a new monk became the responsibility of the vihara where he'd been ordained. It was not at all uncommon for beggars to show up on their doorstep, so they had to be very careful who they took in. Although Sarnath was an important pilgrimage place, the era of mass tourism had not yet arrived. Conditions there were basic, pilgrims were few, and funds scant. They would have to look elsewhere.

Slightly reassured, they told themselves that this was just one more trial, one more test. Satyapriya remembered hearing of a Buddhist monk who lived at the Hindu University back in Benares. Maybe he could advise them.

This kind and corpulent man, Jagdish Kashyap, listened sympathetically to the story of their travels and without hesitation suggested they move on to Kusinārā, the place where the Buddha died. The Burmese monk who lived there, U Chandramani, was renowned for his kindness and generosity. Surely he would grant their wish.

Monks at Last

Thou art not dead, nor dost Thou even sleep
Here on this solemn couch of flower-strewn gold;
But lying plunged in meditation deep
Dost with a peace ineffable enfold
All who with pilgrim footsteps wend to Thee
Sick of the world, and longing to be free.

Couched on my knees before Thy figure vast,
Soothed by the stillness of this silent place,
After much striving I behold at last
The lamp-illumined beauty of Thy face,
And, trembling, feel around, below, above,
The pulsing of Thy vibrant peace and love.[94]

One hundred and thirty miles! A challenge by any standards. To have attempted the trek from Varanasi to Kushinagar at the height of a record-breaking Indian summer, when people were dying from heat exhaustion, was bordering on madness. But travelling from dawn till midday, taking an occasional rest and shelter from the sun beneath the dense foliage of mango trees, they made their way from the site of the Buddha's first sermon to the place of his final passing away. As they begged their food and a little space on an ashram floor for their nights, the journey was a pilgrimage, a test of faith, and a last desperate throw of the dice for Satyapriya at least. For him it was Kusinārā or bust. He'd decided that, if U Chandramani wouldn't ordain them, he would give up his quest for ordination within the Buddhist world and continue his spiritual journey as a Hindu. For Dharmapriya that was out of the question.

These were early days for the Buddhist revival in India. If Bodh Gaya and Sarnath were largely undeveloped, and certainly not equipped to cater for the millions of pilgrims who would arrive in the coming decades, Kusinārā was a rural backwater, its pathways and crumbling buildings playing host to the vegetation with which nature was reclaiming it. It had gone forgotten and ignored for centuries until being rediscovered by Victorian scholars at the turn of the century. Any developments that had taken place since then were due to the efforts of one man. U Chandramani, a devoted Burmese monk, had lived there for fifty of his seventy-one years, along with (at that time) a tiny community of just one monk and ten women who had taken the *anagārika* vow under his supervision.

It speaks to the neglected position of Buddhism in India back then that a significant figure such as U Chandramani should be living under such simple conditions. By then the senior-most Buddhist monk in India, he had translated foundational Buddhist texts into Hindi and established a vihara at Sarnath before settling in Kusinārā. Unheralded and under-resourced, he had dedicated his life to work that called for patience, devotion, and humility, qualities he fortunately had in abundance, along with the kindness he showed our two travel-weary pilgrims.

Little did U Chandramani know it, and not that he would have bothered about such things, but the twenty-four-year-old Englishman asking him for ordination would make a suggestion in a few years' time that would forever associate U Chandramani's name with a dramatic turn in Indian Buddhist history – of which more in due course. For now, as he listened to the two friends, he was minded to take them seriously on the basis of their sincerity and the considerable efforts they'd made to reach him. Even so, he questioned them closely about how much they knew of the Dharma, and whether they'd performed the required preliminaries incumbent on a Buddhist layperson of having recited, at least once, the formulae of the Three Refuges (to the Buddha, Dharma, and Sangha) and the five ethical precepts in the presence of a monk. Fortunately, Dharmapriya had met this requirement back in London when he took *pansil*, as it was termed, at the Buddhist Society Wesak event during the Blitz. The presiding monk, the volunteer stretcher-bearing U Thittila, was also Burmese and U Chandramani even knew him.

Having heard enough, and while making it clear that he was in no position to support the pair or to offer them continued training, he agreed to ordain them as novice monks, *śrāmaṇeras*, in a few days' time.

It was an auspicious setting. They passed the days meditating, strolling among the stupas, and sitting before the giant reclining Buddha in the temple, preparing for the step they were about to take.

The occasion at which the two friends received their *śrāmaṇera* ordination was also a Wesak festival, organized by locals from the surrounding area. Held early in the morning, their ceremony was something of a sideshow for the majority of festivalgoers, but it was over before the brass band opened up. The proceedings were run strictly according to tradition, with U Chandramani insisting on correct pronunciation of Pali words, and getting Dharmapriya to repeat some of the phrases several times until he'd got them right.

When it came to the announcing of names, the names they would carry for the rest of their lives as monks, Satyapriya became Buddharakkhita, meaning 'He who is protected by the Buddha', and Dharmapriya was given the name Dharmarakkhita. Immediately, though, someone pointed out to U Chandramani that a monk called Dharmarakkhita not only lived nearby in Benares, but was actually sitting there, witnessing the ceremony.'"Oh well," said our preceptor, dismissing all this fuss and bother about names with a gesture of good-humoured impatience, "Let *him* be Sangharakkhita!" In this unceremonious manner was I placed under the special protection of the sangha, or Spiritual Community.'[95]

Somewhat dramatically, the moment the ceremony came to its end, the heatwave came to an end too with a sudden clap of thunder and a torrential tropical rainstorm. To the festive crowd, so much rain after a drought was a miracle, even if it dampened the celebrations. If they noticed it at all,

Buddharakkhita and Sangharakkhita, now finally ordained as Buddhist monks, would have taken it as a wonderful climax to their quest, and an auspicious omen.

Within a few days, they were on the move again. Not being one to miss an opportunity, U Chandramani asked the two novice monks to travel a little further north and spend time preaching the Dharma among his Newar disciples in southern Nepal. This would give Sangharakshita his first sustained experience of the Himalayan region and its people. It would also introduce the two novices to the etiquette and formalities of life as Buddhist monks among laypeople.

Wearing robes and wielding their lacquered begging bowls, they set out into a new life. Buddhist tradition dictated they should carry no money and beg their food as they travelled. They could accept only *cooked* food, moreover, which they had to obtain by standing patiently, in silence at the doors of Buddhist households. They were obliged to accept whatever they were given – while being prepared to receive nothing. Often made up of a random assortment of dry and liquid offerings, their lunchtime meals could look extremely unappetizing, but they didn't let that put them off. Siddhartha Gautama, the future Buddha, had vomited after eating the first meal he'd begged after leaving home; surely they could give it a try, and in fact they got used to it surprisingly quickly. Following tradition, they'd eat in silence a little way apart from their benefactors, but inviting them to come in close once they'd eaten so they could offer a little Dharma teaching. Before long they were being asked to preside over rituals and, most important of all,

Monks at last: Sangharakshita (L) and Buddharakshita at Kusinārā, May 1949

to lead their benefactors in reciting those Three Refuges and lay precepts.

In this way they were made welcome wherever they went. For they were bhikkhus, and here, as in any Buddhist context, the act of supporting a monk was considered highly meritorious. In time Sangharakshita came to see his ochre robes and his bowl in the way they are described in the scriptures, as a pair of wings, allowing him to go anywhere within the Buddhist world, free from social ties. Who knew what the future might bring?

Study and Self-Knowledge

In less than a week I was feeling perfectly at home in
my new surroundings, and had embarked on the course
of study that was to keep me busy – almost without
interruption – for seven of the quietest and happiest
months I have ever known.[96]

The Venerable Jagdish Kashyap lived in a simple house on
the extensive campus of the Hindu University in Varanasi
(Benares). He was employed to teach Pali, Sanskrit, Buddhist
philosophy, and logic. Knowledgeable and kind, it was he
who'd directed their path towards U Chandramani and
ordination in Kusinārā. Now, back in Varanasi, the two friends
decided to pay him a visit. Sangharakshita was still recovering
from an illness he'd contracted in Nepal, and Buddharakshita,
who had no passport problems, was still minded to head south
and see if he could enter a monastery in Sri Lanka. All the
same they asked Jagdish Kashyap whether he would take them
on as student-disciples, at least for a while.

With characteristic generosity Kashyap-ji, as he was known,
said he'd be happy to take them, and even had a spare room in
his home for one of them. As Sangharakshita was convalescing

it was obvious that he should be the one to take up the offer. Rightly or wrongly, Buddharakshita suspected that Kashyap-ji wanted only Sangharakshita as a student, and announced that he would proceed to Sri Lanka alone. Their two year fellowship was to end.

On a practical level it had been an enormously valuable arrangement. Buddharakshita was an Indian national, spoke the languages, and knew his country's ways. He was fundamentally warm-hearted, had enormous energy, and liked to get things done. Their friendship had been based on a shared dedication to a spiritual ideal and mutual loyalty through an important phase in their lives. Perhaps there was 'attraction of opposites', but it's worth remembering that Sangharakshita had his own uncompromising, even stubborn, character trait that had allowed him to step out of the army, burn his passport, and walk untold miles barefoot in the blazing sun.

As an instinctive educator, Sangharakshita had seen in the politically driven Brahmin a challenge not to be missed. Their parting provoked mixed feelings: 'Though I was sorry to lose my warm-hearted but irascible companion, once the actual parting was over my predominant feeling was one of relief. Living with Buddharakshita had at times been a nightmare, and it was only now that I was once more on my own that I realized how great the strain had been.'[97] It is worth noting that Buddharakshita would spend the rest of his life as a respected, if notoriously peppery, Theravāda monk.

Living with Kashyap-ji was something else altogether: 'Extreme corpulence gave him an air of mountainous imperturbability. At the same time, the expression of exceptional intelligence that played upon the strongly-marked features of the dark-brown face created an impression of vivacity, even as the look of gentle benignity that beamed from them seemed to invite confidence and trust.'[98]

Like U Chandramani, Kashyap-ji was a humble but significant player in the Indian Buddhist revival. It was while studying Pali in Sri Lanka as a step towards a doctorate in Buddhist philosophy that he'd taken the unexpected turn of becoming a monk. He was a scholar-monk, to be sure, lecturing in Sri Lanka, Malaysia, and India, while transliterating into Devanagari and translating major tracts of the Pali canon into Hindi. But, unlike most of the monks around him, indeed most Theravādin monks of his day, he also maintained a daily meditation practice and had respect for the Bodhisattva figures of the Mahāyāna world.

Despite the differences in age, nationality, and learning, they saw eye to eye. If Sangharakshita had questions about the way Buddhism was practised in Sri Lanka, a 'Buddhist country', Kashyap-ji remembered his own encounters with the unthinking 'orthodoxies' of Sri Lankan monks: 'Sangharakshita-ji,' he said, speaking slowly and deliberately, and with evident feeling, 'they are a set of monkeys [...] sitting on a treasure [...] the value of which [...] they do *not* understand'.[99]

His professional position was precarious. Although the university's millionaire benefactor had decreed that there should be a professor of Pali and Buddhist philosophy, the university authorities were not obliged to supply him with students. In fact, to ensure that Pali and Buddhist philosophy could not be taken as alternatives to Sanskrit and Hindu philosophy, regulations dictated that Pali could only be studied *along with* Sanskrit. As a consequence, Kashyap-ji rarely had more than two or three students to teach, and sometimes none at all.

Sangharakshita made himself comfortable in his room, which, with nothing more than a bookcase, a string mattress, and a frayed carpet, was as spartan as his teacher's. But, given the way he'd been living for the last couple of years, that was good enough. Now, his mind was firmly devoted to the study of Pali, Buddhist philosophy, and logic. He'd never had much of a head for languages, so progress with Pali was slow. Even so, in time he was able to follow, and make his own translations of, the *Dhammapada* and some of the oldest texts. To follow and recite Buddhist suttas in a language close to the Buddha's own was a joyful act of devotion.

The hours spent with logic and philosophy were another matter. To have uninterrupted time to read, reflect, and bask in their byways, and the luxury of an expert mentor sitting or dozing in the room next door, was sheer heaven. Since arriving in India, almost all his philosophical conversations had been with Hindus. Now, finally, he could enjoy the opportunity to talk about nothing but the Buddha-Dharma.

Although faithful to Buddhism since his experience at the age of sixteen, he'd resonated with the depths he'd sensed in some of those Hindu swamis, just as he'd resonated with the *Dao De Jing* and the literature of Christian mysticism. This was in disappointing contrast to the narrow orthodoxy, and occasional mean-spiritedness, he'd encountered among some of the Buddhist monks he'd met. But in Jagdish Kashyap he'd found a refined, intelligent, broad-minded, and kind exemplar of the Buddhist life. Alone, and in conversation as they took their regular evening strolls, he had an opportunity to clarify his thinking and discover what sort of Buddhist he was.

The essays he published during his time at 'Buddhakuti' give us a glimpse of the twenty-four-year-old novice as he worked things out. In 'Philosophy and religion in original and developed Buddhism' he spread his wings to encompass the evolution of Buddhist thought from the earliest Pali sources, through the Madhyamaka and Yogācāra, to later Chinese and Japanese developments. Drawing too on his familiarity with the Indian Vedantists and ancient Greek philosophers, he sought to demonstrate how the central principle of conditionality, 'dependent origination', underpins and unifies the evolution of Buddhist philosophy *and* practice, so making Buddhism, uniquely, a philosophy *and* a religion.

As a philosophy it refuses to propose any kind of self-existent, unchanging absolute reality, whether a force or a god, in relation to which everything and everyone else is relative, even unreal. The Buddha expressed his vision in terms of *paṭiccasamuppāda*, conditionality, one vast process of interdependent processes that includes everything, from the dust at our feet to whatever spirits might inhabit other realms, to the way our minds form ideas and attitudes. As a religion it teaches that the same principle of conditionality, according to which suffering arises in dependence on conditions, with our conscious collaboration and wise effort, makes progress possible towards higher states of consciousness and being, from suffering to happiness to joy and ultimately to wisdom and freedom.

The essay is not an easy read, but maybe that crude sketch is enough to help us imagine Sangharakshita sitting in his room, popping next door occasionally to check his thinking with Kashyap-ji, striving to clarify and articulate how it was that his insight experience could never find a home in any other religion.

Another preoccupation revealed by his essays of the time had to do with the issue of lifestyle. He was now a Buddhist monk. This had been his heart's dream for years, the monk's life exemplifying the kind of renunciation to which he'd felt drawn. Even so, perhaps because he'd spent so much time in a society so troublingly stratified by Brahmanical decrees on the day-to-day duties of a Hindu, he was minded to think through the relationship between commitment and lifestyle.

In a dramatized dialogue, 'Is Buddhism for monks, only?', he asserted that the Buddhist path is open to all, irrespective of lifestyle. The Buddha's threefold way, of perfecting ethical life, engaging in meditation, and accumulating insight, is open to anyone who, through reflection and effort, aligns themselves with that progressive current within conditionality. The monk's life, he suggested, provides excellent conditions for that work, for those people willing and able to live that way. But external conditions alone do not turn anyone into a superior being, nor does their observance give anyone exclusive 'ownership' of the Buddhist path. He would return to these reflections many times in the coming years.

Reading, writing – poems as well as essays – reflecting on the Dharma as he gazed at monsoon rains, it was a delightfully nourishing interlude. He was even gaining attention as a writer on Buddhist philosophy and as a poet. But there was a price to pay. This period of undistracted reflection was giving him a chance to notice a tension, even a conflict, between two rival aspects of his nature, which he termed 'Sangharakshita I and Sangharakshita II':

> Sangharakshita I wanted to enjoy the beauty of nature, to read and write poetry, to listen to music, to look at paintings and sculpture, to experience emotion, to lie in bed and dream, to see places, to meet people. Sangharakshita II wanted to realize the truth, to read and write philosophy, to observe the precepts, to get up early and meditate, to mortify the flesh, to fast and pray. Sometimes Sangharakshita I was victorious, sometimes Sangharakshita II, while occasionally there was an uneasy duumvirate. What they ought to have done, of course, was to marry and give birth to Sangharakshita III, who would have united beauty and truth, poetry and philosophy, spontaneity and discipline; but this seemed to be a dream impossible of fulfilment.[100]

A climax came one day when the ascetic side of his nature took control and set fire to two notebooks of poems he'd written during his first years in India. It was a shocking moment from which both sides of his nature recoiled. It didn't resolve the conflict, but it made him accept that there was no denying either of the two Sangharakshitas. Somehow he'd have to find a way to live with them both, awarding each the time and attention they needed.

Lurking behind this and other conflicts was, as he would put it, the issue of getting beyond the ego:

> We revolve within a vicious circle from which there seems
> to be no possibility of escape. The man who thinks, 'I
> am Enlightened' is equally far from Nirvana as the man
> who thinks, 'I am rich'. The saint may be more attached
> to his sanctity than the sinner to his sin. In fact a 'good'
> man's core of separative selfhood is often harder and more
> impenetrable to the infinite light of Amitābha than that of
> a 'bad' man shattered into humility and repentance by the
> consciousness of his sinful deeds.[101]

For Sangharakshita, the issue of the ego was much more than a theoretical problem. How, he wondered, did one 'get around it, or get rid of it, or get beyond it'? A book by Thomas Merton, the Trappist monk, poet, and contemplative, contained a practical suggestion that 'the disciple should surrender his will absolutely to the will of his spiritual superior'.[102]

This was something he believed he could do, a precept he was willing to observe. For the rest of his time with Jagdish Kashyap, therefore, he went along with whatever his master wished, and as a consequence 'I had no troubles, and experienced great peace of mind.'[103]

In later years, Kashyap-ji would maintain that in some respects he had learned as much from Sangharakshita as his disciple had learned from him. The two of them clearly enjoyed each other's company and respected each other's spiritual integrity.

After seven months they left Buddhakuti for a period of travel, visiting holy places and meeting Buddhists in Bihar. For Kashyap-ji this had been planned as a sort of vacation. The break gave him some space to accept that the time had come to retire from his compromised situation at the university and give himself back to meditation and the life of a monk. During their travels Kashyap-ji was therefore keen to find out whether Sangharakshita's success with the begging bowl among U Chandramani's Newar disciples could be replicated here. Without any difficulty it was. This discovery, that even in these modern times one could live the traditional life of a monk and depend on the generosity shown towards a monk, struck Kashyap-ji with the force of a revelation.

As their travels took in the holy places, particularly Bodh Gaya, where the Buddha gained Enlightenment, and the 'Vulture Peak', a 'dizzy eminence' where the Buddha was wont to meditate, the poet and monk in Sangharakshita joined hands in a mood of sustained devotion:

> As we gazed, even as the Master must have gazed, first at the valley 1,000 feet below – once a populous city, now an impenetrable jungle – then at the blue encircling hills, and finally beyond the hills to the green and fertile fields, the

mud-walled villages, the pleasant mango groves, of ancient Magadha, the modern Bihar, a prayer went forth from my heart. I prayed that not only in this land, the Land of the Great Disciples, but in every land, men might hearken to the Voice of the Buddha, as it sounded from the unseen heights of the spiritual Vulture Peak. I prayed that they might set their feet on the Path leading to their own and others' Enlightenment. Finally, I prayed that I too might one day be enabled to help in some way towards this end.[104]

Their travels reached their farthest point in Kalimpong, a hill-station in the foothills of the Himalayas. They stayed in a Buddhist meeting house in the centre of town, and received their meals from a well-off Buddhist businessman – until, that is, they got a distinct feeling that they were straining his generosity beyond its limits and moved on.

For Kashyap-ji, this meant leaving Kalimpong and heading for northern Bihar where he planned to go into retreat. Whether or not this had been part of his original plan, there was no arguing with the impulse. He was already sitting in the jeep that would take him away when he handed his obedient disciple Sangharakshita one last instruction: 'Stay here and work for the good of Buddhism.'[105]

And so he did stay in Kalimpong, for the next fourteen years. He would work for the good of Buddhism for the rest of his life.

Living in the Presence

I feel like going on my knees
To this old mountain and these trees.
Three or four thousand years ago
I could have worshipped them, I know.
But if one did so in this age
They'd lock him in a padded cage.
We've made the world look mean and small,
And lost the wonder of it all[106]

◆

And the colours! [...] Sometimes, indeed, they glowed with
such intensity that everything seemed to be made of jewels.
And all the time, above the mirth and the music, above the
life and the colour, above the steadfastness of nature and
the security of civilization – above everything – there were
the snows... With the blue of the valleys at their feet and
the blue of the sky above their heads, the shimmering white
masses stretched from end to end of the horizon majestic
beyond belief.[107]

Kalimpong runs along a saddleback, a rounded ridge between
two higher hills, about thirty miles from Darjeeling. Being in

the foothills of the Himalayas the climate is mild, the rainfall moderate, the air cool and clear. Tucked between the Indian, Bhutanese, Sikkhimese, and Tibetan borders, the town hosted a cosmopolitan community of 20,000, and its bazaars resounded to the calls of Lepchas, Bhutia, Tibetans, and Nepalese traders. Soon it would be offering a staging post and a first refuge for thousands of Tibetans fleeing the Chinese invasion.

This bustling town would be Sangharakshita's home, a base, a complete world in whose life he would play a full and active part. There would be complications, opportunities, and challenges, but throughout the years his sense of wonder to be living in constant sight of those snowy peaks and blue, blue skies would never desert him. This was a deeper experience than one of being uplifted by a beautiful view. His imagination soared. Whatever the demands and duties of his everyday life, the poems that poured from his pen through those years suggest that the monk and poet came together in a shared communion with the surrounding natural world bordered by those glistening heights. In the interaction, not only were those warring aspects of his character unified, but, at times, his entire environment presented itself as a living symbol, pointing the mind towards all that is highest, purest, and worthy of reverence. It was a charmed realm.

Down on the ground, though, what really struck him was that for the first time in his life he was on his own, answerable to no one but himself. Undaunted, even thrilled by this freedom, he settled into the 'Dharmodaya Vihara', the first of five residences he'd pass through over the years. Each morning he would set out equipped with his begging bowl to receive offerings of food. This alms round not only sustained life but gave him a chance to familiarize himself with the town, albeit in a rather particular way:

> Since I went on my alms-round with lowered head I did not see much of Kalimpong on such occasions. Apart from the road immediately in front of me, all I saw was legs. Some of the legs were short and thick, of the colour of weak tea, and with enormously developed calf muscles, almost like footballs. These, as I knew, were the legs of Nepalese porters, dozens of whom could be seen at any hour of the day straining beneath the weight of enormous loads borne on their backs in cone-shaped wicker baskets. Others were black and stick-like, with ends of off-white dhotis flapping above bony knees. Some legs were sheathed in tight-fitting white jodhpurs or were encased in Western-style trousers, while others were decently concealed behind the skirts of black, brown, or blue gowns or heavy maroon robes. [...] For my own part, going and coming, I did my best to maintain the modest, measured gait considered appropriate to the alms-gathering monk.[108]

Taking his daily circuits ever further afield, he soon got to know the locals. And, as they got to know him, they realized they'd been blessed with a knowledgeable and approachable teacher. Soon and without any particular effort, Kashyap-ji's parting instruction to stay and work for the good of Buddhism was taking form, and Sangharakshita was turning into something of a local figure, increasingly immersed in the life and dramas of his adopted home town. As people discovered his skills as a speaker, he'd receive requests for talks from Kalimpong and beyond. He'd given many talks before, in Singapore, Calcutta, and especially in Muvattupuzha. He always enjoyed talking about the Dharma, and experienced this aspect of his life as a practice, as important as his study and meditation.

Almost from the outset he'd been drawn to ordination and a life of renunciation, assuming that was how a true follower of the Buddha should live, at a distance from the world, seeking wisdom and ultimately liberation from the realm of suffering. The ideal of a renunciate life had suited his spiritual instincts. Now that he was older, more confident, and more familiar with Mahāyāna teachings, he realized they were drawing him without conscious effort towards a life lived as much for the sake of others as for himself.

This isn't to say he'd never thought in such terms. Even as a sixteen-year-old he'd seen, albeit on his level, that 'awakening', as represented at its fullest pitch by the Buddha's Enlightenment, opens the heart as well as the inner eye. His own experience, as precipitated by *The Diamond Sūtra*, had revealed that wisdom and compassion are not so much two separate aspects of Enlightenment, but emerge spontaneously, completely intertwined, each being intrinsic and inevitable to the other.

'The unity of Buddhism', the article he wrote at the age of eighteen, was a kind of manifesto. In it he demonstrated that he had things to say about 'Buddhism' that the Western world needed to hear. What *The Middle Way*'s readers made of the article we don't know. At best, some of them might have valued it as an interesting contribution to the conversation. What few readers would have realized, given the generally intellectual character of interest in Buddhism at the time, would have been the author's passionate concern, even then, for the proper introduction of the Dharma as nothing less than the unique cure to the world's ills. Now, his visits to neglected holy places, his failure so far to meet more than a handful of Buddhists who'd impressed him during his travels in the East, and finally his serendipitous encounters with U Chandramani and Jagdish Kashyap, those under-resourced pioneers of an Indian Buddhist revival, had alerted him to the scale of the challenge. The magazines he was editing and contributing to gave him a voice in the Buddhist world. Being able to broadcast his opinions in this way was a start, but it was at a remove from the real work required.

The future of Buddhism, he knew, lay in its young people. They had energy and looked at things with fresh eyes. So, very soon after arriving in town, he established his first Buddhist organization: 'The Young Men's Buddhist Association' (YMBA). They'd meet at the vihara, make friends, enjoy film nights, play ping-pong, hear a little about the Dharma, and receive some extra pre-exam coaching from Sangharakshita. Knowing how much he'd enriched his own life by educating himself, he relished the opportunity to encourage others to explore that path. Along the way he made an important discovery:

At the microphone in Nepal, 1951

I happened to be explaining Shelley's 'The Cloud' to three or four students who were preparing for the Intermediate Arts examination. They were all very attentive, there was a good rapport between us, and I found I was able to go more and more deeply into the meaning of the poem. The more deeply I went into it, the profounder and more universal that meaning seemed to be. After a while, as I plumbed depth upon depth of significance, the thought suddenly struck me that I was not simply elucidating Shelley's poem: I was teaching the Dharma. It was not that I was using the poem as a hook on which to hang an exposition of the Dharma, I had given myself to the poem. I had plunged into it as into an ocean, and the ocean had yielded up the pearl of the Dharma, a pearl that was already there, hidden in the depths, only waiting to be discovered. However, it was because I was already acquainted with the Dharma that I was able to recognize it when I encountered it in the poem. Indeed, if one was acquainted with the Dharma, and looked deeply enough, one could encounter the Dharma not just in Shelley's poem but also in other works of Western literature as well, perhaps, in painting and sculpture, and even in musical compositions.[109]

These sessions, and the opportunity they afforded to marry his love of art and literature with the Dharma, took him an important step further into the 'mystical marriage' between Sangharakshitas I and II. A series of lengthy essays and articles he wrote at the time, 'The meaning of Buddhism and the value of art', 'The religion of art', and 'Advice to a young poet', reveal the journey he was on, and his determination to challenge the idea that art, beauty, and imagination have no place in a Buddhist life, whether his own or that of others.

He would also write a great deal of poetry throughout his time in Kalimpong. He would write about the place, the mountains, the beauty of nature, usually in his traditional neo-Georgian style, though sometimes he would allow himself to experiment with poetic forms. Many of his poems sang of the natural beauty around him; others emerged from the inner world of his meditations, a shaft of insight or a mood of devotion to the Buddha. Sometimes a poem would speak directly to the dilemma he had been living with:

> I questioned, in my greener age,
> Whether it were best for me
> To blossom Poet or burgeon Sage;
> But now in riper days I see,
> And with what gladness know it:
> The Poet is the truest Sage,
> The Sage the sweetest Poet –
> The piper his own best tune;
> And laugh that I could ever
> Have striven thus to sever
> The moonlight from the moon.[110]

Not all, but many of his poems made a point. 'I used to feel that a poem ought to have an uplifting message, a moral.' But no matter how earnest or didactic the poem, he rarely strayed far from his urge to honour beauty, though never just for its own sake:

> I believe that the concept of beauty is very important and valid. We are all susceptible to beauty. And one of the characteristics of appreciation of beauty is that it is quite disinterested. When you see a beautiful flower, you appreciate it just for its beauty. You don't want to do anything with

it. You don't want to own it, possess it, take it to pieces, or analyse it. You just want to contemplate it and appreciate it. In this way it lifts you out of your usual preoccupations, it lifts you even beyond your ordinary usual self, into a different kind of world, in which one is concerned with values rather than with interests in the economic sense.[111]

This understanding of the place and value of beauty in life allowed him to land on a definition of art that satisfied him: 'Art is the organization of sensuous impressions into pleasurable formal relations that express the artist's sensibility and communicate to his audience a sense of values that can transform their lives.'[112]

The impulse to break down the barriers between Buddhism and art, even to see the two as being positively intertwined, would carry through into the rest of his life. He would never fail to stay in touch with his sources of inspiration. And as a teacher in the East and West, he would encourage his disciples to seek and honour beauty with a quiet but revolutionary zeal:

Modern man, whether of the East or of the West, is suffering from starvation of beauty, and until he again receives and assimilates that divine pabulum there is little hope of his being restored to spiritual health. Before World War II, the Moral Rearmament movement was launched in England. The inauguration on a global scale of a movement for Aesthetic Rearmament, the launching of a worldwide Battle for Beauty, is today no less necessary. Until an outlet for the emotions of man is found on those higher levels of experience, to which art and religion alike give access, they will continue on the lower their turbulent and destructive career. Like the two wings of a bird, reason and emotion are both indispensable to the spiritual flights of man.

Higher still and higher
From the earth thou springest
Like a cloud of fire;
The deep blue thou wingest,
And singing still dost soar,
And soaring ever singest.

The spiritual aspirant is like Shelley's Skylark: while his understanding soars, his emotions sing. It is in this singing and soaring, in the simultaneous expansion of the understanding and the emotions, that we find the meaning of Buddhism and the value of art, and, in fact, the secret of spiritual life.[113]

Although his ideas about the nature and relevance of the monk's life, even about the nature of the spiritual life itself, were on the move, he still aspired to become a full monk. So when he received an invitation to attend the dedication of a new vihara in Sarnath, he accepted, adding a personal request: with so many monks attending the event, might it be possible to receive his higher ordination while he was there?

His request was granted, and on 24 November 1950, in the presence of the requisite quorum of monks and witnessed by an international, multi-sectarian gathering of visiting monks, he was ordained as a bhikkhu. The ceremony, he records, was businesslike, much of it pronounced in the Burmese version of the Pali language. But it had happened: his long-held wish to become a monk was fulfilled.

A wish, an ambition fulfilled, for sure. Even so, the hidden significance of the event would emerge more fully in a few years' time and in quite an unexpected way, as we shall see. But for now his outer life was taken up with his friendships and duties in Kalimpong, while his inner life was still absorbing the implications of 'working for the good of Buddhism' on his own and, culturally, as an outsider. Although working effectively, inspired by the environment and fascinated by the people he was meeting, on some level he was feeling the strain.

In the course of his visits to Mumbai (Bombay), he had come to know a remarkable Parsee gentleman. Dr Dinshah Mehta, founder and leading figure in the Society of Servants of God, had acted as one of Gandhi's physicians. Now, he ran a health centre and, in the depths of his meditation sessions, claimed to receive guidance directly from God. Over time he accumulated disciples who gathered around, seeing him as a direct channel to the Supreme Being.

Sangharakshita would stay with the Doctor when he was in town, and developed friendships, with him and some of his followers, notably Mrs Dinoo Dubash, a Parsi woman with whom he would keep up a lifelong friendship and correspondence.[114] Although he could not believe that the Doctor's pronouncements came from a supreme being, the man's experience of being guided by a power beyond himself provoked some significant reflections:

Though I had been meditating for a number of years, my achievements in this field were far from commensurate with my aspirations. There were experiences of the bliss and peace of the lower dhyānas [states of meditative absorption]; there were visions, usually of the Buddha or Avalokiteśvara; there were flashes of insight, not always in connection with the meditation itself: and that was about all. What I now had to do, I felt, was to achieve a level of meditative experience which would enable me to receive whatever might be the Buddhist equivalent of Dr. Mehta's 'guidance', for [...] I was well aware that for real spiritual progress to take place the ego [...] needed to open itself to the influence of what I was later to call 'the transcendental outpourings of the Absolute'. Just how that deeper – or higher – level was to be achieved was not clear, but I trusted that if I was able to stay long enough in the lower dhyānas the inherent momentum of those states, together with my intense desire to be truly guided, would be sufficient to carry me further.[115]

His duties in Kalimpong being light at that time, he decided to remain at Mehta's 'Nature Cure Clinic' and take a five-week meditation retreat. A few excerpts from the diary he kept offer a glimpse into the jouney:

Concentrated quite easily.

Neither quite in nor quite out of ordinary mind.

Experience of positive peace in crown of head. This descended and spread throughout whole body.

Experience of ascending and descending at same time.

All kinds of movements and explosions of energy in the body, though not exactly in the physical body. As though some healing, at the same time destructive, force, was pulling and stretching and kneading the mind.

Later, while absorbed in meditation, he would entertain a series of internal 'dialogues', testing his mind, his depths, for the guidance he sought:

Concentrated. Feeling of total dissociation between past and present life. Doubt. [...] Decided to ask more questions, as follows:

Q. What should be my attitude towards surroundings after returning to K.?

A. Absolute detachment. This detachment is positive. Must be detached even from the Buddha. Detachment as taught by the Buddha transcends both attachment and detachment in the ordinary sense.

Q. How behave towards people?

A. Buddha first and everyone else second. – Awareness of shortcomings in this respect.

Q. What about acquiring land etc?

A. This will be settled after your return. You must be ready to be anywhere and nowhere.

Awareness of the Buddha's presence, though rather faintly [sic]. Reflected whether these awarenesses were genuine guidance. Concluded that since they were in agreement with the Scriptures and were not unreasonable they could be accepted.

> Good concentration. Sensation of positive peace descending.
> Asked, 'What should I do?' Awareness of answer came at once: 'Nothing'.[116]

The account he would come to write about just half his time in Kalimpong fills two substantial volumes of memoirs plus a couple more books covering key thematic elements of his time there. By now he had blossomed into a confident, curious, and compassionate young man, deeply versed in the Dharma, ready to engage with the colourful procession of people who crossed his path: shopkeepers and farmers, maharajas and maharanis, princes and politicians, Christian missionaries, fellow Buddhists, fellow writers, kindred spirits, and wily enemies.

An especially important friend, and another source of guidance, though through the medium of friendship, was the German writer and painter Lama Anagarika Govinda:

> One of the most important friends I made through that magazine was Lama Govinda. As we began to correspond, we found that our ideas about Buddhism were very similar. He had experience of several forms of Buddhism, and did not wish to identify himself exclusively with any one form. As for me, even though I had been ordained as a Theravādin Buddhist monk, I accepted the whole of Buddhist tradition, in all its richness.[117] Theravāda, Mahāyāna, Tibetan Buddhism, Zen, Shin – in principle I accepted everything. In 1951, after we had been writing to each other for a while, Lama Govinda came to Kalimpong and spent some time

with me. The friendship that then sprang up between us lasted for many years – indeed, the last letter I received from him was written just four days before his death.[118]

In some ways it was more than a friendship. Sangharakshita always described Govinda as a 'kindred spirit'. He was a poet, Govinda was a painter. The conversations and correspondence through which they explored the relationship between their lives as Buddhists and their commitment to art no doubt fed significantly into Sangharakshita's thinking:

> I tend to think that we need, as it were, a sort of synthesis, if that is the right word, between the two positions. We need a person who is not a lama in the sense that he doesn't represent just the religious absolute nor can we simply have the writer or the artist in the old sense as an absolute, breaking all the rules, breaking all the boundaries etc., etc. We need a new sort of person. And then it occurred to me that Lama Govinda was a bit like that, because Lama Govinda was an artist, at the same time he was a sort of mystic but there was nothing absolute about him. He seemed to synthesise the two very, very well, without any conflict, and he was able to do that by being an artist and a writer and a poet as well as being a Buddhist. [...] I feel that the days of the religious absolute are finished, and we don't really need any longer teachers, whether they are Christian or whether they are Muslim or whether they are Buddhist who stand for a religious absolute. Nor do we need any longer artists, painters and writers who stand for the

aesthetic absolute and who refuse to consider moral and spiritual considerations.[119]

◆

At that moment in its history, Kalimpong was exerting a magnetic pull, out of proportion to its size, as some of the world's more eccentric people showed up there along with some of its wisest. As Sangharakshita became more well known from his writings, travellers and scholars from Europe and America began to correspond with him and even pay visits, some staying a few days, some for months: Marco Pallis, John Driver, John Blofeld, familiar names in the early days of the West's awakening to Buddhism. George Roerich was a neighbour, while Herbert Guenther and Edward Conze were correspondents and regular contributors to Sangharakshita's magazines.

Some of the locals became his students, some became his teachers. Over time and as Sangharakshita's reputation as a monk, writer, and editor spread, he made contacts in the more refined and connected echelons of Kalimpong society. Prince Peter of Greece was a frequent visitor, turning up on his chestnut horse in full cowboy gear, while Prince Lattikin, heir to the now defunct throne of Burma, was a friend, his landlord for a while, and a financial supporter. During this time, he struggled to keep his magazine *Stepping Stones* afloat while keeping a roof over his head. He would move through three temporary residences until he finally arrived at 'the Hermitage'.

Very basic, and initially bordering on dereliction with its leaking roof and walls full of gaps, this five-roomed bungalow would be his home and the base of his activities for much of his time in the area. Although waiting to be rediscovered and restored, the surrounding grounds offered, as well as an orchard of fruit trees, a little paradise of bamboo orchids, magnolias, chocolate palms, and camellias, buried in which was a little summer house where he could meditate.

Throughout his time in Kalimpong he kept detailed diaries into which he'd jot down accounts of day-to-day incidents and pen portraits of the characters who flowed in and out of his orbit. The sheer detail, humour, and compassionate eye with which he described these people, even the worst of them (and some were pretty bad), communicated a warm and strengthening maturity.

Just as his lessons in literature were helping him to merge the dreaming poet and the monk, Sangharakshitas I and II, his life in Kalimpong would soon bring a new element into the mix, one that would take the marriage deeper and move his experience of spiritual practice into a new dimension

◆

Those who have hid themselves on heights of snow,
Face to face with
the stars and the silver moon,
Shall read upon the rocks the Ancient Rune
And thus decipher secrets. They shall know –
Far from the lips of any earthly lover –
What the mists hide and what the winds discover.[120]

Apart from a few days' leave in the Himalayan region back in his army days, he'd had little or nothing to do with Tibetan Buddhism or Tibetan Buddhists. Now he was living in their corner of the Buddhist world, and it would not be long before the influence of their art and archetypes exerted their pull. During a visit to the Darjeeling area one day, he visited a temple devoted to Padmasambhava:

> As I entered the temple [...] I saw in front of me, three or
> four times larger than life, the mighty sedent figure of the
> semi-legendary founder and inspirer of the Nyingmapa
> tradition, a skull cup in his left hand, a staff topped with
> skulls in the crook of his left arm, and the celebrated
> 'wrathful smile' on his moustached face. All this I took in
> instantly, together with the 'lotus hat', the richly embroidered
> robes, and the much smaller flanking figures of his two
> consorts, one Tibetan and one Nepalese. Having taken it
> in, I felt that it had always been there, and that in seeing
> the figure of Padmasambhava I had become conscious of a
> spiritual presence that had in fact been with me all the time.
> Though I had never seen the figure of Padmasambhava
> before, it was familiar to me in a way that no other figure on
> earth was familiar: familiar and fascinating. It was familiar
> as my own self, yet at the same time infinitely mysterious,
> infinitely wonderful, and infinitely inspiring. Familiar,
> mysterious, wonderful, and inspiring it was to remain.
> Indeed, from then on the figure of the Precious Guru –
> Guru Rimpoche – was to occupy a permanent place in my
> inner spiritual world, even as it played a prominent part in

the spiritual life and imagination of the entire Himalayan region.[121]

Over the coming years his connection with Tibetan forms of Buddhism would go much further and deeper, as the more influential locals, among them the beautiful Princess Pema Tseduen of Sikkhim who dazzled the eye in her traditional dress, introduced him to some of the revered Tibetan Buddhist teachers who either lived in the area or were passing through it.

This was a world of 'incarnate lamas'. According to traditional rebirth doctrine, such figures, tulkus as they are known, are the reborn spiritual descendants of notable teachers from the past. Some, such as the Dalai Lama, Tomo Geshe Rimpoche, Rechung Rimpoche, Pabongkhapa, Dudjom Rimpoche, Jamyang Khyentse, and Dilgo Khyentse, were widely revered. Others, like Kachu Rimpoche and Dhardo Rimpoche, were less well known but able to demonstrate exceptional levels of awareness, intuition, and compassion. Over time, Sangharakshita got to know a number of them well, as friends, as English students, as teachers, or as all three.

The rough-hewn 'layman' Chatrul Sangye Dorje, neither a monk nor an incarnate lama, but admired as a man of legendary accomplishments by everyone, not only became a friend and teacher, initiating him into a meditation on Green Tara, but correctly prophesied that Sangharakshita would one day have a place of his own – a vihara – to be known as the Triyana Vardhana Vihara, the 'monastery where the three traditions meet'.

Some of these renowned figures would initiate him into a number of important Vajrayāna meditation practices. Until then, and for his first ten years as a meditator, his regular practice had been the *ānāpānasati*, the mindfulness of in-out breathing. Now, in a series of initiations – ritualized introductions by experienced teachers to the details and spirit of each practice – he was granted access to a realm of illumined imagination where Buddha and Bodhisattva figures, embodying the many various qualities of Enlightenment, are always accessible, ready to communicate their blessings and influence directly into the heart and mind of the receptive disciple.

Up until then, he once said, alongside his formal meditation sessions he had made an effort to keep the Buddha, or some aspect of his teaching, in his mind all the time. When the Buddha Amitābha, the red Buddha of the western quarter, had appeared to him in Ramana Maharshi's mountainside cave, it had been as if a refined but accessible dimension of the enlightened mind was rewarding his efforts and reaching out to him. Now, under the guidance of these Tibetan teachers, he was being offered a way to maintain and deepen that level of connection.

From Jamyang Khyentse he received initiations into Avalokiteśvara, Green Tārā, Mañjughoṣa, and Vajrapaṇi (he also instructed one of his disciples to give him the Padmasambhava initiation). From Dilgo Khyentse he received initiation into Kurukullā and Jambhala, as well as into the *phowa* practice – a preparation for the transference of consciousness at the time of death. From Dudjom Rimpoche he received the Vajrasattva practice and several days of personal instruction and explanation. There were more friends and teachers who guided his way into this charmed realm. Unlike some of the enormous crowd initiations that can occur, in most cases Sangharakshita's initiations and commentaries were intimate, one-to-one affairs. After their time together, Jamyang Khyentse commissioned a thangka for him – a scroll painting illustrating the lineage he had introduced him to. Dudjom Rimpoche came down from his seat to sit on the floor beside the young man, drawing elaborate diagrams into his notebook as he explained the connections between the figures of his lineage.

On giving him the *phowa* initiation, Dilgo Khyentse stated that there was just one man in the region with whom he should discuss this practice. That man was not Tibetan but 'Yogi Chen', a short, stout, cheerful Chinese follower of Chan who lived alone on the edge of town. A virtual hermit, he spent his entire day in meditation, except for the half-hour he would devote every day to writing pamphlets on aspects of meditation practice. Somehow, given his strict and largely secluded regime, he and Sangharakshita enjoyed a warm friendship, and at one point, when the English monk Khantipalo[122] was spending a few months living with Sangharakshita, he let the two young Englishmen pay him a visit each week. They would distil the fruits of their conversation in a book: *Buddhist Meditation, Systematic and Practical.*

Quite how Sangharakshita managed the various elements of his life is something of a marvel. He was now performing a range of meditation practices, writing articles, editing the *Maha Bodhi Journal* as well as his own magazines, running the YMBA, and giving talks around the area. In time he did acquire a place of his own, which became the Triyana Vardhana Vihara. He had his garden, land, and orchards to tend. He was also maintaining connections and friendships throughout the region and corresponding energetically with people around the world.

It was during his time in Kalimpong that he transformed a series of introductory talks on Buddhism into *A Survey of Buddhism*. This book offered an overview of the Buddha's foundational teachings as well as a comprehensive and sometimes critical outline of the relationship between those teachings and the many schools and branches of the Buddhist tradition that evolved in the following millennia. Over the following decades, some of Sangharakshita's ideas would develop further as he found ways of communicating the Dharma in new places, but it was in *A Survey of Buddhism* that he laid down the foundations of his synthetic approach to the foundational Dharma and the development of the Eastern world's Buddhist schools. To this day the *Survey* remains an important entry point to the Buddhist universe, and an essential introduction to Sangharakshita's approach to it.

Fourteen years was a long time, long enough also to lay down drafts of what would become *The Three Jewels*, *The Eternal Legacy*, and the beginnings of his first volume of memoirs, *The Rainbow Road*.

Between Two Worlds

1. Dhardo Rimpoche

The Enlightenment experience is not self-contained in a
one-sided way. The Enlightenment experience contains
an element of 'communication', and contains, therefore,
an element of spiritual friendship, even 'transcendental
friendship', or friendship of the highest conceivable level.[123]

One day in 1949, Dhardo Rimpoche, twelfth incarnation
of that name, and abbot of the Tibetan monastery in Bodh
Gaya, was taking the air on the building's flat roof when to
his astonishment he saw a white man, a European wearing
the robes of a Buddhist monk. 'Look!' he marvelled to his
attendant, pointing out the distant figure, 'See how far the
Dharma has travelled!'

The European was Sangharakshita making his first visit
to the place of the Buddha's Enlightenment. By the time
Sangharakshita had established himself in Kalimpong,
Dhardo Rimpoche had been living there for a while, teaching
his disciples in the region, presiding over rituals at nearby
temples, and establishing the Indo-Tibetan Buddhist Cultural
Institute. Actually, the school was a small cluster of buildings
on a tiny patch of land in the heart of town. With some

prescience, the lama's vision had been to create a space where young Tibetan refugees would have a chance to engage with their own Tibetan culture. In the mornings his young pupils would grapple with the prescribed Indian school curriculum, while afternoon sessions were devoted to Tibetan language, religion, art, and music.

Dhardo Rimpoche and Sangharakshita got to know each other when the latter became involved in helping to sort out a local land dispute. A little later, the Rimpoche proved himself an invaluable mentor as Sangharakshita helped a Tibetan friend to write an article on Buddhism in Tibet for a book being prepared by an American publisher. Through his work on the article, and especially through the connection he made with the Rimpoche, he would receive a comprehensive grounding in the history, schools, doctrines, and practices of Tibetan Buddhism.

The year 1956 marked the 2500th anniversary of the Buddha's death (or *parinirvāna*). As a way of marking the occasion, the Indian government hosted fifty 'eminent Buddhists from the border regions' on a tour of the Indian Buddhist holy places, rather surreally interspersed with visits to hydroelectric dams and similar infrastructural marvels. It was on this journey that a friendship between the Rimpoche and the English monk was sealed, rooted in profound mutual respect. Of Dhardo Rimpoche, Sangharakshita would write:

> I saw that he was adaptable, but he did not stand on his
> dignity as an incarnate lama [...] and that he had a lively

sense of humour. Above all, I saw how uniformly kind he was, how unfailingly mindful. His mindfulness consisted not merely in an absence of anything resembling forgetfulness or inattention, but also in a degree of foresight and preparedness that was almost supernatural.[124]

Sangharakshita would enjoy telling people of the time when the 'eminent monks' found themselves at an important holy place, having been told beforehand that they'd be spending the day at a factory. This was a terrible shock since none of them had come prepared with the candles and incense essential for the offerings they should make at such a place. Well, none except one. Without hesitation, like a magician, Dhardo Rimpoche pulled from the folds of his robes enough candles and incense for everyone.

Many years later, when I visited the Rimpoche at his school, I saw him produce a small blackboard from within those robes. We'd come across a tiny girl, lost and crying in a corner of the playground. As he murmured encouraging words and drew letters from the Tibetan alphabet on the board, her tears turned to chuckles and then into laughter.

As well as giving Sangharakshita another Tārā initiation, the Rimpoche also acted as his witness-preceptor when he took the Bodhisattva vow.

In the Mahāyāna and Vajrayāna worlds, the Bodhisattva embodies the ideal Buddhist life, a life fully committed to the spiritual path not simply for one's own sake but, crucially, for the sake of all beings. The Bodhisattva's life is an uninterrupted

With Dhardo Rimpoche, Kalimpong, 1967

act of altruism, no less energetic for being rooted in the paradoxical insight that there is no such thing as an individual 'self' to liberate and therefore no beings to save. Down on the ground, in the here and now, the vow manifests in the purity of the aspiration, and one's attempt to act out its implications among the everyday realities of life in samsara.

Life in Kalimpong was very full and not always easy, not least when some of the people around Sangharakshita got caught up in gossip or conflict. At such times he could feel isolated, and would turn for guidance and inspiration to the literature of the Bodhisattva ideal, 'one of the sublimest spiritual ideals that humankind has ever seen'.[125] He'd felt inspired to take the Bodhisattva vow for some time, but was reluctant to take it as a merely ritual act. The vow would only have its true impact, he believed, if he made it in the presence of someone he considered to be a Bodhisattva. As time went by, and as he got to know the Rimpoche, he knew he'd met such a person.

For his part, Dhardo Rimpoche's impression of Sangharakshita was of someone wholeheartedly dedicated to the Dharma with an exceptionally sharp mind, able to grasp Dharma points very quickly:

When we talked about profound aspects of Buddhism he had no difficulty at all in understanding them – with ease. Not only this but, at the same time, he was able to put it all into practice and teach others. Ordinary people cannot understand deep points of Dharma so easily and are not in a position to teach to others. His high level of motivation and dedication to the study of Buddhism encouraged and inspired me to study Buddhism even more seriously and in greater depth.[126]

Their friendship would thrive and bring them great joy for the next ten years. When the Rimpoche and I met in 1982, he mused on an unexpected effect of the friendship: 'I have many Tibetan disciples, here and in Tibet. But I could not teach them in the way I could teach Sangharakshita, or at least not as quickly as I could teach him. For them I am the high lama, they see me as "up there", so although they listen to my teachings, it can take them a long time to understand what I am trying to communicate. But as Sangharakshita and I became friends I found I could teach him very easily and quickly, at least in part because we were close friends. This was something I hadn't experienced before, and I found it very interesting.'

2. Dr B.R. Ambedkar

What will you say to those
Whose lives spring up between
Custom and circumstance
As weeds between wet stones,
Whose lives corruptly flower
Warped from the beautiful,
Refuse and sediment
Their means of sustenance –
What will you say to them?

[...]
Or these dim shadows which
Through the pale gold tropic dawn
From the outcaste village flit
Balancing on their heads
Baskets to bear away
Garbage and excrement,
Hugging the wall for fear
Of the scorn of their fellow men –
What will you say to them?[127]

Whether or not any of those fifty 'eminent Buddhists from the border regions' realized it, something significant took place in Delhi when they paused there. At Sangharakshita's suggestion, they paid a visit to Dr Bhimrao Ramji Ambedkar.

One of the twentieth century's outstanding heroes, Ambedkar was at the time of Independence the undisputed leader and voice of India's 'untouchable' masses.

In Hindu India, to be born into an 'untouchable' subcaste condemned you to the lowest stratum of society. Your touch, and even sight in some cases, was considered polluting. Forbidden any kind of education, religious or secular, you would live on the outskirts of the town or village, your allotted role being to perform the most degrading tasks with no hope of uplift. The arrangement had persisted for so long that scholars still debate its origins – so long that the Buddha is recorded as condemning its early signs 2,500 years ago. The British defined these people, who made up some 17 per cent of the Indian population, as 'Scheduled Castes or Classes'. Gandhi rebranded them as 'Harijans', the 'Children of God'. They referred to themselves, and still do, as 'Dalits', 'the oppressed'.

By 1956, the newly drafted constitution of independent India had made the practice of untouchability illegal, and reserved a set percentage of educational opportunities, seats in Parliament, and jobs in government service for members of that community. Almost incredibly, the committee that drafted the constitution was chaired by a man who had been born an 'untouchable' in 1891. This was India's first law minister, Dr Bhimrao 'Babasaheb' Ambedkar.

Thanks to his father's position in a regiment of the British imperial army, the support of a benevolent maharaja, and above all his exceptional mind, the young Bhimrao achieved an unprecedented level of education for a person born into that community. Even to matriculate was rare enough to spark a major celebration in his locality, but Bhimrao went further, to a degree in economics and political science at Bombay University and then to Columbia University in New York, and finally to the London School of Economics.

With a range of degrees including a DSc in economics, and an LLDS (Doctor of Laws), he earned his living as a barrister while devoting most of his time and immense resources of energy, intelligence, and, it has to be said, outrage to the liberation of his people from the 'hell of caste'. He wrote books, founded social-welfare and educational projects, unions, a political party, and fought innumerable battles as a lawyer and campaigner. Unlike Gandhi, who saw the traditional arrangement of Indian society along caste lines as a basis for stability, Ambedkar abhorred untouchability and the sickness of a society that so complacently accepted, promoted, and depended on it.

Outwardly, the constitution he drafted went some way towards setting things right, but, with 80 per cent of the Indian population still living in villages, the practice of untouchability continued unabated, unchallenged by local authorities or law-enforcement agencies. Ambedkar tried to get more reforms through Parliament, but, when he failed, and then lost his ministerial position, he refocused his attention on a radically different strategy.

Years earlier, in a speech delivered before his political prominence, he'd vowed, 'Unfortunately I was born a Hindu, but I will not die a Hindu.'[128] It was now time to redeem that promise and lead his people out of the Hindu fold to a place where they might find dignity, self-respect, and confidence. He'd once said: 'My social philosophy may be said to be enshrined in three words: liberty, equality and fraternity. Let no one, however, say that I have borrowed my philosophy from the French Revolution. I have not. My philosophy has roots in religion and not in political science. I have derived them from the teachings of my Master, the Buddha.'[129]

In principle, Buddhism was the obvious choice. Founded by a human being who through his own efforts had awoken to a state of moral and spiritual perfection, it spoke not just to the dignity of the individual but to the potential lying within us all, irrespective of race, class, or caste. But to meet the scale of the challenge, were the Dalits to convert to Buddhism, he saw that Buddhism, as an institution at work in the world, would have to be reformed, reborn even. It needed a new generation of teachers, willing to practise what they preached and to get out into the world to preach with conviction. Looking around, he saw little or no sign of any candidates. Worse, the president of the Maha Bodhi Society, the most prominent Buddhist organization in India, was a Hindu Brahmin.

While he delayed announcing his decision to convert to Buddhism, he was energetically courted by representatives of the other major religions, as well as by the Communist Party. He had about 80 million followers, after all – why wouldn't they seek his favour? Incredibly, no senior Buddhist figures sought him out or showed any interest when he made contact with them. Even so, he couldn't shake off his leaning towards Buddhism, and wrote an essay for the *Maha Bodhi Journal*: 'The Buddha and future of his religion'.

Sickened by his encounters with the practice of untouchability, whether in villages or ashrams, Sangharakshita had been aware of Ambedkar and his mission for a while. After reading the Doctor's article in the *Journal*, he wrote to him, outlining the experiences that had led him to found a Young Men's Buddhist Association. If Buddhism had a future in India or anywhere else, it would call on the fresh energy of a new generation, uncorrupted by the complacent formalism of existing Buddhist institutions.

'What can your Maha Bodhi Society do for us, with a Bengali Brahmin as its president?' was Ambedkar's opening sally when the two of them met for the first time in Bombay. But when Sangharakshita assured him that the situation at the Society upset him just as much, relations turned warmer, and they settled into a friendly conversation about the state of Buddhism in India, Ambedkar's hopes, and Sangharakshita's projects. They parted on good terms. It would be a couple of years before they'd meet again.

By now ageing visibly and racked with arthritis, Ambedkar had made his final decision to convert to Buddhism. He wanted to set a movement of 'mass conversion' in motion by organizing an initial event for hundreds of thousands of his followers. How though, he asked, did one actually *become* a Buddhist? Sangharakshita explained that it would involve a simple ceremony, led by an ordained monk, consisting in the recitation of the Three Refuges, the traditional formula expressive of one's commitment to the ideals and values of Buddhism, along with the five 'lay precepts', an ethical training of refraining from killing or harming living beings, taking the not-given, sexual misconduct, false speech, and taking intoxicants that cloud the mind.

Hearing that any ordained monk could officiate at such a ceremony, Ambedkar asked the young Englishman whether he could perform it. But Sangharakshita's response was to urge Ambedkar to approach U Chandramani, the Burmese monk in Kusinārā who had conducted his own *śrāmaṇera* ordination. U Chandramani was the most senior Buddhist monk in India, so his participation would give the ceremony the necessary impact and attract attention from the wider Buddhist world. After all, the new Buddhists would need all the help and support they could get.

Sadly, the invitation arrived late. Sangharakshita was in Gangtok, committed to spending time with the maharaja of Sikkhim. He was thus unable to be in Nagpur on 14 October 1956, when Dr Ambedkar recited those refuges and precepts in U Chandramani's presence, before turning to 380,000 of his followers and leading them in reciting the same formula. He also led them in reciting an additional twenty-two vows he'd composed, representing a thoroughgoing rejection of Hinduism and untouchability and a clear commitment to practise the eightfold path of Buddhism.

Even though critics tried to dismiss these conversions to Buddhism as a political stunt and claim that they were merely nominal, Ambedkar's vows underlined the spirit of his vision. The plan was about social transformation on the basis of personal transformation. At a stroke he had unleashed a peaceful 'Dhamma Revolution'.

It was just a few weeks after the ceremony when those fifty eminent Buddhists gathered around the Doctor in the garden of his Delhi residence. They'd come to congratulate him, but found him weary almost to death and in despair at his failing physical energy. The end couldn't be far away.

He spoke so softly that only Sangharakshita, leaning in very close, could hear him. There was so much to do, he said. What would happen to his people if he wasn't there to guide them? How could they possibly understand the significance of what they'd done? It wasn't enough to have converted in a single ceremony. They'd have to be taught, helped to *become* Buddhists and live as Buddhists if they were to derive the benefits from their conversion, not just for themselves but for the good of India. His voice was so quiet, his mouth so close, the conversation so intimate in its way that Sangharakshita experienced it as a kind of transmission, the passing on of the burden.

Amazingly, Ambedkar's health rallied briefly over the following days, allowing him to visit Kathmandu on 20 November to deliver a talk on 'Buddhism and Karl Marx'.

But three weeks later, just six weeks after the first mass-conversion ceremony, Sangharakshita was back in Poona, staying with Dr Mehta, when he felt an unaccountable impulse to visit Nagpur, the heartland of Ambedkar's movement. Dr Mehta strongly advised against the idea, claiming he'd received a divine message that Sangharakshita should definitely stay. Sangharakshita ignored the warning and took a train, reaching Nagpur just a few hours before terrible news arrived – that 'Babasaheb', Dr Ambedkar, had died.

Silence is just not known in an Indian town or crowd. The effect of tens of thousands of people walking in complete silence from the town's Buddhist localities towards Kasturchand Park, a large public space in the heart of town, created an eerie atmosphere. There was nothing stage-managed about it. It was a silence of utter grief and despair, of having nothing to say, nothing anyone could think of saying. Dr Ambedkar had been more than a leader or politician, he'd been a saviour and a father. The grief was visceral, as was the fear that all hope was gone.

The affliction spread to the movement's leaders. Witnesses remember how, one by one, they'd get up to address the crowd but couldn't speak. Their grief and the sense of hopelessness were just too great. But then they saw an English monk climb onto the seat of a rickshaw, doing what he could to offer encouragement. He reminded them that Ambedkar's legacy was in their hands. It was now up to them to follow Ambedkar's leadership and take advantage of his final, most profound gift. They'd taken the step of freeing themselves from their 'untouchable' status in the Hindu world. Now, the riches of the Buddha's teaching and example were open to them. There was no reason for the Dhamma Revolution to die along with their great leader. 'At that moment, we didn't want to hear about politics or anything of that sort. People were very much afraid that Babasaheb's death might be some kind of punishment. There was a conversion, yes? And then, suddenly, there was a death, yes? People had great fear. They wanted more than anything to be given some confidence in the Dharma.'[130]

Here and over the next three days, during which he gave more than thirty talks, he did what he could to keep hope alive, vowing that he would help the new converts to make their conversion meaningful. Of those few days he would write:

> My own spiritual experience during this period was most
> peculiar. I felt that I was not a person but an impersonal
> force. At one stage I was working quite literally without any
> thought, just as one is in samādhi. Also I felt hardly any
> tiredness – certainly not at all what one would have expected
> from such a tremendous strain. When I left Nagpur I felt
> quite refreshed and rested.[131]

From then on his year would be split between Kalimpong and extended visits to the plains where, with very few other monks taking any interest, he gave hundreds of talks, conducted conversion ceremonies, and developed a connection with Ambedkar's close followers that would endure for the rest of their lives.

On the plains, his energy amazed people. They'd struggle to keep up as he walked from locality to locality, village to village, to visit people, give talks, and offer guidance. Out on the road he'd eat anything, sleep anywhere, on a stubbly field or in a cow barn, on hot days and cold. In between, whenever he was in Bombay, he'd stay with Dr Mehta and enjoy some comfort and access to modern conveniences. I asked his regular translator of the time, and a good friend, Dharmarakshita, what his Buddhist friends thought of him staying with a rich Parsee:

'None of us had any money or food, so he was doing us a favour by finding his own lodgings. Anyway, so long as we could use him, why should we worry where he stayed?'

But didn't it seem strange that one of the most prominent monks on the scene should have been an Englishman?

'Why should it seem strange? Very few monks were Indian anyway. They came from Burma, Thailand, Sri Lanka.... Naturally, we assumed they came from England also.'[132]

These tours cemented a relationship with Dr Ambedkar's followers that would occupy his last ten years in India – and indeed the rest of his life. For it would be just ten years after the first ordinations in England that members of Sangharakshita's new order would start activities in India and establish what is now a major branch of the Triratna Order and Community in that vast land.

Sangharakshita's connection with Ambedkar, his writings, and his movement of mass conversion ignited his appreciation of the Dharma as a force for social change. He had always known as a fundamental axiom that Enlightenment expresses itself as wisdom *and* compassion. He knew too that the Buddha had told his first sixty disciples to go forth, no two in the same direction, to teach the Dharma for the happiness and welfare of the many. But he would say in later years that it was only when he encountered Ambedkar that he truly came to appreciate the depth, even inevitability, of the relationship between Buddhism and the transformation of society – that the formula 'wisdom and compassion' can be equally expressed in terms of liberation of self *and* world.

At that time, Sangharakshita had no way of knowing that his Western disciples would one day continue his work among Ambedkar's followers. In fact, at the time he had no idea that he would ever have Western followers. So far as he knew, he would be spending the rest of his life in India.

But that would change when he received a letter from Christmas Humphreys, high-court judge, author and president of the London Buddhist Society. The tiny English Buddhist community had got itself tangled in a factional split, and Humphreys wondered whether Sangharakshita, being the senior-most monk of British origin, might pay a visit and bring things back into harmony. Sangharakshita sat on the invitation for a while, but in 1964, after fourteen years in Kalimpong, he boarded a plane for London.

A Visit to England

Inside, the panelled room was full
Of ladies and gents so refined,
All talking about their previous births
And how it was all in the mind.

They talked so loud, and they talked so long,
That they never even heard
What I'd come five thousand miles to say –
No, not a single word.

For they only wanted to sit and gaze
At my yellow robe so exotic,
And watched the gradual growth of my hair
With a fascination neurotic.[133]

As the taxi reached its destination, Christmas Humphreys
made the suggestion that Sangharakshita could think of
himself as 'the Buddhist vicar of Hampstead'. For this
pleasant and wealthy corner of London was where the English
Sangha Trust, ostensibly a Theravāda organization, had
located its Vihara in hopes of attracting the intellectuals who
supposedly roamed its streets. One wonders what Humphreys
was expecting. Indeed, what was anyone expecting? They

were hoping Sangharakshita would heal the tensions running through the British Buddhist community, but none of them knew him very well.

Humphreys could probably remember his surprise on meeting the eighteen-year-old responsible for the *Middle Way* article on 'The unity of Buddhism' back in 1943. He'd met up with him briefly a few times during visits to India, even in Kalimpong. He would have known too that Sangharakshita's passage through the Eastern Buddhist world had been less than usual. In Kalimpong, Sangharakshita's path had carried him from the Burmese Theravāda lineage of his preceptors into the Chinese Mahāyāna with Mr Chen and into the major Vajrayāna schools with Dhardo Rimpoche and a host of Tibetan teachers and initiators. His involvement in Ambedkar's movement of mass conversion had associated his name with a nascent social revolution. From his contributions to Buddhist magazines and *A Survey of Buddhism*, they would have known him to be knowledgeable, broadly experienced, and well recognized in the East as a writer and commentator. But he was also something of a one-off. How would it work out?

As for Sangharakshita, even before coming face to face with the opposing parties in the rift, his journal-reading and correspondence had alerted him to the divide. Actually, the nature of the divide hadn't surprised him, for it was the product of certain conditions, endemic to the Western approach to Buddhism, that he'd already noticed. There would be those, influenced by a post-Reformation distrust of religious rites and rituals, who would be attracted by what they saw as Buddhism's philosophical, ethical approach to life, refreshingly free, or so they thought, of idols, rituals, and 'religious clap-trap'. Others, seeking an antidote to the alienating effect of modern life, would be drawn by the hope of otherworldly experience. This being the case, he once said, 'One might well have predicted, at the end of the last century, which forms of Buddhism would be most popular in Britain during the first half of the twentieth century: Theravāda and Zen – Theravāda as representing a code of ethics, and Zen as representing experience.'[134]

It was just such a split that had prompted Humphreys to invite Sangharakshita to visit England. The key protagonists were two prominent Buddhist institutions, the staunchly Theravādin Hampstead Buddhist Vihara, funded by the English Sangha Trust, and the Buddhist Society, an inter-denominational society devoted to encouraging the study and practice of Buddhist principles, but at that time leaning towards a fascination with Zen.

Sangharakshita was expecting to stay in England for about six months. He'd do what he could to bring harmony, and in the meantime contribute to the spread of Buddhism in his native land. Based on his reading and conversations, his best estimate was that, aside from immigrants from Buddhist countries, there were at most 200 people in Britain engaged in Buddhist practice.

Settling into the Vihara, he was disappointed if not particularly surprised to find the resident community, a small, multinational handful of monks with a couple of lay supporters, as complacent and self-indulgent as some of those he'd met out East. From the outset he was virtually ignored, the focus of attention being the charismatic figure of Ananda Bodhi, a Canadian monk, five years younger than Sangharakshita, and ordained like him within the Burmese Theravāda tradition. In *Moving Against the Stream*, Sangharakshita recorded his memories of breakfast the day after his arrival:

> There was a choice of four or five different hot drinks, and at the centre of the table, besides jam, marmalade, and honey, there were various spreads quite new to me. In my own monastery in Kalimpong we drank only tea, and jam had been seen on only one occasion when, plums being unusually cheap that year, we had made a couple of dozen jars of it. As I was going upstairs to my room after the meal I heard the oldest of the novices ordering supplies on the phone. 'You've only two kinds of salmon?' he was saying. 'Then send the more expensive kind.'[135]

As it turned out, breakfast was the only time when the Vihara's residents came together. The conversation was dominated by Ananda Bodhi, who'd recently appeared as a guest speaker at the Fifth International Congress of Psychotherapists in London, where he'd mixed with luminaries such as Julian Huxley and R.D. Laing.

Perhaps this measure of worldly attention had prompted him to expect a position as the focus of attention as his natural right. Sangharakshita sat quietly by as Ananda Bodhi regaled his listeners with tales of his encounters with the populace beyond the Vihara's doors. Apparently, he'd interrupted a session of the Psychotherapists' Congress in order to assert the effectiveness of meditation as a cure for schizophrenia; on another occasion he'd sprinkled his audience at the Cambridge University Buddhist Society with jelly.

As Ananda Bodhi told his stories, Sangharakshita was ignored, an extraordinary lapse of monastic etiquette, he being not just the senior-most monk present but now the Vihara's incumbent. In such a Theravāda setting, where points of etiquette matter almost more than anything else, it was astonishing. On a personal level, Sangharakshita took it easily in his stride. He'd been an outsider of one kind or another for much of his life, and found the position generally offered more benefits than difficulties. And for now, in this new setting, he was content to observe the dynamics, get a sense of the people, and let his intuitive faculties feel the mood. Within hours of entering the country, he was getting a first-hand glimpse of the conditions at play behind one side of the rift he'd been asked to heal.

When Ananda Bodhi had confronted those psychiatrists with his claim for the healing power of meditation, he would have been talking about the particular practice he focused on. This was an intense but, in Sangharakshita's view, crude variation on a traditional meditation practice from the Burmese insight tradition. Bringing a refined level of mindful attention to the flow of conditions surrounding even the simplest of physical and mental actions, one could, in appropriately supportive conditions, and with experienced guidance, begin to recognize and deconstruct the reactive mechanisms behind the habit, ultimately, of imagining a fixed *self* directing those actions. In Ananda Bodhi's sessions, ready or not, the participants were thrown into a pressure cooker of all-day silence, long meditation sessions, and retreats during which they'd get just four hours of sleep a night. For Westerners, unused to sitting still for long under any circumstances, let alone cross-legged on the floor, physical pain could be a constant companion. Those who complained about their pain would be assured that it was a sign they were on the brink of transcendental insight into the Noble Truth of suffering. Among his new duties Sangharakshita found himself visiting a few of Ananda Bodhi's former meditation students in mental institutions.

Despite eccentricities, such as a preponderance of books on Christianity and the occult in the Vihara's library, the place was set up along traditional Theravādin lines. This is why, in the end, one of the monks, perhaps less in thrall to Ananda Bodhi than others, pointed out that Sangharakshita should be treated with more respect, and offered him the leader's embroidered sitting cushion in the shrine room. Then, when an indignant Ananda Bodhi took himself away on a teaching trip, Sangharakshita was moved into the 'abbot's room'. Before long, Ananda Bodhi moved out altogether, first establishing a retreat centre in Scotland and then returning to Canada.

With his admiration for Zen and championing of D.T. Suzuki, Christmas Humphreys was thought by some to be rebranding the ecumenical Buddhist Society as a Zen monoculture – with Zen being presented as a split-off from Buddhism, a path in its own right. Things hadn't gone too far yet, but they'd gone far enough to sow not only turbulence within the Society, but hostility towards the Theravādin dogmatism of the Vihara.

The fading of Ananda Bodhi's influence and his departure had gone some way to calm the tensions. Now Sangharakshita made a point of giving talks and meditation classes at the Society as well as at the Vihara. He would also give talks on neutral territory, at the London College of Psychic Science, and visit Buddhist groups up and down the country. Although his ecumenical approach offended a few extremists on each side of the divide, the moderates were relieved and appreciated his willingness to make himself so available.

Those of his talks that have been preserved on tape offer a sense of the direction he was taking. Many of them dealt with reliably basic topics such as the three *laksana*s ('marks' of conditioned existence) and the twelve *nidāna*s (links of conditioned co-production), and they included a series of talks on Zen. These latter, with their alluring titles, would have whetted appetites for the kind of Zen magic that was popular at the time: 'A special transmission outside the scriptures', 'No dependence on words and letters', 'Direct pointing to the mind', and 'Seeing into one's own nature and realizing Buddhahood'. What his listeners received as he located the Zen tradition clearly within the total tradition, was an authoritative, challenging invitation to the heart of the Buddhist life. In 'Buddha, God and man' and elsewhere, he explored some of the Christian cultural assumptions that lead to misconceptions about Buddhism. Another talk, 'Evolution, lower and higher', saw him experimenting for the first time with a model he'd apply in years to come as he looked for ways to naturalize Buddhist discourse in this new environment.

As for those tensions in the Buddhist community, his main conclusion was that they had their origins in the intellectual or emotional preferences of people who, when it came down to it, knew very little about Buddhism and had practised it even less. The unifying antidote, he decided, would be an emphasis on practice, but appropriate to their level of experience.

As a matter of urgency, he wanted to give people an alternative to Ananda Bodhi's rather extreme approach to meditation teaching, and the disturbing mental states his variant could lead to. 'Alienated awareness' was the term he coined for such a state – one in which the meditator's close *attention* to an experience, of taking a step or lifting a teacup, say, became so wilfully prioritized that the practitioner would fail to *experience* the actual felt sensations of the movement. He therefore guided people into a more gentle meditation on the breath, and for balance introduced sessions of the *mettā bhāvanā*, the development of loving-kindness.

On weekend retreats and at the Buddhist Society's annual summer school he also introduced a 'sevenfold puja', a devotional practice involving the recitation of verses drawn from Śāntideva's *Bodhicaryāvatāra*, recited in call and response, and interspersed with the chanting of the Three Refuges and five lay precepts in Pali. Through the puja, practitioners would be guided in an imaginative journey into the heart-mind of the Bodhisattva, the ideal Buddhist, an archetype of absolute compassion. The popularity of these sessions, which brought a new level of emotional and imaginative engagement to their Buddhist lives, surprised some of the old guard who'd never thought such things would be tolerated on our shores, especially not the burning of incense.

Sangharakshita was reassured, though, to find there was an appetite for real Dharma practice in England waiting to be tapped and nurtured in the right way. Writing in *The Buddhist* in 1965, not very long after arriving in England, he was ready to share his thoughts. In essence he was defining an approach to the introduction of Buddhism that, he believed, could work in the West:

> While an English Buddhist might feel attracted to one
> form of Buddhism more than others [...] his loyalties are
> not exclusive, and occasional lapses from grace apart, he
> refuses to carry with him over into Buddhism the narrow
> sectarianism which disgusted him in Christianity and which
> was, perhaps, one of the main reasons for his abandoning
> that religion.
>
> Such liberalmindedness may disappoint, even irritate,
> those Eastern Buddhists who, failing to understand both the
> spirit of Buddhism and the realities of the current situation,
> would like to see their own school of Buddhism and their
> own version of the Dharma established in the West to the
> exclusion of all others; but for the English Buddhist, with
> his wider (sometimes deeper) knowledge of the Buddha's
> Teaching, and his greater objectivity, no other attitude than
> one of liberalmindedness is possible. [...]

The English Buddhist has, most often, been attracted to Buddhism on account of the spiritual principles of which it is the embodiment – principles which he tries, with varying degrees of success, to put into practice in his own life. He is much less interested in the various national cultures wherein, throughout the traditionally Buddhist countries of the East, these principles are embedded. Generally he tends to believe that, as the Dharma becomes acclimatized in this country, it will tend more and more to express itself, through the mouths of its qualified native exponents, in terms of the best indigenous thought and culture. English Buddhism, he hopes, far from remaining a frail transplant carefully sheltered from the chill northern blast in some secluded pseudo-oriental hothouse, will in time develop into a sturdy and vigorous growth true both to its own high spiritual ancestry and the conditions under which it has now to live and propagate its kind. [...]

Time will no doubt show (and the next few decades will probably be decisive in this respect) that the Buddhists of this country, drawing upon the streams of all available Buddhist traditions, and resolving their differences at the highest attainable level of spiritual experience, are capable of creating a form of Buddhism which, finding comprehensive expression in terms of the best of Western thought and culture, will be able to meet the deepest spiritual needs of Western man.[136]

The above was a rather flattering analysis and vision, given the stage things were at, but Sangharakshita knew what he was doing. His vision would have inspired his friends and followers, even if his words might have offended those who neither agreed with his analysis nor felt ready to embrace the developments his words were pointing to. In the following years, whenever asked why he thought the English Sangha Trust had effectively sacked him, he'd usually explain that his broad take on the Buddhist tradition and his willingness to work with members of both the Trust *and* the Buddhist Society had offended extremists on both sides.

No doubt that played a part, possibly a major part, in the story. But that wasn't the whole of it.

14

Of Monks and Men

What we really need to defend is not the technicalities
of the Vinaya, or the validity and meaning of bhikkhu
ordination, but the fundamental principles of Buddhism
and the significance and value of the spiritual life.[137]

Six months turned into two years, and he was now thinking seriously of staying on to work in the West. His talks, meditation sessions, and retreats were well attended; people were drawn to him and to what he was offering. A few were becoming good friends, and some were helping out at the Vihara. For his part, he was engaging wholeheartedly in the creative challenge of communicating the Dharma in a new context.

Some years before, after initiating him into a meditation practice devoted to Padmasambhava, Kachu Rimpoche had given him an extra name, associated with Padmasambhava: 'Urgyen'. This connection with the great 'Guru Rimpoche' – the spiritual genius who had played a critical role in introducing Buddhism to Tibet – was something Sangharakshita had taken seriously, just as he had taken seriously the Bodhisattva vow he'd made in the presence of Dhardo Rimpoche. Now, fate was confronting him with the opportunity to honour both the name and the vow.

To stay in the West would mean teaching in a post-industrial context, in places where the Dharma had never been taught before. It was an alluring prospect. He was by no means the first person to envisage the renaissance that might come about if Buddhism were to exert its influence on the West. He was certainly aware of Schopenhauer's thoughts on the matter. Now, here he was, a Buddhist and a Westerner. He was equipped and qualified to play a part in making such a thing come about.

Meanwhile, he was living at the Hampstead Buddhist Vihara and directing its affairs. As the embroidered-cushion episode had shown, he was working in a context where details of form, status, and tradition outweighed most other considerations. Even at the Buddhist Society's summer school his decision to dine with the laity rather than in the partitioned-off area reserved for 'members of the sangha' caused ripples. Was this the kind of life he wanted? Was this the kind of Buddhism the modern world needed?

He had taken ordination in Theravāda contexts. In his spiritual heart, though, things had never been so straightforward. He respected the Theravāda tradition but he was not uncritical. He felt uncomfortable with the triumphalist claims of orthodoxy made by some of its contemporary exponents, and the extent to which it prioritized external forms over commitment. His thoughts on these matters had been amply recorded in his writings.

He was deeply inspired by the Bodhisattva ideal, as well as by the philosophical perspectives of Mahāyāna schools. With the support of his Tibetan teachers, his curiosity and spiritual impulses had flowed naturally and without inhibition towards Vajrayāna meditations and rituals. At his Triyana Vihara back in Kalimpong, he embodied a Triyana approach, not out of confusion but as a matter of spiritual principle:

> As the years went by I increasingly found that the more
> I related Buddhism to the spiritual life of the individual
> Buddhist the more I saw it in its deeper interconnections
> within itself, and the more I saw it in its deeper
> interconnections within itself the more I saw it not as a
> collection of miscellaneous parts but as an organic whole.[138]

Despite living in a tiny bastion of Theravāda orthodoxy, he was clear about what needed to be done and the way he wanted to teach. He saw no need to be limited by the expectations that came with the Vihara package.

He never doubted his devotion to the Buddha or the Buddhist path. And there had been a time in his life when he'd wanted, with an unbearable intensity, to become a monk. But living as a monk in a Theravādin setting came with such a burden of detail: what time of day one could eat, which shoulder should be covered by the robe and which exposed, who sat where, who spoke when... These were matters of great importance. They were considered the best way to live as a true follower of the Buddha in this impure world. They also signalled the continuity of an unbroken lineage, and so confirmed a monk's qualification to 'make merit' for lay supporters by accepting their donations. It was more than personal idiosyncrasy that had prompted U Chandramani to insist on the correct pronunciation of Pali words during Sangharakshita's ordination ceremony. The details mattered in that world, but how much did they matter in this one?

Sangharakshita would have pondered these questions under any circumstances. They had to do with important issues of principle, of general interest and concern. But there was something more personal that gave his reflections an extra edge.

The legitimacy of his higher ordination at Sarnath hung on the details as much as anything. Following prescribed custom, the ritual ordination arena, the *sīmā*, had been specially consecrated, and a specific number of monks, spotlessly pure with regard to the monastic rules, had been required to form a quorum. When, some years after the ceremony, he discovered that at least one of the monks had not been 'pure', in that he had a mistress, 'The discovery left me in a quandary. If the supposed *bhikkhu* was not really a *bhikkhu* then I was not really a *bhikkhu* either, his presence within the *sīmā* having invalidated the entire proceedings and rendered my ordination ceremony null and void.'[139]

All the same, he carried on with life as before on the reasonable assumption that he was a monk because he felt like one, wanted to live like one, and had after all been seen to go through an ordination ceremony. However, it occurred to him that, if such a thing had happened to him, then it must have happened to others countless times through the ages. If the presence of just one impure monk in an ordination *sīmā* rendered the person or persons being ordained impure, and therefore themselves technically unqualified to participate in a *sīmā* for someone else, then, through a network of chain reactions, it had to be recognized that the fabled purity of the lineage, and thus the charismatic basis of a monk's status within that world, was rooted in a myth.

In a way, none of this really mattered. After all, nobody talked about it, and Sangharakshita could hardly have been alone in noticing this inconvenient truth. There were still plenty of good, sincere monks living under the Theravāda banner. Nor did these considerations dent his respect for renunciation, the fellowship of monastic life, or the debt Buddhists owed to Theravādin monastics down the ages for their commitment to preserving the teachings and making them known. The system worked, and in most ways worked benignly, so long as there were good monks in the mix and so long as the laity drew comfort, inspiration – and merit – from supporting the sangha.

But here, in a country with no Buddhist history and no historical relationship with Eastern lineages and orthodoxies, he had to wonder what part monastic ordination and monastic purity would, even should, play. It seemed significant that the first Buddhist monk he'd ever seen, at that Blitz-time Wesak celebration, was U Thittila, who spent his nights in overalls searching for survivors in bombed-out buildings. According to monastic discipline, his failure to wear robes made him a bad monk, but without question he was a good Buddhist.

These were among the questions running through Sangharakshita's mind. They had to do with the future of

Buddhism in the West, for sure, but they also had something to do with him. How much would it help and how much might it hinder if he wore robes and kept his hair cropped, didn't eat beyond midday, and so on? Would that attract people to the Dharma or would it put them off? What was the appropriate balance between one's commitment to the Three Jewels and such details of lifestyle? These were serious and timely thoughts. But at the Vihara, even among members of the Buddhist Society, he was on his own with them.

And this is when Terry Delamere comes into the story. A *deus ex machina*, a muse perhaps, certainly a catalyst for change.

15

Terry Delamere

The time has come
For us to lay aside the masks
Painted hieratic masks
The time has come
For us to hang up the gorgeous costumes in the greenroom
cupboard
To leave the brilliantly lit stage
The applause
And to go home
Through deserted streets
To a quiet room
Up three flights of stairs
And to someone perhaps
With whom we can be
Ourselves[140]

Ten years younger than Sangharakshita, which would have made him around thirty at the time, Terry was a photographer working for a successful advertising agency. Suffering from recurring depression, he experienced his marriage and life in general as meaningless. When Terry was ten, his father had made him kill rabbits every Saturday morning, ready to be sold in his butcher's shop. The memory still haunted him, as did his bitterness and a nagging sense of inferiority thanks to being taken out of school at the age of fifteen. His parents, for and from whom he'd never experienced any feelings of love, had decided that more education wouldn't make any difference to his prospects. His marriage collapsed into atrophy and then divorce when his wife admitted she'd been having an affair with his closest friend at work. He turned for help to psychiatry. Despite the more progressive approaches coming on the scene in the early 1960s, the treatment he was offered included electroconvulsive therapy, carried out under ether. Quite unexpectedly, though, what happened as the ether took hold of his mind set him on a new path. In his memoirs Sangharakshita recalls how Terry described the experience:

> The feeling he had was one of exquisite fineness – a
> fineness he at one stage described as the point of a needle.
> Yet knowing that there was the climax of 'no point' still to
> come he waited and observed. Whereupon he experienced
> a sensation of 'standing in pure knowledge' – a moment of
> total comprehension – that represented a human being's
> perfect and total development. But even this moment of 'no
> point' contained a subtle experience of knowing. It therefore
> was not the absolute experience, which was.... But what it
> was Terry was never able to say.[141]

The experience had been blissfully liberating. Although short-lived, it gave him a glimpse of something absolute, something essential, something that would be totally liberating – if he could only give himself to it. Such glimpses might be triggered, he realized even as he came out of the experience, by accident, as had happened to him under ether; or, he wondered, was it possible that the realm he'd only glimpsed could become one's permanent 'home', perhaps after lifetimes of effort? The very thought of such a long-term path implied so much struggle that, even as he surfaced from the ether-dream, he burst into tears. Even so, he took up Transcendental Meditation and widened his intellectual horizons at the School of Philosophy and Economic Science's London branch. Then, one day, he came across an advert for a talk on 'Buddhism and the problem of death'.

Sangharakshita spoke for ninety minutes on Tibetan attitudes to death, and in particular gave an overview of the *Bardo Thodol*, more commonly known as *The Tibetan Book of the Dead*. Afterwards, Terry waited his turn to have a word. '"I just wanted to tell you",' he said, "that I have seen the pure white light." [...] So unassuming was the young man's demeanour, and so frank and trustful his gaze, that it was impossible for me not to believe that he spoke the truth.'[142] A few days later Terry visited Sangharakshita at the Vihara and shared an account of his life, his ether experience, and his explorations so far.

He was at the next public talk, on 'Mysticism', and afterwards offered Sangharakshita a ride back to the Vihara in his Volkswagen campervan:

Not wanting to trouble him unnecessarily, and thinking that perhaps he could drop me at a convenient Underground

station, I asked him how far in the direction of the Vihara
he was willing to drive.

'I can drive you as far as you like,' was the cheerful
response.

'Could you drive me to India?' I asked, the words
springing unpremeditated to my lips.

'Yes,' he replied, his face lighting up, 'I could.'

Thus began a friendship that was to have 'important consequences for the rest of my life and, through me, for the
future of British Buddhism'.[143]

Before long Sangharakshita would be spending several
evenings a week at Terry's flat, often staying over for the night.
On retreats they'd 'slip away', as Sangharakshita would put it,
after the day's final meditation or puja to find a place where
they could talk, often into the early hours. It was a strong,
intimate friendship, an instant and mutual attraction, and a
meeting of emotional needs. What was going on, and why was
it so important?

There was, and in some quarters remains, a well-worn
narrative that the unguarded intimacy that grew between
them prompted 'the old ladies of Hampstead', as Christmas
Humphreys described them, to assume they were in a homosexual
relationship. Is this what lay behind Sangharakshita's reference to
'important consequences for the rest of my life and, through me,
for the future of British Buddhism'? For it was this atmosphere
of suspicion that led, very possibly more than anything else, to
his rejection by the English Buddhist establishment.

Years later, I interviewed Sangharakshita on the place of sex in the spiritual life.[144] It was a relaxed conversation that veered naturally on and off the record as he talked about sex in general and with easy transparency about his own sexual experiences. When I asked him, point blank, whether his friendship with Terry had involved sex, his immediate response was to laugh: 'But Terry was a complete ladies' man! Sex was never involved.'

Given the decisive role those rumours played in his life, it might seem surprising that Sangharakshita never challenged the rumours. His response, though, was quite matter of fact: 'Well, no one ever challenged me to my face. Nobody asked or told me what they thought. And I considered it beneath my dignity as a monk, which I still was at the time, to raise the subject myself.'

Terry, assailed by depression and suicidal thoughts, yet convinced there was a plane of being on which all mundane struggles are transcended, no doubt talked about himself, his states, his worries, his fears and dreams. He also believed that his relationships with women were hobbled by his lack of sexual responsiveness.

What might Sangharakshita have talked about into those early hours? An instinctive educator, one can imagine him sharing anecdotes of his life, recommending books, enthralling Terry with his knowledge of Buddhist philosophy and metaphysics. And there was probably more. Considering his life up to that point, as a child, as a young man in India, and now in the stifling atmosphere of the Vihara, it must have been liberating to feel able to share himself in his native language with someone who was interested in him as a person, a kindred spirit, rather than as 'the monk'. He might have felt in Terry's burning hunger to be united with 'the clear white light' something that resonated with his own hunger for truth. And as Terry talked about his issues with sex, it's not hard to imagine Sangharakshita's relief in feeling able, finally, to talk to someone about his own. As he wrote many years later,

> In my own country, as in other countries, any kind of homosexual activity was a criminal offence, and there were countries in which it was punishable by death. It therefore behoved me to be very careful what I did or said, or even how I looked at other men. This was not without its consequences for my emotional life. Keeping my feelings to myself became a habit, especially when those feelings were very strong and directed to another man. Many years were to pass before I was able to give expression to such feelings even to a limited extent.[145]

For several reasons, Sangharakshita had felt like an outsider since late childhood, and yet, immersing himself in the words and worlds of Dr Johnson, Goethe, Matthew Arnold, the Romantic poets, not to mention the Greek and Roman philosophers and dramatists, some part of him had been primed for a 'particular friendship', an elective affinity as Goethe put it. It maybe helped that Terry was a good-looking man, but one would be missing the mark by a country mile to assume that the avidity with which they took up their friendship was based on sex.

Terry remained indifferent to Sangharakshita's status as a monk and his role at the Vihara, or for that matter his vision of a Buddhist movement. He was simply drawn to Sangharakshita as a fascinating, wise, and empathic friend, and called him Dennis, or 'D'. He encouraged him to let his hair grow and wear ordinary 'civilian' clothes, at least while staying at the flat. One day they went out and bought a jacket and trousers, the first items of clothing Sangharakshita had owned since selling or burning his possessions in Kasauli. Now he could walk about in London without being the centre of attention. Far from feeling he was living a double life in Terry's company, he was allowing himself an experience of wholeness he'd not known before.

None of this suggests he was any less of a Buddhist or any less committed to the project of teaching the Dharma. Whether he was giving a talk at the Vihara or sitting alone in a pub sipping a Guinness, watching people, feeling his way into the English world and the English mind, he was being himself and feeling free to be himself.

Terry's campervan, or the 'Little Bus' as they called it, was their magic carpet, whisking them not only to and from retreats but also out and about, to Oxford, Stonehenge, Lichfield (an obligatory pilgrimage to Dr Johnson's birthplace), and beyond as Sangharakshita tapped into the culture, ancient and modern, of his new context.

The 'bus' also took them on an extended trip around Europe, to France, Italy, Turkey, and Greece. Day after day

Sangharakshita feasted on galleries, cathedrals, and museums. Regarding contemplation of 'the beautiful' as an intrinsic part of a spiritual life, his capacity to commune with the art and architecture they encountered was insatiable. His memoirs recall in meticulous detail where they camped, what sites they visited, which paintings, statues, frescos, mosaics, or buildings made what kind of impression.

To be in Delphi was a sublime experience. It

> was not holy by virtue of its association with a particular event, at least not of the historical order. Delphi was itself holy. It was not a holy place simply because it was there that Apollo's temple and oracle were located. Temple and oracle were located at Delphi because Delphi was a holy place. It was as if the very earth was holy, and as if this holiness penetrated the rocks and the trees and permeated the air, so that one felt it in the warmth of the sun and drew it in with every breath. Though the temple was in ruins, and though the oracle had been silent for more than a thousand years, Delphi was still a holy place and its influence could still be felt.[146]

Yes, felt by the aesthete and the animist in Sangharakshita, but not by Terry. Terry was finding it tough going. He couldn't keep up, couldn't begin to match his companion's capacity to absorb such a relentless cascade of culture. Labouring, at Sangharakshita's recommendation, with Kant, Schopenhauer, Suzuki (D.T.), and *The Laṅkāvatāra Sūtra*, he struggled with exhaustion and feelings of inferiority. The buildings, paintings, and statues were starting to leave him cold, bored, on the edge, and sometimes over the edge of depression.

Sometimes they'd pass an afternoon in an olive grove or parking lot. This gave Sangharakshita time to read histories, biographies, novels, and dramas, drinking in the cultural heritage of whichever region they were passing through. Relief came for Terry when village lads stopped by to chat with them. Despite the lack of a common language, Terry relished their company and Sangharakshita noticed the change:

> This was only partly due to the obvious inoffensiveness
> of the intruders, if such they could really be called. It was
> also due to the fact that, as could be safely assumed, they
> were not more educated and more knowledgeable than he
> was and that there was no question, therefore, of his being
> at a disadvantage with them. Even had they happened to
> be more educated and knowledgeable, in the absence of a
> common language this would not have become apparent.
> Thus there was no danger of my friend being made to
> feel inadequate and inferior, as sometimes was the case in
> England. [...] The truth was that Terry really liked people,
> and became anxious, and therefore stiff and reserved,
> only when he felt threatened by their superior education
> and knowledge. There were times when I thought he felt
> threatened even by me, though the fact that in certain fields
> he was the more knowledgeable of the two should have
> been enough to rule out any feelings of this kind. I might
> know more about religion and philosophy, but he knew more
> about the practicalities of modern urban living.[147]

Although Sangharakshita might have found it hard to understand how someone could tire of beauty, which for him was a source of constant delight and nourishment, he wasn't blind to Terry's episodes of depression or lacking in sympathy. With what he describes as their 'little chats', which were more likely hours of patient listening and talking, he would coax Terry back onto solid ground.

Terry himself doesn't seem to have resented the imbalance, or rebelled against the situation. The friendship continued undiminished, and deepened over the months. Intriguingly, they even spoke of 'doing something together', as if Sangharakshita could envisage working in some kind of partnership with Terry, despite the latter's lack of interest in the idea of a Buddhist movement.

On their return to England, Sangharakshita gave himself back to his work, supervising the affairs of the Vihara while teaching classes and giving talks there and elsewhere. He kept up his meditation practice, but with so many visitors and so much correspondence he had little or no time for literary work. In some part of his mind, though, he was coming to a decision. He would return to India, but only for a farewell tour. From now on the primary focus of his work would be in the West.

In September 1966 he and Terry were therefore on the move again, not in the 'Little Bus' but on a plane to India. Their first destination was Sarnath where, among other things, Sangharakshita would meet with the Dalai Lama and share his impressions of the Buddhist movement in the UK. When, during the journey from Bombay, the train had stopped in

The farewell tour to India, 1967

Ahmedabad, their carriage was besieged by a host of cheering, chanting Ambedkarite Buddhist converts, jostling to catch a glimpse of Sangharakshita and passing cups of tea and garlands through the carriage windows. One can only imagine what Terry must have thought and how he would have felt to see his friend in this context.

In the coming years, Terry's razor-sharp colour slides would provide the climax to the FWBO's early festival events: there was 'Bhante', as he was known, with the Dalai Lama, with Dhardo Rimpoche, with Kachu Rimpoche, Jagdish Kashyap, Lama Govinda and Li Gotami, Mr Chen, and

Dilgo Khyentse... interspersed with shots of places they passed through. Meeting up with his old friends and teachers, Sangharakshita would tell them about his work, his plans, and his hopes for the future of Buddhism in the West. He asked for and received their blessings for his plans.

Meanwhile, back in England, people were talking and the forces were gathering. Arriving in Kalimpong, he made his way to the Vihara, where a pile of mail was waiting for him:

> One of the first letters to be opened was from the English
> Sangha Trust. It was dated 1st November and was signed
> by George Goulstone in his capacity as one of the Directors
> of the Trust. After assuring me in the most fulsome terms
> of the Trust's deep appreciation of my services to the
> Dharma in England, he went on to inform me that in the
> opinion of the Trust and my fellow Order members my long
> absences from the Hampstead Buddhist Vihara, together
> with what he described as my extramural activities, were
> not in accordance with the Theravāda's high standards of
> discipline and ethics. Moreover, I had not comported myself
> in a manner fitting the religious office that I held in the
> Order. The Trust had therefore decided to seek elsewhere
> for an incumbent of the Vihara. As my work in India was so
> dear to my heart, the letter continued blandly, I might think
> that my allotted task was to remain and serve Buddhism
> in the East. Should I, on careful reflection, consider that
> my work lay in the East, this would be acceptable as a
> reasonable ground for my resignation, and notification to

this effect would be made to the Buddhist Authorities in the West. Should I not feel disposed to take this step, the trustees would feel regretfully obliged to withdraw their support from me. In so doing, they felt sure of having the agreement of the Sangha authorities in England.

'Do you know what this means?' I asked Terry, when I had finished reading the letter. 'It means a new Buddhist Movement!'[148]

It wasn't that he'd never considered the possibility of starting something completely new. He'd discussed the matter with Christmas Humphreys, but given the situation within the English Buddhist community they'd agreed that another Buddhist organization on the scene might just add to the confusion. Until reading that letter he had felt a moral duty to work within the existing context. Now things were different.

He had left for India just a few months before on a wave of goodwill, of being told how much people were looking forward to his return. Indeed, so far had he been from telling anyone that 'his allotted task was to remain and serve Buddhism in the East' that he'd given his solemn word that he would return. Now he was being told his services were no longer required and financial support was no longer available. It was quite a turnaround. At the same time, he saw in an instant that he was free to start something new.

In later years he'd often insist that he'd never thought of himself as an ideal or even suitable person to start a new Buddhist movement. But in one way or another he'd been preparing to accept this challenge ever since he'd written 'The unity of Buddhism', perhaps even since his encounter with *The Diamond Sūtra* at the age of sixteen.

When he arrived back in London in March 1967, his close friends and supporters gathered round, one of them even expressing relief that he'd arrived in one piece, as if he'd even been fearing for Sangharakshita's safety. A trust, established by an English industrialist sympathetic to Buddhism, provided some welcome financial support, and for a while he and Terry shared a flat until Terry moved in with his girlfriend. They saw each other a few times every week, however, and their friendship continued undimmed.

A good friend, a regular at his Vihara classes, ran Sakura, a shop specializing in Asian ornaments and ritual objects, in central London. The building had a tiny basement, but perhaps big enough to offer space for some small meditation classes. Within days a rent was agreed and a lease signed. A few weeks later, on 6 April 1967, twenty-three people crammed into the twelve-by-fourteen-foot space to hear Sangharakshita dedicate the 'Triratna Buddhist Centre' with some lines of dedication composed for the occasion. A new Buddhist movement had been born, and for Sangharakshita a new phase was beginning.

16

A Fresh Start and
a New Kind of Order

Let us do away with the divisions between monastic and
lay Buddhists, between men and women Buddhists, and
between the followers of different sects and schools of
Buddhism. Let us have an integrated Buddhism and an
integrated Buddhist community. Let us base ourselves
firmly and unmistakably upon our common Going for
Refuge to the Buddha, the Dharma, and the Sangha.[149]

A new phase hardly does it justice. It would call on his energy,
faith, imagination, whatever skills and talents he had to offer,
and whatever spiritual qualities he'd developed so far.

Inadequate as he felt, his aspiration was nothing less than
to make the Buddha, Dharma, and Sangha living forces
in the religious and cultural life of the West. And given his
commitment to a non-sectarian approach he would effectively
be doing it on his own.

Getting down to work, he gave his talks and lectures in hired
rooms as before, and ran meditation classes and discussion
groups in the little basement room. Sitting beside the shrine,
with the gaping void of a 'coal hole' behind him, concealed

by a curtain, he introduced people to the mindfulness of breathing and *mettā bhāvanā*, led sevenfold pujas, and answered questions. Those who were around in those days say the place felt warm and quiet, conducive to stilling the mind. With Sangharakshita at its heart, it felt magical and somehow vibrant, with a significance that belied the miniature scale of the setting and Sangharakshita's following.

There wasn't much money to spend on publicity, but people showed up week by week, and some came back for more, so it wasn't long before his former supporters were supplemented by a new batch of regulars. Within a year, he felt confident that there were three women and nine men who had been practising sincerely under his tutelage and whose understanding of the spiritual life resonated with his own. So far as he could tell, they were committed to their practice and to the path. He therefore decided to ordain them. In doing so he would make his new Order, this core community of similarly committed, kindred spirits, a reality.

As historic events go it was modest. It took place on 8 April 1968 with an audience of thirty, in a hired room in central London. Modest, perhaps, but radical, even in some ways revolutionary, for right from the outset he was establishing not only a new Buddhist order but an order composed of men and women with equal status. To underline his conviction that this new Western Buddhist Order was an authentic if non-sectarian addition to the Buddhist tradition, he invited a Zen monk, a Shin priest, and two Theravāda monks to attend and witness the proceedings. Afterwards he wrote:

The twelve people who made up the Western Buddhist Order had 'taken' the Three Refuges and Ten Precepts from me, – had been ordained as *upāsaka*s and *upāsikā*s by me – and their understanding of the meaning of Going for Refuge coincided with mine, at least partly. Like one lamp lighting a dozen others, I had been able to share with them my realization of the absolute centrality of the act of Going for Refuge, and henceforth that realization would find expression not in my life only but also in theirs. Not that the realization in question was something fixed and final. It could continue to grow and develop, and find expression in a hundred ways as yet unthought of.[150]

It was quite a leap. It's unlikely that any of the twelve quite realized what they were taking on, but, as some of Sangharakshita's closest friends and colleagues have commented, he had always tended towards an instinctive preference to relate to people in terms of the potential he saw in them. Even so, the Order was now a reality.

◆

Until the modern era no society had been exposed all at once to scriptures, teachers, and practices from every corner of the Buddhist world. Nor had Buddhism been introduced into such 'global' communities. Buddhist teachers arriving from the East were therefore faced with a set of options. One would be to work faithfully in the style of their 'home tradition', teaching practices and conducting rituals, even building temples in strict conformity with their home heritage. Another would be to start out more or less within the style of their Eastern lineage while gradually adapting their approach to suit Western conditions as time went by.

Or perhaps there was a third possibility, of something traditional *and* new: a practice community grounded firmly in commitment to the Buddha's vision and essential teachings, free from the outset to express itself anew and evolve according to circumstance, and willing to take intelligent advantage of the experience and wisdom accumulated over 2,500 years.

Actually, in Sangharakshita's mind, this third was not just one option among others: it was what the task had always been. In fact it was what the spiritual life, whether of the individual or of an evolving spiritual community, should essentially be about. 'I was simply following an ancient pattern that we find again and again when we look at the history of Buddhism. We find that teachers arise; they study whatever Dharma teachings are available in their time; they then give their own presentation and that attracts people and that develops into a Sangha, into a school or a tradition.'[151]

Those pioneers who established a branch of the Buddhist tradition in new cultures were effective because they managed to understand and address the temperaments and latent spiritual yearnings of the people they met. This was imaginative, sensitive, and intelligent work. It took time, detailed care, constant reflection, and patience. As a result, new sects and schools emerged with distinct practices, new ways of talking Dharma, new myths and new rituals as teachers captured the interest and imagination of their disciples.

So, as the Dharma became naturalized in new countries, its rhetoric and outward manifestations came to reflect not just national dress or national architecture, but the characteristic psychological and spiritual needs and temperaments of people living in those places. Those needs and temperaments varied from place to place, and consequently the way Buddhist missionaries taught, the aspects of the path they emphasized, would vary too. The outcome after 2,500 years of development was an array of schools, each in geographical isolation, differing remarkably in appearance, emphasis, and character. And yet, like so many fingers pointing at the same moon, they were all born of the same intention: to help people reach towards Enlightenment, the ultimate potential of any human being, anywhere.

From the earliest days of his Buddhist life, Sangharakshita seems to have understood this and related to the Buddhist tradition as an organic whole. Something about his initial experience with *The Diamond Sūtra* had allowed him to see through the confusing assortment of Buddhist schools to the essential animating impulse the Buddha had set in motion when he first communicated his experience to others.

Given this core integrity at the heart of Buddhist tradition, why shouldn't the contemporary Buddhist take intelligent advantage of those ways in which gifted teachers had addressed the varieties and levels of human experience?

Of course, handled crudely and carelessly, such an approach could lead people into an eclectic maze. To work as an effective method of spiritual discipline, such an approach would require a continuing effort of selection, experiment, and organization. Those who took up such a path would need education, support, and feedback. They'd also need to know themselves deeply enough to be sure they weren't getting lost or distracted by novelty. The advice Ramdas had so often repeated in his talks at Anandashram might have been on Sangharakshita's mind: to remember the goal at all times – and know what one needs to do right now, today, to attain it.

This isn't something that comes naturally to many of us. We don't always know ourselves as well as we might, or see ourselves as others see us. So, as he brought the FWBO world to life, Sangharakshita encouraged his followers to cultivate the kind of friendships that would keep them on a path rather than lost in a maze. To the extent that he could encourage and enable it, this would be a world of 'spiritual friendship', of *kalyāṇamitratā*.

Looking back to his time with Bannerji/Buddharakshita, even when their connection was fraught with differences and tensions, Sangharakshita remained a loyal friend. He clearly valued that friendship, learned from it and enjoyed sharing his spiritual journey with another person as a common endeavour. He'd thrived during his time and friendship with Kashyap-ji, and in Kalimpong he'd made strong connections with a number of local characters. Bhikkhu Khantipalo wrote warmly of the months he spent with Sangharakshita there, and above all stood Sangharakshita's ten-year friendship with his teacher Dhardo Rimpoche. For Sangharakshita, the Sangha Jewel was more than an optional extra. He enjoyed and truly honoured the experience of spiritual communion as an essential aspect of his spiritual life.

It therefore followed that his new movement would have to emerge from a culture of engaged spiritual friendship. He repeatedly reminded his followers of the Buddha's response to Ananda, that spiritual friendship is 'not half but the whole of the spiritual life', and his advice to the youthfully naive Meghiya on the importance of seeking out 'good friends in the holy life'. Without doubt, he upheld the Sangha Jewel as an ideal in its own right; but he also saw it as an essential working ground: 'We tend to expect that adopting a spiritual life should make everything go more smoothly for us, but that certainly does not always happen. The spiritual life may be a happy one, but it is by no means necessarily easy or free from difficulties and suffering. A properly functioning spiritual community will help to carry us over these hurdles.'[152]

The Order at the heart of his movement would be a vibrant core community, an expanding circle of clearly committed men and women bound by a network of friendships. One could say, as he once put it to me, that the movement, the project, was *about* that community. The Order would be a resource, a priceless refuge for those seeking a path of practice and kindred spirits to share it with. The wider movement would hopefully act as a benign force in the world, but its essential *raison d'être* lay in its function as a bridge between the 'world' and the Order for those seeking such a community.

Now it was time to get organized. Fortunately, this seems to have been something Sangharakshita was well suited for. We've met Sangharakshitas I and II, the monk and the poet. They represented powerful sides of his character. But there was another element in the mix, which now joined the fray. It turned out that he was an exceptionally capable organizational thinker, with an energetic eye for the minutest detail.

So far he'd had few opportunities to develop this aspect of his potential. He'd proved himself a useful administrator during his brief involvements with the Ramakrishna Mission and the Maha Bodhi Society. In Muvattupuzha he'd increased the Ramakrishna Society's membership subscriptions considerably, and he once told me with pride how, in Kalimpong, he'd transformed a neglected orchard on the vihara's land into a valuable source of income. It was now time to direct that side of his mind to the emerging shape and needs of a new Buddhist community.

The facts, that the president of the Maha Bodhi Society had been a Brahmin and that Bodh Gaya, the site of the Buddha's Enlightenment, was governed by a committee dominated by Hindus who regarded the Buddha as an incarnation of Vishnu, had taught him what can happen when an organization is governed by anyone other than those deeply committed to its core aims and values. In his new movement there would be no institutional, subscription-paying membership; anyone who came along would be considered a 'friend'. Any power or directing responsibility would rest in the hands of the spiritually committed. This would be the foundational keystone of the movement's architecture. Everything could follow from that.

He knew that much, but there would be countless more issues to resolve as time went by. Even as he ordained its first twelve members, and for some time afterwards, he was working out the form the Order might finally take, and where it would stand in relation to its historic forebears and its more traditional contemporaries. After all these years, he was still unpacking the implications of the discovery that his higher ordination had been technically invalid, and reflecting on the themes of ordination, lineage, and orthodoxy. Now he had to work out how these questions related to the community he was establishing in the West. Perhaps, above all, would his movement follow tradition and split into a world of laypeople surrounding and supporting a core community of monks and nuns, or emerge as something quite different?

Those first twelve men and women were ordained as *upāsaka*s (m) and *upāsikā*s (f), a label applied in the Eastern context to lay followers. In a talk he gave shortly after the ceremony he allowed himself to think aloud about the possibility of adding three extra levels to the mix: the *mahā upāsaka*, the bodhisattva, and the bhikkhu/bhikkhunī. He did experiment with the two intermediate stages, ordaining a woman as a *mahā upāsikā* and one man as a bodhisattva, but he never did it again. With increasing momentum, his thinking drew him towards a crucial matter of principle, that there can only be, should only be, one clear moment in one's life when one makes that commitment to the spiritual life, one life-defining act of going for refuge. Hence there should be just one ordination.

A central part of his *śrāmaṇera* ordination ceremony in Kusinārā had been the recitation of the formulae of going for refuge, of commitment to the Buddha, Dharma, and Sangha. Significantly, this did not form part of his higher ordination ceremony, the ceremony that actually made him a bhikkhu, a full monk. Instead the formulae he'd recited in call and response on that occasion had to do with the details of a monk's lifestyle, and he knew for sure that he wasn't going to replicate a system that prioritized lifestyle over commitment.

In the context of his own life, to follow the renunciate aspirations of his youth and the discipline of a monk's life had brought him great happiness and satisfaction. At times it had also brought tension, not just in the wrestling match between Sangharakshitas I and II, the scholar and the dreamer, but sometimes in the struggle between the spirit and the flesh. He had found the challenge of sublimating mundane instinct and impulse to be an important and creative working ground. For many years, as his poetry and essays demonstrate, he'd considered that work a positive, even indispensable, aspect of his spiritual life. But, no matter how valuable, that had been a practice, a working-out of his commitment to the Three Jewels, not the commitment itself.

With Terry's encouragement, he felt free to loosen the restraints. Living a monk's lifestyle was not the way he wanted to practise. The future would involve constant organizational demands, untold numbers of people to engage with, countless triggers for creative reflection. There would be other challenges to meet. At this moment in his life, the current of his commitment was encouraging him to be free.

The lengthening hair and 'civilian' clothes didn't represent any weakening of his commitment to the Three Jewels or to the project. Nor did his friends and followers seem concerned by them, even if a few of them knew enough about Eastern Buddhism to recognize the extent of the shift he was making. On the whole it drew them closer. Challenging convention was what the sixties were all about, surely.

Before long, though, they'd have another shift to absorb.

A Walk on the Wild Side

There was never any question of sex between Terry and I. He would simply not have been interested and that was not the nature of our friendship. But my contact with him did help me to move away from even my own, by then, very attenuated version of Theravāda Bhikkhu-hood and therefore predisposed me to take the final step away from celibacy as a mere discipline.[153]

There were rumours. Perhaps there had always been rumours. Sangharakshita had made no secret of his occasional struggles with the vow of celibacy, especially, he said, in his early days in Kalimpong. Some of the poems he wrote at the time speak not only of the struggle but also of the goal he strived for, of sublimating those drives and desires:

How sweet is love's austerity,
How fiercely sweet, when it denies
My hands the bliss of touching thee,
The heaven of looking to mine eyes.

With no more sweets to seek and find
Love wanes as bright full moon above;

But this harsh abstinence shall grind
A finer point upon my love.

A point so fine, an aim so true,
Upon my passion shall there be,
That it will pierce like lightning through
The veiled heart of Reality.[154]

He wrote 'Love's austerity' in 1959, in Kalimpong. In 1967, on the brink of a new kind of life, he was in a different mood:

I want to break out,
Batter down the door,
Go tramping black heather all day
On the windy moor,
And at night, in hayloft, or under hedge, find
A companion suited to my mind.

I want to break through,
Shatter time and space,
Cut up the Void with a knife,
Pitch the stars from their place,
Nor shrink back when, lidded with darkness, the Eye
Of Reality opens and blinds me, blue as the sky.[155]

It was on a summer afternoon in 1968 that he arrived at Sakura to find some of his friends milling about on the pavement looking bewildered and generally disapproving of a shabbily dressed young man in their midst.

His name was Carter. He was an American traveller who'd got talking to the proprietor of the shop upstairs the day before.

Hearing that he had nowhere to stay, the proprietor, one of the first twelve Order members, had suggested he could spend the night among the mats and cushions downstairs. Unfortunately he fell asleep while reading by candlelight. The candle tipped over and set fire to the shrine and part of the building.

Sangharakshita wasn't particularly taken by this careless stranger, but nevertheless offered him a place to stay at his flat, at least for a while. Although he offered Carter a choice between the floor and the bed, that night, somewhat unexpectedly but naturally and mutually, they got into the same bed.

Given the life-changing effect of the baseless rumours that had surrounded his friendship with Terry, I once asked Sangharakshita how deeply he'd considered the consequences of allowing himself a sex life. As usual, his answer came from a broader perspective: 'Well, perhaps I could have continued to live a life of chastity, but of course that would have led to a very different kind of Order and movement.'

The fact of the matter was that, good Buddhist though he knew himself to be, he no longer wanted to live the prescribed life of a monk. It was time to relax the tension, see what it would be like and what he might learn if he allowed himself to live differently. Essentially, he was reconfiguring what it meant, for him, to be a fully committed Buddhist. As he confirmed some years later, 'It was only after I started having serious doubts about the bhikkhu life itself that I started having a different attitude to the possibility of becoming sexually active. Those doubts and that possibility went along together.'[156] As for the gossip and those 'old ladies of Hampstead', he told me, 'Well, I decided I might as well be hung for a sheep as for a lamb.'

He once put it to me that the life of a Buddhist monk should be seen not so much as a matter of identity but as a *practice* available to those wishing to take on certain disciplines for a period, maybe for life, maybe not. It's akin, he said, to going on retreat. He had chosen to spend seventeen years living in a particular way with a particular range of challenges and disciplines. Now he was coming out of retreat, full of ideas, energy, and imagination, and looking to do things differently.

There was nothing secretive about the development, nor did it seem to cause waves among his close followers. As those who were around at the time have put it, Sangharakshita was such a radical character, and so obviously a genuine Buddhist, that whether or not he was living like a monk wasn't an issue. If anything, the development made him more interesting, perhaps more in tune with the spirit of the times.

◆

Carter never became involved with the FWBO, but they enjoyed an open sexual relationship for a couple of years. It was also with Carter that he tried marijuana and, just a few times, LSD. Being an inveterate writer and diarist, he chronicled his experiences in an essay, '1969–1970: a Retrospect'.[157]

When Carter returned to the USA, it wasn't long before Sangharakshita began another relationship, again with someone uninvolved in the FWBO. Over the following years, from his mid-forties to mid-sixties, there would be five or six extended sexual relationships, as well as periods of what he termed 'healthy promiscuity'. Through those years, with those two early exceptions, his partners were men involved with the FWBO.

Perhaps some people were confused or put off the FWBO by the transformation of its founder. And for them there was a burgeoning array of more traditional options, as Eastern or Eastern-trained teachers established their Buddhist movements. Whatever gossip was circulating in the world he'd left behind didn't seem to concern him. Teaching and working as he now was with members of a younger, less conventional generation, after his time in the middle-aged, middle-class worlds of the Buddhist Society and Hampstead Buddhist Vihara, he felt energized and optimistic for the future of Buddhism. So, as far as his new disciples were concerned, he was just doing his thing while they were doing theirs.

After living alone for a while, he set up house in North London with a couple of young art students. They were familiar faces at FWBO meetings but didn't seem to relate to him in quite the way others did. As he once put it, 'They don't want anything from me. They're happy to let me be myself.' That was his experience of those times.

Graham (now Siddhiratna) remembered it slightly differently when we spoke informally: 'We had a kind of routine. We'd get up, meditate, and have a bit of breakfast. Then he'd take his cup of tea into a tiny little room, not much bigger than a broom cupboard, where he worked. He'd painted it purple, lime green, and yellow ochre – absolutely crazy colours. It was awful! I'd sometimes go in and draw him while he sat there writing his lectures. After lunch he'd listen to the radio, always Radio 4, and read the newspapers before getting back to his writing.

'I was so in awe of him. I thought that anything I might say would just be imbecilic and uninformed. I could ask him to pass the salt, or ask if he wanted another cup of tea, but as for what was going on in the country, or what I needed to do to make my meditation better, I couldn't go there. I felt too stupid.

'One night a group of people came round for dinner, about six regulars from the meditation classes. God, it was blocked! Nobody could say anything. It was excruciating! They were suffering from exactly the same symptoms as me, when you're so tongue-tied you can't think of anything to say that won't sound crass or stupid. After that night, if anyone came round, and if there were more than two of them, he'd slip me a five-pound note and send me to the off-licence for a bottle of wine to loosen things up.'

In the late 1990s, a decade or more since he'd brought the sexually active phase of his life to an end, stories emerged online and in *The Guardian* newspaper of inept or insensitive approaches, and in particular of one relationship, his longest, which his partner claimed, in some detail, to have been coercive. Even though the allegation surprised some of us who'd been around at the time and witnessed the relationship close up, more stories from other sources began to surface. Over the years it became evident, certainly more evident than it had ever seemed at the time, that Sangharakshita had made some damaging mistakes and misjudgements.

Perhaps we shouldn't have been surprised. He was a complicated man with a passionate nature who entered the realm of sex and sexual relationships during the fabled 'Summer of Love' with no previous sexual socialization. An outcome of this was that he got things wrong at times and had done some harm.

Did his position and status in the FWBO add a coercive, even predatory, element to the mix? He began his first relationship with someone involved in the movement in 1970, when there were about a dozen active Order members in the world. His last ended in the late1980s, when there were about 120. Several of his partners have been happy to admit that they felt no physical attraction but were nevertheless willing to respond to his obvious longing for, and capacity to give, human warmth and intimacy. Others were attracted by the possibility of getting close to such an intriguing person with quite an extraordinary energy, and took his approaches as an opportunity not to be missed. But for sure, even if the FWBO was small at the time, his position as its founder, his age, and his sometimes overwhelming personal presence must have made it hard for some people to say no. Either way, whether his power was based on need, personal charisma, or his position as head of our tiny community, it clearly brought confusion and pain to some, and has left his followers with a tangled legacy.

As mentioned earlier, in 1987 I interviewed him on the theme of 'Sex and spiritual life' for the movement's magazine. By then he'd brought the sexually active phase of his life to an end. In our pre-interview conversation he used the word 'experimentation'.

'But was it really that?' I asked.

'What do you mean?'

'Well, surely there was appetite involved.'

He looked astonished, 'Well, of course there was. But what's wrong with that? What's wrong with a healthy human appetite?'

Soon after the interview was published, he quickly accepted that 'exploration' would have been a more fitting word to use. However, to this day the word 'experimentation' has not been forgotten or in some minds forgiven. Some people wonder: was it an evasion, the first draft of a whitewash? But that seemed entirely out of character. What seemed more likely, and more characteristic of the man, was that he was trying to suggest something very important about the way he was approaching life at that time. Sex was part of a much bigger experiment, or exploration, with himself, with life, with communication. He certainly wasn't trying to claim that he'd brought a detached mood of scientific enquiry to the proceedings – when all he was doing was enjoying sex.

As he moved beyond his life as a monk and started teaching in 1960s England, perhaps everything felt like an exploration, and more than that – an opportunity. At this particular moment in British cultural history, he found himself standing on the threshold of a vast project, while his circumstances allowed him, you could say, to live, act, and teach in whatever way felt right. His vision of the spiritual life was increasingly one that involved, and ultimately integrated, his entire being, bringing all his qualities, energies, and resources into the picture:

> Therefore will I, all I can,
> Build up complete the Fourfold Man,
> Head and heart, and loins fine,
> And hands and feet, all made divine.
> Banish single vision far!
> With double vision ever war!
> Fourfold vision night and day
> Light and guide you on your way.[158]

◆

His friendship with Terry Delamere, which had played such an important part in supporting these transformations, continued as close as ever throughout those early years. They saw each other several times a week, their friendship undiminished by Sangharakshita's relationship with Carter, or the fact that Terry was now living with his girlfriend. More than ever, though, their conversations revolved around Terry's increasingly desperate mental states. He spoke frequently about the pull of suicide, the temptation to shrug off the pain of his blighted earthly life and immerse himself once and for all in the pure white light he'd glimpsed under the influence of ether.

Driving the 'Little Bus' back to London after the Easter retreat in 1969, with his Portuguese partner Mafalda and Sangharakshita sitting next to him on the front seat, he confessed that he was fighting an almost overpowering urge to drive the van at high speed into a brick wall. He managed

With Terry Delamere at Keffolds, 1968

to restrain himself, but it was only a temporary reprieve. The next morning he did commit suicide.

The letter he left for Sangharakshita spoke of his hope that maybe another time, in another life, they would meet and 'work miracles together'. The letter ended:

> We will always be together.
> What happiness!
> Yours ever,
> T.[159]

Sangharakshita's grief was immense. He wept, he writes in *Moving against the Stream*, every day for six months, and could still weep when talking about it twenty years later.

Those who were around him at the time speak of that grief, but also of the way he carried on with his work, not so much compartmentalizing his feelings for Terry, as letting them nourish his commitment to the Three Jewels and his work for the good of Buddhism. As he sat meditating on the day after Terry's death, some words came to him:

Pain shall be transmuted into joy,
suffering into ecstasy,
When to the eternal life of Buddhahood
We all awake.[160]

18

Talking Dharma in the West

A wind was in my sails. It blew
Stronger and fiercer hour by hour.
I did not know from whence it came,
Or why. I only knew its power.

Sometimes it dashed me on the rocks,
Sometimes it spun me round and round.
Sometimes I laughed aloud for joy,
Sometimes I felt a peace profound.

It drove me on, that manic wind,
When I was young. It drives me still
Now I am old. It lives in me,
Its breath my breath, its will my will.[161]

◆

It was a very rich, fruitful, creative period and I had a lot of
energy that expressed itself in all sorts of ways, including the
sexual, as well as in Dharma talks, poetry, etcetera. Some of
the things going on might have been seen as incompatible,
but they were not, so far as I was concerned at the time. It all
seemed right and natural.[162]

Since the fire at Sakura, Sangharakshita and his band of followers had been homeless, meeting once a week in a succession of hired rooms. By now, he wasn't in robes, except sometimes when teaching or leading a puja. He could wander London, especially its bookshops, and bask in anonymity.

Describing their first encounter with him, some speak of feeling disappointed, unimpressed; others found him fascinating, eccentric, fearless, mysterious, even in one case 'royal'. As one person put it, 'Even to be in the same room as him was to pick up on an energy that was absolutely different. And it wasn't just charisma.' At times he could seem oddly distant – he had an unsettling way of shaking your hand while looking in the exact opposite direction. And yet without inhibition he could focus on someone, say a latecomer at the meditation class, with unnerving intensity, as if he was reading them down to their very soul.

As a beginner on my first retreat, I remember him coming into the library, sitting down across the room and watching me. Not knowing what to make of it – it certainly didn't feel sexual – I kept my eyes pinned to my book until, after about five minutes, he got up and left.

To be around him was like being in the company of a bigger presence in a bigger universe. Despite, or perhaps because of, the extreme mindfulness of his movements and diction, his knowledge, refinement, and wisdom, there was something almost unnervingly different about him, something deliberate, conscious, but quietly untamed; one knew he wasn't civilized in the normal way. There was something unmistakably refined but implicitly and directly challenging about him. It was something you couldn't shake off. To use a term upon which he would come to heap a world of significance, he was a 'true individual'.

His talks, and there were a good many of them, were an education and an enchantment. In his lecture on the mantra *Oṃ maṇi padme hūṃ*, for example, one of eight talks he gave on themes from *The White Lotus Sūtra*, he took us first to the Tibetan plateau, where the traveller sees the mantra inscribed on stupas or painted onto old stone walls; he then guided us into the Mahāyāna world of the sūtra, and finally into the inner life of the mantra itself. It was a rite of fascination delivered with simple but engaging authenticity. Drawing on an extensive reservoir of knowledge and talking from experience, he could take us to places we'd not been to before and make the mythic seem real.

Purna, a New Zealander, remembers hearing tapes of his talks: 'This was just fantastic material. It completely opened up the world of myth in a positive sense. I thought, "This man is onto something in a way I've never met in any other Buddhist teacher", and I'd been involved with Buddhism for quite a few years. He was of a completely different calibre.' Another friend put it more simply, 'He always surprised me. He always had something fresh and unexpected to say. And this would always take the discussion to new and deeper places.'

His fortnightly question-and-answer sessions were dazzling. No matter how efficiently our questions displayed the extent of our ignorance or naivety, he would educate and thrill with the generosity of his replies. Alongside Buddhist sources, he could draw on English literature, Renaissance art, the Bible, or the Western philosophical tradition. Like the merchant in a bazaar throwing one gorgeously patterned carpet after another across the floor, he would entrance and inspire as he revealed the wonders of his native world, infecting us with his feeling for the higher life and easing our path as we took our first steps in that direction. Despite the range of illustrative references he added along the way, you knew he was simply trying to share his experience of Buddhism with us. For no matter how widely he roamed in search of fitting cultural parallels or references, his intention was to make the Dharma feel as relevant and natural to us as it had ever been in the East, and as it was for him.

His talks would introduce themes from all three major branches of the tradition, many focusing on what he'd call 'basic Buddhism' – the essential, foundational teachings and systems that populate those lists generally found in the Pali canon. As he spoke, he'd redeem them from the dusty pages of their Victorian translations and breathe life into them, adding his own interpretations and emphases along the way, the fruits of his time with Jagdish Kashyap and his rainy-season reflections in Muvattupuzha or Kalimpong.

Translating *sammā-diṭṭhi*, for example, the first 'limb' of the Buddha's eightfold path, as 'perfect vision' rather than the more common but less accurate 'right understanding' (by no means his most radical gloss), he brought the teaching out of the classroom and into alignment with whatever glimpses or intimations had drawn us into his orbit. By highlighting a traditional division of the path into a 'path of vision' and a 'path of transformation', he turned what might have seemed like another list into a comprehensive existential challenge.

Many Buddhists take the teaching of the four noble truths as the Buddha's enjoinder to remain focused on the facts of impermanence and suffering. Sangharakshita preferred to emphasize the positive, highlighting not so much the suffering, but the formula's effectiveness as an illustration of the central Buddhist principle of conditionality. Yes, we suffer, but just as our suffering arises out of conditions – which we can learn to recognize – so also there is a path that leads to its end – which we can follow.

The formula of twelve *nidāna*s, or links of *cyclical* conditionality (from ignorance... to contact, to feeling, to craving... and ultimately to old age, sickness, and death), features in many important texts, not least in accounts of the Buddha's Enlightenment. The list is well known, widely taught, and colourfully illustrated in the Tibetan wheel of life. Canonical, but far less well known, is another list of twelve links operating within a progressive dimension of conditionality. Here, suffering can lead to faith, and faith to joy, to bliss... all the way to 'seeing things as they really are' and the liberation of Enlightenment.

This leaning towards positive models, an upward-facing rhetoric of spiritual life and practice, would play a prominent role in the choices he made. He felt it necessary to counter the unhelpful way Buddhism had been promoted by early Western commentators. Inadequately communicated and wrongly approached, its references to suffering, cessation, freeing oneself from the wheel of life, and 'extinction' could fall on new ears as something remorselessly negative, even nihilistic. Set against the promises of salvation, redemption, and eternal life found in other religions, it came across as the honest but poor relation. And yet for Sangharakshita, Buddhism – with its profound insights into the heights of human potential, and into the way in which deep, but crucially workable habits of our conditioned minds define our experience of reality – was not only an affirmation of our potential for change and freedom, but a treasure house of advice, guidance, and support for those willing to reach towards it.

◆

There was a time in human history when the idea of a *universal* religion, as opposed to the unifying myth of a single tribe or ethnically homogeneous society, was unknown. As for a universal religion with no conception of a supreme being, even today that is such an unfamiliar idea that many Westerners or Easterners find it too puzzling to engage with.

Christianity is a universal religion, with followers around the entire world, which revolves around the belief in a god. Everything flows from that, including an entire religious vocabulary. When in the mid-nineteenth century the West 'discovered' Buddhism, there was no vocabulary fit and ready to express Buddhist principles and truths in a Buddhist way. Inevitably, the first translations of Pali and Sanskrit texts, and the first introductory books on Buddhism, were framed in words and metaphors drawn from the existing local religious vocabulary. But words and metaphors are not neutral; they come with baggage.

This was something Sangharakshita had always been keenly aware of. The opening pages of *A Survey of Buddhism* broached the topic immediately and head-on as he critiqued the available translations of Buddhist texts. So, as he set out on a new project in a new environment, he would bear in mind, and frequently quote, Confucius: 'The one thing needed first is the rectification of terms.' He was referring to a statement found in the *Analects*, which is worth sharing in full, albeit from another translation:

> If names be not correct, language is not in accordance with the truth of things. If language be not in accordance with the truth of things, affairs cannot be carried on to success.
>
> When affairs cannot be carried on to success, proprieties and music will not flourish. When proprieties and music do not flourish, punishments will not be properly awarded. When punishments are not properly awarded, the people do not know how to move hand or foot.
>
> Therefore, a superior man considers it necessary that the names he uses may be spoken appropriately, and also that what he speaks may be carried out appropriately. What the superior man requires, is just that in his words there may be nothing incorrect.[163]

Devising new metaphors and models, a language, and even words that might be suitable or at least salvageable for use in a

Western Buddhist context was something this lifelong disciple of Dr Johnson might have approached with relish, not that this made the task easy. This book is liberally sprinkled with the word 'spiritual'. Sangharakshita once defined '*spiritual* practice' as practice aimed at, or conducive to, states of consciousness higher than the ordinary, arising, for example, in meditative absorption, even in transcendental experience. His decision to settle on that word was just one conscious outcome of the choices he had to make, but even in doing so he knew it was not ideal. It was and is a work in progress.

A few original terms, such as *karma* and *nirvana*, were already naturalized, and probably a few more would follow. But for the time being it was impossible for Sangharakshita to ignore the scale of the task ahead, and he worried when he saw Western writers, even Buddhist groups, approaching the issue lightly: 'They underestimate the power which old meanings retain. Already some Buddhist groups seem more like psychotherapy gatherings, or those of humanists, or even of thinly disguised Christians. The importance of creating and safeguarding a clear vocabulary for the expression of the Dharma is obvious.'[164]

So this was a vast field for experiment. In early talks, he'd speak of the Buddhist life in terms of making the transition from 'reactive mind' to 'creative mind'. An edited transcript of a lecture he gave on the subject tied with *The Essence of Zen*[165] to be the first publication to come out of the movement. It is still in print and much appreciated.[166]

His first comprehensive attempt to communicate the Buddhist path in terms and concepts accessible to the Western ear was the metaphor of the 'Higher Evolution'. Over the course of sixteen lectures, he gave a poetic twist to the theory of evolution, aligning it with a developmental approach to the Buddhist life. It portrayed the spiritual life as a consciously willed journey not made by the species but open to any human being thanks to the (biological) evolutionary accident of 'reflexive self-consciousness'. The journey of Higher Evolution is one that takes the motivated individual from ordinary human consciousness to self-aware individuality, to ever higher levels of awareness, sensitivity, and being, culminating in the infinite, or 'absolute consciousness' of Enlightenment. The terminology might have been new to Buddhism, but in Sangharakshita's view the vision behind it was thoroughly traditional:

> In one form or another, the concept of the Path has always been central to Buddhism. The Path consists of steps or stages. These steps or stages represent, essentially, states of consciousness, or of being, which are progressive, leading the individual from ignorance to Enlightenment, from the condition of *pṛthagjana* [worldly person] to that of *arhat* or Buddha. One could therefore say that the conception of spiritual development, or spiritual *evolution* (what I call the higher evolution of Man) is central to Buddhism.[167]

This was not the way in which we usually thought of Buddhism, but it was what Buddhism essentially was. In Buddhism there were many doctrines and disciplines, many

moral rules and devotional observances, but they were
all secondary. Even meditation was secondary. What was
important, for Buddhism, was that [a human being] should
grow and develop – that he should evolve. Buddhism was not
a matter of thinking and knowing, or even of doing, but of
being and becoming. In other words Buddhism was a matter
of following the path of the Higher Evolution.[168]

Some of his choices around language were offered as a
corrective. He'd heard Christmas Humphreys evoking the
Buddhist life in terms of climbing a mountain while hacking
off 'great bleeding lumps of self'. The image had repelled him,
and more to the point it didn't communicate the principle of
anattā in any useful way to people who wouldn't know what
notion of a 'self' the Buddha was challenging. That such
language could encourage spiritual bypassing or foster an
atmosphere of nihilism was also a factor.

Sangharakshita was of course fluent in the traditional
language of *anattā*, of breaking through the delusion of
'selfhood', to the 'extinction' of nibbāna. But his experience,
his character, and his spiritual intuition directed him towards
stressing the positive nature of the spiritual path. For those
who might think he was ignoring the traditional teachings on
anattā, he had an answer:

We talk in terms of 'development'; we talk in terms of the
'higher evolution', but this is not any different really from
talking in terms of *anattā*. Do you see this point? Because for
change to be possible, for development to be possible, real,

radical development, there can be no unchanging self, which is the whole point of *anattā*. So to say that you believe in the development of the individual, to say that you believe in the higher evolution, is tantamount to an affirmation of the principle of *anattā*, except that you're affirming it in a more dynamic way and more in terms of life and experience and not in an abstract, as it were static way.[169]

Sometimes he would speak in terms of *expanding* the sense of self to include others rather than losing it or cutting it off. This was nothing more revolutionary than the language of the Mahāyāna, of the Bodhisattva ideal. As he once put it, if the spiritual life culminates in the dissolution of the subject–object or self–other dichotomy, then presumably one can work at the 'other' end of the formula just as effectively as one can work at the 'self' end. Perhaps, when talking in this way, he would have had one of Dhardo Rimpoche's maxims in mind: 'If you have any doubts about what you need to do, just do something for others.'

Unlike his recently converted Buddhist friends in India, who approached the Buddhist life very much in social terms, Westerners, he saw, were more preoccupied with themselves and their personal psychology. And yet, so many of them, especially those who tended to haunt Eastern spiritual movements, seemed actually to be out of touch with themselves, their emotional life, even their bodies. To offer them the language of no-self and cessation, he believed, would leave many of them more confused, even more alienated from their experience than they'd been before.

◆

Within a few years, he'd given talks and lecture series on the most fundamental teachings and most major trends within Buddhist history. He'd introduced devotional and ritual practices as a regular feature of his class sessions and retreats, along of course with meditation. And he'd stressed again and again the centrality of the act of going for refuge, how one's commitment to the ideals and practices of Buddhism are the key to the spiritual life, more essential than the taking up of any prescribed lifestyle.

Looking back on the talks he'd given in the first few years of his movement's life, he realized that they 'constituted not only a systematic exposition of the fundamentals of Buddhism, interpreted from a non-sectarian point of view, but at the same time a total synthesis of traditional spiritual wisdom and modern scientific knowledge as represented, in particular, by biology, anthropology and psychology'.[170]

He gave many of his talks on the Higher Evolution and *The White Lotus Sūtra* around the time of a visit to America, where he took up a visiting professorship at Yale University. His lecturing duties there were light, which gave him time to visit old friends and contacts from the Kalimpong days and to make new ones, especially among the students. The enthusiasm and energy of the young people delighted and energized him. After-lecture discussions raged for twice as long as the timetable dictated. He ran extramural meditation classes and 'communication exercises', which were well attended and surprisingly fruitful thanks to the wholehearted way people took them on.

Interviewed for BBC Radio, London 1968/1969

There was something very appealing about the spaciousness of the American landscape and the minds he was meeting. But when a Mongolian friend from his Kalimpong days, Geshe Wangyal, author of the remarkable *Door of Liberation*,[171] begged him, almost in tears, to take over the monastery he had established in New Jersey, he knew he had no intention of letting down his friends in England, and returned.

This loyalty to his English disciples was rewarded when he saw how well things had gone in his absence. Three of the new Order members had kept classes running, and there were plenty of new faces showing up at talks. Even so, he couldn't help noticing the difference between his English friends and the people he'd got to know in the New World.

English people 'seemed less interested in things, less enthusiastic, less alive. [...] Nevertheless, I did not despair, and by way of both precept and example strove to infuse new life and energy into the movement.' More optimistically he wrote, 'In the case of a few of those most closely associated with me, I knew that their lifelessness represented a definite stage in their development and that as such it was more apparent than real. Increased awareness had dissolved the old unconscious, conditioned motives for action, but new ones – freer, more spontaneous – had not yet emerged.'[172]

He was particularly struck by the effect of his talks on the Higher Evolution:

> Several members of the audience were on occasion in a
> state of evident shock, having only now realized that the
> light-hearted spirit in which they had taken up Buddhism,
> or the spiritual life, or the Higher Evolution, was in no way
> justified by the seriousness of the enterprise. It was as if
> they had awakened from a dream and now saw, for the first
> time, how precipitous was the ascent, how lofty the peaks
> they proposed to scale, and how terrifying the abysses that
> yawned on every side.[173]

19

Time to Get Serious

Pack your suitcase, catch the train,
Eastertide has come again.
Now at last your way lies clear
From Waterloo to Haslemere.

Typewriter, textbook, left behind,
To higher things you tune your mind,
Solaced, between the well-kept stations,
With tea and Govinda's 'Foundations'.

Free, down elm-shadowed lanes you wend,
Where British blackbirds call 'Attend!'
Making your way, with quiet elation,
To 'Keffolds', brown rice, and meditation.[174]

'Is your left hand yin or yang?'
　'Oh, yin.'
　'Ah. Right. Thanks.'
　The sixteen-day summer retreat was the highlight of the FWBO's year, and a conversation of that kind (overheard in the kitchen) says something about the times and the people who were there. It was 1971, the FWBO was four years old, still largely unformed in anyone's mind except perhaps Sangharakshita's.

The retreat was lively, colourful, fun, and laced with substantial bouts of practice. About eighty people passed through it, with fifty or so on-site at any one time. Among them, not that it would have been easy to notice, were three or four of the original twelve Order members, and a tiny handful of men and women who'd been ordained in the intervening years.

Even though he didn't regret those first ordinations, and had conducted them in good faith, it was already apparent that few of the first twelve had fully understood the implications of the step they were taking. In some respects those implications were still dawning on Sangharakshita himself, so this was hardly surprising.

A committed Buddhist life involves bringing every aspect of life under the influence of the Dharma. This isn't easy and it doesn't come naturally, not least if you are on your own. Even if few of the first people to be ordained had fully understood what was being asked of them, he wanted future Order members to be more prepared for the challenge, and sufficiently bonded with each other to form a vibrant and supportive community.

Those extended Easter and summer retreats and the occasional weekend retreats were breeding grounds, not just for deeper practice, but for strong and special friendships. There would be four or five hours of meditation each day, yoga and karate sessions, discussion groups, and dreamwork groups. Meals were plentiful and lentil-full, leaning as they did towards the macrobiotic. In the evenings, Sangharakshita would perch himself cross-legged in an armchair and laugh at his own jokes as his recorded lectures issued from a gigantic reel-to-reel tape machine. At times the place would resound to shouts, screams, and tears as he led us in those communication exercises that had worked so well during his time at Yale. The days would finish with a sevenfold puja.

As one regular participant put it, 'We'd get to know each other, and ourselves, in ways we'd never experienced before. That amount of meditation alone could take us newbies through some strong ups and downs. But Bhante [as we called him] was holding the situation, and the overall context was so friendly that we'd come through and look forward to the next time.'

Sangharakshita and most of his immediate followers were still living in London, so it was natural to carry on deepening connections at Dharma classes, yoga and karate classes, as well as meeting up in each other's homes. Perhaps the lack of a permanent base had a timely bonding effect. Each week the word would get out, often at the last minute, announcing where the weekly gathering would be held. Something that could have been a bit routine instead felt like an underground adventure.

◆

How did he come across in the midst of this developing scene? For how he appeared to us as we got to know him, how he engaged with us as we learned from him, and how he interacted with us as we built a movement would be the primary business of his life from then onwards.

In those early years, he was invariably friendly, tolerant, and patient, happy to discuss our practice, our love life, our problems, even our LSD experiences. But if you thought he might be interested, impressed even, to hear about a 'trip' you'd taken over the weekend, you'd come away a little chastened. This wasn't because he'd disapprove – rather, you'd realize, even while you were talking, that your drug-based experiences were giving you no more than a brief, puny glimpse of the realms he coursed in. He'd give you his attention and then murmur something like, 'Well, it all depends on the context', implying that whatever had happened was only useful if it had taught you something. How did it fit into the serious business of life? Was it really such a big a deal?

He would seem so grounded most of the time, approachable, reasonable, even rather normal; and then he would say something, do something, or even look at you in a way that would alert you with a shock to the depths in which he lived.

He'd sometimes compare himself to a gardener, happy to watch and wait, ready to prune the occasional excess, but mainly concerned to nurture healthy developments. He watched us, listened to our stories, and tried to work out what made us tick. Then he'd find gentle ways of encouraging us to see things in a broader and deeper context. What did we want our lives to be about? Did we have any real sense of purpose? Were we 'goal-oriented' or 'problem-oriented'? From time to time he would let his teeth show. Coming into lunch one day on retreat, after a series of private interviews, he announced, 'Right, we're going to have a moratorium on problems!' When someone asked what he meant, he replied, 'We're just not going to have them any more.' It was a light-hearted exchange, but it carried weight. As he pointed out in one of his talks, a guru is neither a father figure nor a therapist. Whether or not he was, or thought himself, a guru is another matter – to which we'll return – but at least he knew he didn't want to be seen as one of those other options.

His life in England, the people he was working with, the doors he was opening were taking him far from the life he'd lived as a monk in India. One might expect it to have knocked him off course, at least for a while, as he allowed new interests and preoccupations to inhabit his mind. But, so far as we could tell, there was nothing distracted or vague about him or his commitment to the FWBO, tiny though it was. There was no diminution in his sense of purpose or his seriousness about the project. If he wasn't acting like a monk in a traditional sense, he was clearly a devoted, knowledgeable, and available Buddhist with the capacity to transmit the spirit of the Dharma in ways that reached us. And he was enough of a guide for our needs. What did most of us know or care about monastic rules? So what if he was in a sexual relationship? If there was some clay in those feet and blood in those veins that we could identify with, then it made the challenges he embodied harder to ignore.

On the last afternoon of the Easter retreat in 1972, he ordained four men in a single ceremony. This was hardly an event to match the mass-conversion ceremonies he'd conducted in India, but it was a big deal for us. All four had been involved for some while, and were well-liked members of our community. One in particular, Hugh, who became Buddhadasa that night, had been the first person to quit his career in order to help Sangharakshita in whatever way he could. The ordinations felt like an affirmation of our generation, the community that had developed in the years since the first ordinations.

At the summer retreat that year, he introduced more and longer periods of silence, and regularly punctuated activities with appeals for greater mindfulness. He'd pace the terrace communicating something that looked, to me at least, like impatience as we sat on the lawns chatting between events. Was it my projection, or was he getting frustrated by our half-heartedness? In question-and-answer sessions he'd challenge the vagueness of a question, or remind the questioner that he'd covered the topic in *A Survey of Buddhism*, *The Three Jewels*, or one of his recorded talks. Somebody asked him, 'Bhante, can you say something about Mahāmudrā?' to which he responded, 'Well, the whole point of Mahāmudrā is that you can't talk about it so I don't think I should say anything. Why don't you wait and see what happens?' Perhaps trying to be helpful or maybe seeking some attention and reassurance, I asked, 'Bhante, could you say something about the idea of going for refuge?'

'It's not an idea,' he shot back. 'It's an *act*.'

He went on to talk more fully about the central importance of that act, but he'd fired another warning shot. He wasn't being unkind, but you could sense he was asking us to get more serious.

One evening, after the puja, I found myself sitting next to him, drinking a cup of cocoa in the kitchen. Earlier on we'd been listening to one of his talks, during which he'd discussed the antidote effect of spiritual practice: mindfulness as an antidote to distraction, *mettā bhāvanā* as an antidote to ill will, and so on. 'Bhante,' I asked, 'what is the antidote to the hindrance of doubt?'

'Commitment,' he said without a moment's hesitation.

'But surely, if you have doubts, how do you know what to commit yourself to?'

'That's right. You don't. You have to take risks.'

Soon after that retreat, he gave a series of lectures on 'Creative symbols of the tantric path to Enlightenment'. He was on form, on fire. They were rich and full of fascinating content. But as he spoke about 'the cremation ground and the celestial maidens', 'the diamond sceptre of the lamas', or 'the symbolism of offerings and self-sacrifice', his agenda was pretty obvious. He was encouraging us to be more real, more engaged, willing to leave our comfort zone and take more risks.

And then he disappeared. Without warning, he took a sabbatical for a few months.

He'd been sharing the leadership at weekly classes for a while now, but he was unquestionably the essential force at the heart of things. So this came as quite a shock. Why had he gone? And why now? Things were taking off. The FWBO had a new base in North London, Pundarika – not huge, but much bigger than the Sakura basement. It was hosting a lively programme of activities for a promising body of regular 'friends'. So what had brought this turnabout? Had he had enough of England? Did he think he'd done his job and could now go back to India?

Settled in a cliffside shack in Cornwall with his companion, Mark, he gave himself a few weeks before writing a 'personal letter' to say he had no such thing in mind. He had now been teaching, planning, and communicating for years. He wanted a change from being treated sometimes like a piece of 'Buddhist clockwork', a dispenser of advice. But mainly, he wrote, he felt it was time to live in a different way, 'to release unprogrammed and unprogrammable energy, long accumulating within me'.

Living quietly by the sea, he meditated, read, and reflected. Working for some of the time on his first volume of memoirs[175] gave him a chance to reflect and revisit the trajectory that had brought him to this place at this point in his life. He was far from his teachers, far from his life as a freelance wanderer and monk, shunned by much of the English Buddhist establishment, and yet on the brink of a major creative enterprise. But, no, there had never been any question of abandoning his new community. A few months later, back in London, he spoke of having vividly sensed our presence when he meditated, as if we were sitting in the shack with him.

By a historical accident, he'd landed in England at a time of cultural upheaval. Established social arrangements, ways of living and working, of doing life, were being challenged and supplanted, not least by the kind of people who were attracted to his classes. They had energy, they were serious about their practice, and, being young, were mostly free of family responsibilities and financial concerns. There could hardly have been a more favourable set of conditions. But he was now approaching his fifties. If he was going to work with these people and initiate the kind of Buddhist movement the times called for, there was much to do and not much time to do it.

He returned from Cornwall in August 1973 and joined a number of us on a retreat we'd put together in his absence. Each evening a few of us would make our way, one at a time, to visit him in his room. He was relaxed, friendly, and interested. To my eyes he seemed to glow with warmth. In each case the conversation would begin or end with a request for ordination.

Within a year or so about twenty men and women were ordained, which meant there were now something like thirty active members of the Order with a good hold on their practice and an effective grasp of his approach to the Dharma. Whether many of us knew what he had in mind is another matter.

Immediately after my own ordination ceremony, in January 1974, he led us five new 'initiates' and the twenty or so Order members who'd witnessed the proceedings into another room. We sat ourselves on the floor leaning against the walls in a kind of horseshoe facing Sangharakshita, who sat before us in an armchair. The first convention of the Western Buddhist Order was about to begin.

20

For the Sake of All Beings

I am the Windhorse!
I am the king of space, the master of infinity,
Traversing the universe
With flashing, fiery hooves!
On my strong back, on a saddle blazing with gems,
I bear through the world
The Three Flaming Jewels.[176]

It was a short and homely gathering, a few days spent in a leafy suburb to the south of London. But it changed thousands of lives if you count those whose lives would be touched by what took place. If it had a theme, it was to do with bringing the Order to meaningful life, not just for our own sake, not even for the sake of Sangharakshita's wider field of followers, but for the sake of the world beyond.

He had now seen a few of us take some first real steps in our Buddhist lives. He'd seen us bring the beginnings of an effective spiritual community to life, founded on the friendships we'd formed as we practised and studied together. But there was further to go. It wasn't enough to approach Dharma practice as an accompaniment to an otherwise conventional, ultimately self-centred life. He wanted to see things go deeper, in our lives and out into the world.

As I write, in 2022, Buddhist centres and practice communities are a recognized part of the Western scene. Buddhism isn't the dominant option, but it's a recognized one, and not just for hippies and cranks. Back in the early 1970s, things were different. The Buddhist Society and the Hampstead Buddhist Vihara had been around for a while, along with a few viharas and temples catering for the ethnically Buddhist population. For a long time that had been about it.

In 1967, the year Sangharakshita founded the FWBO, Chögyam Trungpa and Akong Rinpoche established Samye Ling, a Tibetan Buddhist monastery in the Scottish Borders. A few years later, Jiyu Kennet Roshi would open Throssel Hole Priory, a Zen monastery on the edge of the Lake District, and soon Lamas Yeshe and Zopa would be asking their disciples to scout England for somewhere to establish what would become the Manjusri Institute. Nor would it be too long before Ajahn Sumedho would establish his first monastery in the UK.

Things were moving a little faster in the United States, but it's important to understand that these were very early days for the introduction of Buddhism as something Westerners might actually practise. All the more remarkable, then, seems the scope of Sangharakshita's ambition. His contemporary pioneers were focusing their attention on developing a single flagship teaching centre: a monastery, a vihara, a priory, or an institute. Sangharakshita, with his new centre in a derelict piano warehouse next to an adventure playground in a corner of London scheduled for demolition, had the vision, the sense of urgency, and some would say chutzpah not only to start a new teaching tradition but to encourage his few close followers, as soon as he felt them ready, to think beyond themselves and conceive of a *movement*, a constellation of public Dharma centres and facilities throughout the world.

So let's return to that genteel London suburb in January 1974, where Sangharakshita was sitting in an armchair, facing twenty-four members of his new Order, most of us in our early twenties and five of us ordained for a matter of minutes.

A good portion of our time was devoted to issues concerning personal practice. But, even while urging us, for example, to spend a month of each year on solitary retreat, his main concern was to talk about the Order's collective life. It was time to set the bar higher.

In tune with the Buddha's advice to his disciples, he urged us to meet regularly and often, for an evening each week and for a day or weekend every month. Allowing ourselves to envisage the geographical expansion of the Order, we talked about meeting on a more subtle plane by practising an 'Order *mettā bhāvanā*'. Wherever we would each happen to be at 7pm GMT on the first Friday of every month, we would direct *mettā*, loving-kindness, towards our fellow Order members. He also proposed a monthly, unedited circular through which we could share news of what we'd been doing, reading, practising, and reflecting on. This way we could stay in close, even intimate connection with each other, and help to keep him in good contact with us. The idea was appealing; someone even came up with a name that won Sangharakshita's approval: *Shabda*, which means something like 'sacred sound'.

He had high hopes, great expectations for what it would mean to be part of this community. Reflecting on his understanding at the time he would write, if rather formally:

> Those who went for Refuge to the Sangha also went for Refuge to the Buddha and the Dharma, that is, they had a common spiritual teacher (or spiritual ideal) and a common teaching (or spiritual principle), and this tended to draw them together, even on the social plane. But what did one mean by 'together'? One did not mean physical proximity, or agreement on doctrinal questions, or even the attainment of the same stages of the spiritual path. It was rather more subtle than that. The 'together' lay in communication, which was not just an exchange of ideas but a vital mutual responsiveness, on the basis of a common spiritual ideal and a common spiritual principle. It was a common exploration, in complete harmony and complete honesty, of the spiritual world. In this way spiritual progress took place.[177]

It's probably a testament to his skill as a leader, given how clear he was about the direction he wanted us to take, that I find it hard to recall which of the initiatives explored during that weekend came from Sangharakshita and which from our general discussion. He was our preceptor, teacher, and mentor, the leader without question, and he was certainly guiding the discussion. But even at that early moment in our history he was starting to share his responsibility with the Order.

Reminding us that he wouldn't be around forever, he encouraged us to take over running all the day-to-day activities at Pundarika, teaching meditation, giving talks, and running Dharma courses and retreats. He strongly encouraged us to think about setting up new centres in other cities, even overseas. He reminded us that one of the first twelve Order members had taken a suitcase of taped lectures with him when he emigrated to New Zealand. As a result, we now had branches of the movement in Auckland, Wellington, and Christchurch. He was even hoping to ordain a few people when he visited the country later in the year.

The world was in desperate need of the Dharma, he said: surely it would be selfish to sit in our own little nest keeping it all to ourselves. That is why he invariably talked in terms of 'the movement'. It was an evocative term, suggesting something of far greater scope and significance than we might imagine if we focused on the day-to-day reality of our nascent community.

The movement, he said, would work on a hierarchical principle, but it would be a hierarchy of commitment, of responsibility, not of power. There would be no central ownership of the movement's assets. Each centre would be legally and financially autonomous, the unifying link between them being the informal network of spiritual friendships and influence alive in the Order – hence the importance of ensuring that the governing councils of FWBO institutions should always be comprised of Order members. Perhaps it was here too that he laid down the principle, adhered to with few exceptions ever since, that decisions should be based on consensus, not on majority vote. With this simple intervention, he'd handed us the lifetime project of staying in effective and harmonious communication with each other, of being willing to keep talking and listening respectfully when we disagreed.

Even as he opened our eyes to this prospect of a 'movement', he affirmed the principle that the spiritual life rests on individual practice and individual vision. No Order member, he said, should feel obliged to contribute to the development of the movement. Nor did he wish to suggest that there weren't other ways of contributing to the welfare of the world. He spoke of his own concern for animal rights, the state of the environment, the fragility of world peace. But at this moment in history, he added, there were so few people in the West trying to communicate the Dharma or making available the resource of a genuine Buddhist spiritual community.

Over the years, he would occasionally say he would have been happy to share the task of building a Western movement with a team of peers. But the work would have required monks with far greater understanding of Western life and the Western mind than he'd ever seen displayed in the monks he knew. Instead, this small band of brothers and sisters seated around him that weekend would be his core team. His contribution would be to help us, and those who joined us, to deepen our practice and our knowledge of the Dharma while highlighting relevant Dharmic principles as we engaged with our projects. If such a collaborative approach could work, then not only would it serve the needs of the world but it could act as the vital catalyst for our personal growth. Over time, and with his constant input, we'd maybe find out what it meant to be Western Buddhists.

It was possibly during that weekend that he first proposed a symbol for the Order: the 1,000-armed Avalokiteśvara, the Bodhisattva of compassion. Avalokiteśvara is awake to the cries of the world and the needs of beings. He stands for that perfect blend of wisdom and compassion that can be released into the world when an effective spiritual community brings the bodhicitta, the 'will to Enlightenment' or 'awakening mind', to life in the world. His eleven heads scan the universe for those in need of help, while his 1,000 arms hold whatever tools, talents, or qualities might serve their needs. As Sangharakshita saw us, we members of the Order were, or would be, those 1,000 arms: a harmonious community of inspired individuals, bonded by a common purpose, each reaching out to the world with whatever skills or qualities we had to offer.

The myth of Avalokiteśvara also speaks to the resolution of the creative tension that can arise between one's developing sensitivity to the cries of the world and the need to keep working on oneself so as to be of help to others. Such a tension presents a kind of kōan, a problem that cannot be solved on its own level. But in the right context, with the right balance of activities, and with good friends around us, the spiritual conflicts we'd experience in our work for the movement, Sangharakshita believed, would trigger the breakthroughs that would keep moving us to higher levels of individual and collective consciousness.

The more we talked that weekend, the more this sounded like an adventure few of us wanted to miss. Those few days with Sangharakshita would set the direction of our lives.

◆

True to his word, Sangharakshita wasn't around forever, or even for long. He was living in a small cottage in Norfolk and would never again teach on a day-to-day basis at any FWBO centre. Apart from his few years in that cottage, where he would receive regular visits from those of us working on the 'front line', his future homes – a flat above the London Buddhist Centre, a study at Padmaloka retreat centre in Norfolk, a flat at Madhyamaloka community in Birmingham, and finally at Adhisthana in Herefordshire – would always be within FWBO/Triratna institutions where he was easily available. Knowing how much we had to learn, and how much needed to be done, he had no plans to fade into the distance. There would be times when he'd take himself off for a few weeks, usually to some country retreat, to recharge and reconnect with the energies and rhythms of his depths, but he would always return and engage.

A great believer in living a regular life, itself a form of spiritual practice, an 'indirect method of raising consciousness', he maintained pretty much the daily programme that Bhikkhu Khantipalo recorded when living with him in the Kalimpong Hermitage for a number of months. Waking

The writer at his desk, Padmaloka, late 1970s

Haiku

How many inkstains
On its chipped surface –
My old wooden desk
– Sangharakshita

early, he'd devote an hour or so before meditating to poetry and creative writing. He'd spend the rest of his mornings writing: essays, books, and papers on Dharma topics. A few hundred words a day of finished, polished prose would be added to a mounting pile of typescript, ready for the press by lunchtime. He spent his afternoons on correspondence, reading the minutes of our various meetings (always twice), and seeing visitors. On most evenings he'd edit transcripts of his talks, while often reserving Friday evenings for an hour or two of classical music. An exceptionally fast reader since childhood, he also managed to read two or three books every week.

◆

At that time there was nobody in the Order or movement who had known him except in this English manifestation, working at the heart of our all-absorbing project. I wonder how often we stopped to consider what it might have been like for him to be living this life, so different from anything he'd done before, and in what must have been for him still something of a new setting. London now was so different from the town he'd grown up in, and England was nothing like India. And as for us, how unlike his Indian friends we must have seemed. I doubt any of us appreciated what a leap he was making from one life to another. His confidence and clarity as he engaged with us made it easy to imagine he'd always been around, had always been teaching here in England. But his own experience must have felt quite different.

One evening, not long after that first convention and during one of his visits to London, he invited himself along to the weekly meeting of local Order members. Taking advantage of his presence, we moved the conversation to the teaching work we were doing at the centre, something to which most of us were fairly new. When the conversation focused on the amount of work involved in leading retreats, he made the remark, 'Well, if you're leading or supporting a retreat you shouldn't expect to get anything out of it yourself.' Someone laughed and said, perhaps a little sentimentally, 'But Bhante, if you go with that attitude you'll probably get more out of it than anyone else.' Quick as a flash, Sangharakshita turned to face him, pointing an admonishing finger and snapped, 'No! Not even that!'

I once asked what he thought his life might have been like had he never received the invitation to visit England. 'Well, I would have been quite happy to spend the rest of my days in Kalimpong writing poetry and books on Buddhist metaphysics.' Anyone who came close to the energy that powered his wish to get out and share the Dharma might find that hard to believe, but maybe there was the occasional day when the Hermitage in Kalimpong felt very far away.

From time to time, on a festival occasion, for example, or because he had something important to say, he'd ask us to hire a hall where he could give a talk. As his reflections on our project developed, many of his talks were designed to deepen our understanding of who we were and what we were doing: 'Fifteen points for old and new Order members', 'Fifteen points for new and old Order members', 'The five pillars of the FWBO', 'The six distinct emphases of the FWBO', 'Buddhism for today and tomorrow', 'The path of regular steps and the path of irregular steps', 'Enlightenment as experience and as non-experience'. As the years went by he'd write extended papers: 'The history of my going for refuge', 'The ten pillars of Buddhism', 'Forty-three years ago', 'Was the Buddha a bhikkhu?', 'Extending the hand of fellowship', 'My relation to the Order'. Some of these latter were offered for public consumption, and some were delivered to an audience of Order members or to people preparing for ordination.

On a number of occasions, he encouraged us to approach the scriptures, whether Pali or Sanskrit, as literature and not just as teachings. When he modelled this approach in his lectures or seminars, you could feel the stories, and with them the Buddha or other great teachers, coming to life. It was a deeply engaging gift, and it was just what we needed. In the late seventies, when so many of us were involved in fundraising and building public centres and retreat centres, he gave two series of public talks, on *The Sūtra of Golden Light* and *The Vimalakīrti Nirdeśa*. As he brought out the mythic dimensions of those teachings, he merged his scholarship and detailed appreciation of Indian Buddhist imagery with core themes at the heart of our lives: morality, economics, the environment, altruistic activity, and social transformation, as we envisaged the possibility of a Buddhist culture in the West.

Less public but possibly more seminal was the fifteen-year period, starting in the early seventies, that he devoted to running more than a hundred study seminars covering a wide range of texts: from the *Dhammapada*, the *Udāna*, the *Sutta Nipāta*, and the *Itivuttaka* to the *Bardo Thodol*, the *Ratnaguṇasaṃcayagāthā*, the *Tiratana Vandanā*, the *Bodhicaryāvatāra*, *Dhyāna for Beginners*, the *Songs of Milarepa*, the *Kālāma Sutta*. With a host of texts, drawn from all branches of the tradition, he handed us the keys to the treasure house. As he guided us through the texts, paragraph by paragraph, he'd explain, illuminate, allowing himself to refer across to themes relevant to our work for the movement or our everyday lives. He was helping us to see through the words and bring these texts to life. Often relating the texts to his own distinctive approach, he taught us to think more clearly, to read more mindfully and where necessary critically, and to be on the lookout, especially in the case of modern commentaries, for misapprehensions, distortions, and 'wrong views'.

No matter how widely we roamed, he would always make a point of relating the material we were exploring to the Buddha's foundational teachings, just as he encouraged us to engage with what they were saying about living a spiritual life right now. Sometimes he'd take up a contemporary book about Buddhism: *Outlines of Mahayana Buddhism* by D.T. Suzuki, *The Buddha* by Trevor Ling, and so on. Sometimes he'd applaud and expand on the ideas they contained, but he would be quick to spot distortions or misrepresentations.

The targets of his critical thinking were not restricted to modern Western authors or commentaries. His critiques of Theravāda triumphalism are on record, but he could be equally critical of triumphalist tendencies throughout the ages demonstrated by any school or sect that promoted its particular emphasis as the 'highest teaching'. He would engage too with the sometimes exhausting hyperbole of some revered sayings from the texts. After a lengthy discussion about the possible meaning of the trope that the true Bodhisattva will hold back from entering the bliss of nirvana until 'every blade of grass has attained Enlightenment', he wrapped up the conversation with the words, 'Beware of cant, even Buddhist cant.'

Introducing us to the wealth available in the tradition, encouraging clear and critical thinking, identifying modern *micchādiṭṭhi*s or 'wrong views' (such as when the *Kālāma Sutta* was presented as the Buddha's advice to test the validity of a teaching by referring always to 'one's own common sense') formed a major portion of the work he did with us on these seminars. But when he took us into the realms of the *Bardo Thodol* (*The Tibetan Book of the Dead*), the Mahāyāna's Perfection of Wisdom or Yogācāra literature, or, say, the *Songs of Milarepa*, the challenges he offered took us far beyond clear thinking, beyond thought, even.

The discussion could soar into the realms of highest meditation experience, or it could come down to earth with his reminder, for example, that the first dhyāna – the first stage of meditative absorption – is the key, indispensable mental state one needs to cultivate and strengthen so as to make oneself available to insight. But, he said, it would be wrong to think of that first dhyāna as 'some highfalutin state'. 'It is the state of mind in which a committed Buddhist should be living *all the time*', he said, indicating a calm, balanced, conflict-free, integrated state of mind of a 'happy, healthy human'.

There would rarely be more than ten participants on a seminar, but the highlights would filter outwards by way of talks, study groups, and a mysterious process of osmosis whereby the core message of the latest seminar would suddenly be on everyone's mind. We were still a relatively small community, many of us living together, so, despite his more remote living arrangements, his teachings, observations, and opinions flowed through our bloodstream if anything more tellingly than ever.

Again and again, two words – 'Bhante says' – punctuated our conversations. Seen from the outside it would have seemed cultish, and, in its own way, triumphalist. But then, Sangharakshita was without question our teacher, with a vastly deeper and broader degree of experience than any of us. What else were we to do as we learned to practise and to teach, except engage with what he had to say, or was rumoured to have said? And then, the simple fact was, whether or not we'd read or studied much Buddhism before or practised with another teacher, we had stayed with Sangharakshita precisely because we'd been attracted to the way he presented the Dharma. He spoke a language and took an approach to the Dharma that suited us, and that we were learning and practising. In time, as our own knowledge and practice deepened, we'd be able to work more creatively with them.

From where he stood, Sangharakshita knew very well that he was in a unique position as a Westerner with a very particular degree of knowledge and experience. He was reflecting deeply and constantly on the way he spoke about the Dharma and the pace at which he could develop his followers' understanding. He knew too that nobody else around in those days was even trying to do what he was doing in terms of 'translating' the language and practice of the Dharma into a Western idiom. So if he did sometimes – actually rather often – feed our confidence by asserting his and our movement's special position as a unique contribution to Western Buddhism, then one could hardly argue that he didn't have a point.

Bearing in mind he'd been an avid student of the available canonical texts since the age of sixteen, and composed *A Survey of Buddhism* while in his twenties, I sometimes wonder what he must have thought of us, so slight was our 'book learning'. But perhaps it didn't worry him too much. One evening back in 1972, when none of us had read much Buddhist literature at all, someone's question prompted him to make a surprising point: 'Probably, any of you sitting here have already read more than you need to gain Enlightenment.' Two maxims he liked to repeat were, 'More and more of less and less' and 'There are no higher teachings, just deeper understandings.' Ravenous autodidact though he was, he was fully aware that the teachings mean very little unless they're reflected on deeply and put into practice.

Mind you, when somebody included the word 'vibes' in a comment, he pondered: 'Ah yes. Vibes. That poor little word! It seems to have to bear half the weight of some people's entire philosophy of life.'

◆

As we've seen, at the time of the first ordinations he was still basing his thinking, at least to some extent, around traditional structures. However, before very long, his continuing reflections and the Order's development transformed his original conception:

> Only much later, after I had realized that the Going for Refuge was the central and definitive act of the Buddhist life, and that commitment to the Three Jewels was primary and lifestyle, whether lay or monastic, secondary, did it become possible for me, taking the feeling I experienced during my ordination ceremony as a clue, to understand what really happened and acknowledge to myself that I had been ordained not as a *bhikkhu* by *bhikkhus* but, in reality, as a Buddhist by Buddhists, and welcomed not into the monastic order but into the Buddhist spiritual community in the widest sense.[178]

As the trajectory of his reflections intertwined with the development of his community, he became fully convinced that there could be only one 'essential' ordination. It would mark the point at which one's understanding and commitment to the path was sufficient, given supportive conditions, to keep moving forward. In time he would develop a language and schema of 'levels of going for refuge'. But in his Order, there would only be one essential ordination.

It was obvious too that most of his *upāsaka*s and *upāsikā*s were fully involved, one way or another, in the life of the Order and doing their best, one way or another, to live a committed spiritual life. Within a year of that first convention, many of us were working within the movement, many of us were living together, and many of us were teaching. By the time of the Order convention in 1976, whose minutes read almost like the record of an extended business meeting, the Order had doubled in size since the first convention, new branches and centres were springing up in the UK and abroad. Given all this, it no longer seemed appropriate to style members of his Order as *upāsaka*s and *upāsikā*s, which in the East suggested they were nominal 'lay followers'. Even so, it wouldn't be until 1982, during a weekend retreat he was running in a suburb of Mumbai, that he announced his decision to restyle them as Dharmacharis (m) and Dharmacharinis (f), simply 'Dharma-farers'.

As for the bhikkhu/bhikkhunī ordination, and its defining characteristic in many minds of celibacy, he never gave up encouraging those who were so minded to take up the practice, or aspire to take it up one day – but as an added training precept rather than as a higher ordination:

> Well, certainly it is true that the celibate life, while it isn't itself necessarily more dedicated, makes possible a greater degree of dedication, because you are free. But it should be viewed as an opportunity, not as an achievement in itself. If someone is just celibate, so what? They're just celibate. What do they do with their celibacy? They can sit down and twiddle their thumbs, or they can get on with an enormous range of activities. Celibacy by itself is just a clearing of the decks for action, it's not the action itself.[179]

What then of Sangharakshita? What was he, and where did he stand on this issue? Although ordained as a monk by a Theravadin elder, in his heart he had never aspired to be anything other than a fully committed, full-time Buddhist. The fact that he was not celibate at the time didn't seem to represent any loss of purpose. In his dreams, though, he'd find himself happily living among monks (some with ochre and some with red robes), and in his waking life he could hardly have been living more simply. Even if he was now engaging in sexual relationships, everyone knew he'd 'walked his talk', and lived a celibate life for a very long time, which was more than any of us had done.

For a number of years I edited the *FWBO Newsletter*, our in-house magazine. One day he gave me a call and asked that we stop referring to him in print as 'the Ven. Sangharakshita'. 'I think we can dispense with the "Venerable" part now', he said. 'I have been the bridge between the old and the new, between the East and the West, and it's perhaps been helpful to maintain that style, with the "Venerable" and my robes, for a while. But I think we're ready to be confident as a Buddhist movement and Order in our own right.'

Building a Buddhist World

I come to you with four gifts.
The first gift is a lotus-flower.
Do you understand?
My second gift is a golden net.
Can you recognize it?
My third gift is a shepherds' round-dance.
Do your feet know how to dance?
My fourth gift is a garden planted in a wilderness.
Could you work there?
I come to you with four gifts.
Dare you accept them?[180]

◆

> Buddhism comes to us wearing an Indian dress, or a
> Japanese dress, or a Tibetan dress, a very beautiful,
> attractive, glamorous, and fascinating dress [...] if we're
> not careful, we're more interested in the dress than what is
> inside the dress, that is Buddhism itself as a universally valid
> spiritual teaching, a teaching which in its essence is neither
> of the East, or the West, but for all time, all space, for man,
> for all forms of sentient life even.[181]

That was Sangharakshita speaking in 1975. As an aside he
hinted that Zen might soon give way to Tibetan Buddhism as

the go-to tradition for seekers of the exotic. By the time I visited his friend and teacher Dhardo Rimpoche in Kalimpong in 1982, Tibetan forms of Buddhism had more or less supplanted Zen in that respect. I wondered what thoughts he might have on the matter. Did he think Tibetan Buddhism could be suited to the West?

We were sitting in the headmaster's cramped study at the school he ran for refugee children. The walls were papered with government notices, probably about health and safety, as well as class timetables, woodblock prints and thangkas, images of Buddha and Bodhisattva figures. Tucked into an alcove near his desk was a small shrine containing a *rupa* (a statuette) of Tārā, the Bodhisattva of compassion. Above her head, set in motion by the heat of a tea light, rotated the Tibetan characters of her mantra: *Oṃ tāre tuttāre ture swāhā*. A weak bulb gave the room some light, but it was a gloomy, cave-like space.

Dressed in his yellow waistcoat and a well-worn, red monk's 'skirt', he leaned forward, squinting in concentration and nodding as he took in the translation of my question. Then he laughed.

'But Tibetan Buddhism is *Tibetan!* It took a thousand years to blend our culture with the Dharma. It now goes so deep you can't separate them, you can't even tell which is which! That is what you will have to do for yourselves in the West.'

It was still early days, but the Rimpoche was describing the enterprise Sangharakshita had embarked on. In terms of Buddhist ideas and terminology he'd made a start, selecting and promoting core teachings, introducing his followers to the riches of the wider tradition, finding new models and metaphors for the Buddhist vision, as well as identifying elements in Western culture and philosophy that aligned, at least to some extent, with the Dharma.

If there was a 'Westernized' master metaphor in his narrative of the Buddhist path, it was still the Higher Evolution. For a good many years its terminology of 'higher and lower', of 'vertical and horizontal', of psychological integration on the level of the Lower Evolution or on increasingly higher levels, and so on, dominated FWBO discourse. Some of us even wore little badges with a silhouette image of a sitting Buddha with the words 'Higher Evolution' printed below it.

If the Higher Evolution was the narrative, then its hero or heroine was the 'true individual', a self-aware person committed to embodying the fullest reach of human potential, which is, ultimately, Enlightenment, Awakening, Buddhahood. The true individual, Sangharakshita asserted, is neither defined by any group nor influenced exclusively by subjective factors such as family and social conditioning or even biological conditionings such as instinct and impulse. Such rare people, whether religious or artistic – and he certainly counted great artists as being on that path – display a positive and refined emotional nature; their energies flow naturally, creatively, and spontaneously without blockage, inhibition, or check. The true individual sees things in depth, sees them as they are. Speaking with his characteristic qualifiers, he declared that the true individual 'is one through whom, as it were, the deeper reality of things, the truth behind appearances, if you like, functions in the world, or is present in the world.'.[182]

To achieve that state of true individuality was in Sangharakshita's view the initial target for the aspiring Buddhist, and its flowering in Enlightenment its ultimate goal. In the early years of the FWBO, the themes and terminology of 'true' vis-à-vis 'statistical' individuality, between individuality and individualism, between the group and the spiritual community, were topics he expanded on regularly, and became as familiar to us as were the terms and themes of traditional Dharma discourse.

In part this was an attempt to 'naturalize' Buddhism, and in part it was Sangharakshita's way of applying a Buddhist perspective to urgent contemporary issues. In his 1971 lecture 'Evolution or extinction: a Buddhist view of current world problems', he revealed the passion behind his focus on the theme. The world's problems, he said, are rooted in the way human affairs have come to be lived almost entirely through the medium of the group. Group collaboration – and competition – has been a vital, defining aspect of our human heritage since the earliest days. However, the groups that now dominate our lives are so extensive, so powerful, and yet so divorced from the everyday realities of our lives that individual human consciousness is submerged in a maelstrom of group conditioning. The individual, he said, must be saved from the 'gravitational pull of the group'. At a time when the interests and power of rival groups were threatening our very existence, he asserted that the reclamation of the individual was key to the survival of the human race.

The transformation of the world, one person at a time, is not the battle cry of a typical revolutionary. But then, Sangharakshita was no average revolutionary. Nor was the man whose work he'd come to admire, and for whose revolution he'd been working in India since 1956. Just a few weeks before he died after a lifetime of legal battles, activism, and politics, Dr Ambedkar explained why he'd entrusted the uplift of India's former 'untouchables' to the taking up of Buddhism, individual by individual:

> There is no use in pursuing a certain path if that path is not going to be a lasting path. If it is going to lead you into the jungle; if it is going to lead you to anarchy, there is no use in pursuing it. But if you are assured that the path you are asked to follow is slow, maybe devious, maybe with long detours, yet if it ultimately makes you reach a safe, sound ground so that the ideals are there to help you to mould your life permanently, it is much better, in judgement, to follow the slower path.[183]

Sangharakshita's vision was one in which 'aspiring individuals' would find each other and form a network of communities, 'free associations of individuals' committed to supporting the higher development of their participants. More than that, such communities, crucially inspired and nourished by Dharma practice, would spark and support the potential latent in others and so, over time, weaken, even undermine, the influence and power of group consciousness, ultimately bringing about the transformation of society.

Idealistic, even messianic, you might think, but it was with such a vision in mind and such language, and with Sangharakshita's influence and close mentoring, that we set about building a 'world within the world', a 'New Society'.

Before long, most core members of the FWBO sangha, whether ordained or not, were living together in 'single-sex' residential communities. This certainly made economic sense; many of us had thrown ourselves into the project after giving up jobs and careers 'out in the world', but we saw ourselves exploring, with varying emphases and degrees of strictness, what it might mean to live with others day to day in a modern Western society, in the light of Dharma practice and Buddhist values.

By the late 1970s we were also setting up small-scale businesses as we graduated from one-off fundraising projects to something more substantial. There were wholefood shops, vegetarian cafes, gardening enterprises, light-removals businesses, and so on. In the UK, an increasing number of people were supported to work full-time as teachers and administrators in the movement's developing network of urban public centres and retreat centres. It had been fun once upon a time to share a stall with Sangharakshita selling bric-a-brac at a 'jumble sale' (a kind of collective 'garage sale') to raise funds for a new London centre, but those days were over.

When contemplating the possibility of a Western Buddhist movement, Sangharakshita had assumed that all its activities would be 'mixed' (co-ed). However, somewhere in the mid-1970s, some men and very soon afterwards some women ran a few weekend retreats just by themselves for themselves. The participants enjoyed them and felt they had a special value of their own, so more single-sex retreats followed, with Sangharakshita's encouragement and when possible his participation. Around the same time, following the example of a men's community next door to the first public centre, one by one, any residential communities around our centres that were still mixed went 'single-sex'.

In the Order, men and women enjoyed equal status, and all classes and retreats at beginner level were open to men and women and run by 'mixed' teams. But, over a short space of time, pretty much every FWBO gathering beyond beginner level was offered on a single-sex basis.

By the end of the 1970s and into the 1980s, most FWBO centres stood at the heart of a 'mandala' of residential communities and businesses. Since the businesses were legally registered as 'co-operatives', we'd speak of our collective FWBO lifestyle as being based on the 'three C's' of 'centre, community, co-op'. Essentially, though, these developments were part of an attempt to find a middle way between monastic and lay ways of living, of being 'in the world but not of it', as the Zen saying has it. It was Sangharakshita who coined the term 'semi-monastic' – and some wag who came up with the alternative, 'semi-detached'.

◆

Sangharakshita watched these developments closely. When he saw something promising, he would be quick to encourage it and to comment and advise at the level of principle. He'd alert us to Dharma texts, such as the *Cūlagosiṅga Sutta*, the story of three monks who live with each other in perfect harmony, or the tale from the *Udāna* of Meghiya, to whom the Buddha explained the importance of living in constant contact with 'spiritual friends'. As businesses got under way, he outlined a simple three-point model for determining their spiritual health. Such businesses should provide an ethical means of support, act as an arena for spiritual friendship, and aim to generate a surplus that could be donated to good causes, which in those days usually meant supporting the work of the local FWBO centre, so that it could keep the cost of its classes and retreats as low as possible.

He described work carried out within such a framework as 'the tantric guru', by which he was pointing out that the everyday challenges and disappointments, those brushes with reality, that people meet in the work setting could be, with the right kind of supporting practices and friendships, at least equivalent to the challenges they met on their meditation cushions, and just as likely to trigger insight.

Sangharakshita made good use of his study seminars to share his concerns and appreciation, thoughts and opinions on the developments taking place. He was, as someone put it rather well, 'talking the movement into existence'. Sometimes he would use a lecture to raise the bar not just higher but to the highest level of principle. Here we find him in 1979, concluding a talk entitled 'Building the Buddha land'. It's a lengthy extract but it offers a textured glimpse of the way he would build his case, working always from Dharma principles, and inspiring his disciples as they went about building a new world:

> The external world is object in the broadest sense. But we're not simply passive in relation to the external world. We do not simply register impressions. The world impinges on us, yes, but we also impinge on the world. We impinge on our own environment, or part of our environment; we impinge on our own selves – on ourselves considered as objects to ourselves i.e. considered reflexively; and we impinge on other people. We not only impinge on the world, we also affect it in various ways. We alter it, we arrange it, we re-arrange it – at least to some extent, however slight. Not only that, we don't impinge on the world at random. We don't alter or arrange, or re-arrange at random. We impinge in accordance with a certain idea, in accordance with a certain pattern or image, or gestalt, or myth, within ourselves, or which is even, ourselves.
>
> This idea is not always consciously realized. In fact, it's very rarely consciously realized. So what does all this mean? It means that our relation with the world is essentially creative. The subject, the human subject is essentially creative in relation to its object. We are creating all of the time. There's no question therefore of anyone not being creative. It's only a question of degree – only a question of greater or less success; greater or less clarity; greater or less positivity; only a question of the quality, as we may call it, of our creativity. We are being creative when we speak; we're being creative when we paint and decorate a room; we're being creative when we write a letter. [...]

Now if our relation to the world is essentially creative, an interesting conclusion follows: it follows that the world, our world if you like, is our creation, that we create the world. There's no question therefore of whether or not we should be creative. No question of whether or not we should create a world. We've no choice. It's only a question of *what* we create. It's only a question of what *kind* of world we create. In traditional Buddhist terms, we can create for ourselves a world of the gods, that is to say a world of refined, sensuous, intellectual, aesthetic, but a rather selfish, rather self-indulgent pleasure. Or we can create for ourselves a world of [...] ordinary human domestic, civic, political and cultural obligations and activities. Or we can create for ourselves a world of the Asuras, or anti-gods: a world of jealousy, of excessive sexual polarization; of over-aggressiveness; of ruthless competition, and covert or overt conflict. Or we can create for ourselves a world of hungry ghosts – that is to say a world of neurotic craving, intense possessiveness, and relationships characterized by extreme emotional dependence. Or we can create for ourselves a world of tormented beings, that is to say a world of pain and suffering – of intense physical and mental distress. Or we can create for ourselves a world of animals, that is to say a world of straight-forward food, sex and sleep.

Or turning our back on all of these we can devote ourselves to developing ourselves as individuals. We can devote ourselves to the Bodhisattva Ideal. We can devote

ourselves directly, or indirectly, to building the Buddha
Land.[184]

◆

We foot soldiers in this enterprise tried to live simpler, less
individualistic lives, adopting the Marxist slogan 'From each
according to his ability, to each according to his needs', or, more
simply, 'Take what you need, give what you can.' The practice
of living with such a maxim launched many discussions as we
lived and worked with it through the yuppy days of the 1980s.

But Sangharakshita was living simply too. Pretty though it
was, his cottage in Norfolk had been small and basic, with an
outdoor toilet. At a time when Bhagawan Sri Rashneesh could
choose which of his ninety-three Rolls-Royces he'd select for
his daily progress among the faithful, Sangharakshita would
be driven from A to B in an ageing, second-hand Ford. That's
not to say he didn't enjoy being driven around; it was and
remained for life one of his pleasures, to sit in the front of a car
avoiding conversation as he reflected and hummed to himself.

If his writings and lectures had a tendency to highlight
the idealism underlying our experiment, his seminars would
give people a chance to discuss what was happening down on
the ground. If you read *The Ten pillars of Buddhism*, you'll be
impressed to discover that 'Within the spiritual community
it is impossible to act in accordance with the power mode,
for by its very nature as a voluntary association of free
individuals sharing certain common goals the spiritual
community is based on the love mode.'[185] However, during

a seminar based on his lecture 'Authority and the individual in the New Society', someone took advantage of the more informal setting:

Question: 'Bhante, Why has power, authority and callous indifference crept, at times, into Sukhavati community and the London Buddhist Centre in general?'

Sangharakshita: 'Well, there's a very general point to be made here: that is to say, within the Movement and Order, even, there are not many Stream Entrants. Now, if you are a Stream Entrant, you will be operating predominantly in accordance with the love mode; but if you are not a Stream Entrant you will be operating predominantly in accordance with the power mode all the time.

'And I think one of the first things we have to do is to recognize that that is our normal way of functioning; that is the way in which people almost always function all the time. So when we come into the FWBO, normally we are creatures of the power mode. Even when we are ordained we are still creatures of the power mode, really. We only operate in accordance with the love mode from time to time in certain circumstances, under, very often, ideal conditions.

'All right, so what happens in a community, whether Sukhavati or any other, whether large or small? [...] In their better moments, [people might] operate in accordance with the love mode; but sometimes it happens [...] that none of them are at their best; they are all operating in accordance with the power mode, and then some quite dreadful things can happen [...]. "Power, authority and callous indifference" do creep in. [...] And afterwards you have just to try to put things right and recognize what has happened; if need be, make amends for what has happened or even apologise for what has happened, whether individually or collectively. [...]

'This is, of course, one of the reasons why [...] people do need to make a really vigorous effort to cultivate [the love mode], because if you are not functioning in accordance with the love mode you will definitely be functioning in accordance with the power mode. [...] I am afraid I see it much more in men than in women. In men it very often takes the form of competitiveness, negative competitiveness. It is a sort of jostling for power and position all the time. [...] Sometimes it seems to be done in a good-humoured, joky sort of way, but [...] there is a power struggle going on all the time underneath; don't be misled by the jokiness and the jocularity and the humour!'[186]

And so on... The process was organic and a bit haphazard. But, as he shared his observations and reflections, Sangharakshita was responding to what he observed, exploring the possibility of bringing into being an effective and intensely lived spiritual community that was neither monastic *nor* lay.

In the summer of 1976, when there were just sixty Order members in the world, undeterred by the naivety of our efforts and fully knowing that the movement was very much a work in progress, he gave a short series of public talks in the seaside town of Brighton entitled: 'Buddhism for today and tomorrow'. During a talk on the Order as 'The nucleus of a New Society', he ended an account of the movement's development up to that time with a certain swagger: 'The rest, we may say, is history!'

Ten years later, a couple of us attended a conference on the state of Buddhism in the USA. As we contributed to the discussions, offering glimpses of the experiment that Sangharakshita was conducting, monks would approach us at meal times to express their amazement. Most of them had been supported by their immigrant lay followers for years. They'd lived in their temples or viharas, observing the Vinaya[187] as good monks, but with all the limitations that had imposed on their freedom to teach, to go out and meet new people. Their ageing supporters were now dying off, leaving sons and daughters who had no interest in Buddhism. They were facing extinction. 'Sangharakshita is so far ahead of us!' they'd say. 'He seems to have thought things through like nobody else!'

But it wasn't quite like that. Somebody once drew up his birth chart:

> According to this chart I had most of my planets below the horizon, which apparently meant that the influences which these planets represented were operating not in the field of consciousness but below it. Though I have never taken astrology very seriously, or indeed had any real interest in the subject, reflecting on this fact I nonetheless came to the conclusion that the course of my life had been determined by impulse and intuition rather than by reason and logic and

that, for me, there could be no question of first clarifying an
idea or concept and then acting upon it, i.e. acting upon it
in its clarified form. An idea or concept was clarified in the
process of its being acted upon.[188]

This is a good way of describing his relationship with
his followers as we created our world. He was always well
informed, he watched developments, read minutes, met with
people, ran the seminars, and listened to our stories. He
seemed to know how and when to comment or, occasionally, to
intervene effectively. He might have been leading from behind,
but he was certainly leading.

Back in 1969 he'd given a talk on 'Art and the spiritual life',
in which he compared the qualities of the genuine artist with
those of the true individual:

We have spoken of the artist as having experienced
something, some higher level of being and consciousness,
and then creating out of that experience. But it is not really
quite so simple and straightforward. It is not that the artist
has the experience itself fully and perfectly and completely
first, before creating. If he had it in that way, fully and
perfectly, he would not be an artist, he would be a mystic,
which is something higher or at least potentially higher.
No, what the artist has is at first a sort of vague sense, an
indeterminate experience of something, and this is his
starting point. He clarifies this, he intensifies this, in the
process of actual creation of the work of art. And we may
say that the original experience of the artist, the creative

experience, is like a sort of seed which is pulsing with life but the nature of which is fully revealed only when the flower, that is to say the work of art itself, stands complete and stands perfect.[189]

In his inner life he might have been a mystic, but in relation to the Order and movement Sangharakshita was the artist, and those of us working under his influence were his material, his medium. On the whole he gave an impression of being patient and content to watch, but he had a calm but unavoidable way of communicating a sense of urgency and the belief that things could always be better. It was a bracing experience to live in this world, under his influence. Even at that early stage in the story, he kept us inspired by his confidence that we were doing something truly significant.

22

Where Angels Fear to Tread

Men like thee, and women too,
Androgýnous, ever-new –
Divine Imaginations free
Exulting in Eternity.[190]

It was 11pm on a summer's night in 1975. A few of us were making final adjustments to page layouts for the *FWBO Newsletter* that was going to press in the morning. It was to be a special issue featuring the Old Fire Station in Bethnal Green, the substantial but derelict, fire-damaged building the FWBO had acquired from the London County Council with permission to turn it into a Buddhist centre and residential community.

Sangharakshita's London-based followers had been fundraising and property-searching for a couple of years. Now, work was well under way as a resident work-team was slowly transforming the place. There was still a long way to go, but it was time to devote an issue of the magazine to the project. There would be photos, drawings, artist's impressions, and articles, letting people know how the four-storey building would be used.

The hope had been that the team running the Centre and teaching there would be composed of men and women, and for a while it had seemed that the building would be spacious enough to accommodate a women's and a men's community, each on its own floor. Jokes about padlocked doors and alarm systems had abounded. But as work got under way, and as the building's potential became clearer, it looked like there would be room for just one residential community. Back in the design studio, none of us knew this, and it was getting quite late when the phone rang. Relishing his chance to utter an iconic phrase, Subhuti was on the line: 'Hold the front page!' He'd just come off the phone with Sangharakshita, who had confirmed that the space above the Centre should house only a men's community.

Sangharakshita had watched the emergence of single-sex retreats and single-sex communities with interest. He certainly hadn't hesitated to offer his encouragement and support for the development, but this felt like a significant moment.

While taking it as a given that single-sex arrangements would offer (heterosexual) people a break from the distracting pull of sexual dynamics, in most of his comments on the single-sex development he preferred to put his focus elsewhere. Men, he said, needed to be more open with each other, able to bring more intimacy to their friendships. They might even break out of the habit of looking to women, *a* woman, to answer all their emotional needs. Across the gender divide he'd observed how ready some women were to accept the role of supporting men rather than taking a lead themselves. He wanted to see them living with confidence, taking more initiative. What he looked to encourage, he said, was a softening of gender polarization within the individual mind, the ultimate goal being one of 'spiritual androgyny'. Over time, his championing of the 'single-sex idea' would firm up as it became for some years a more or less normative aspect of the Order's collective life.

At this time in our history, most of us were relatively young, single, and open to sexual relationships. When a few men set up a remote retreat community in Wales devoted to meditation practice, with an explicit house rule of chastity, there were few takers. That pretty much took care of the 'neither monastic' end of Sangharakshita's equation, at least for the time being. But what about the 'nor lay' end?

The Buddha once suggested that if nature had implanted in us another desire as strong as that associated with sex and procreation, then Enlightenment would have been out of the question. The story of his 'going forth' from home and family into homelessness is a revered and universal Buddhist archetype. It represents the challenge the individual will face on a number of levels, when he or she strives to go beyond the pull of habit and social, even biological, conditioning.

Throughout history, monastic life has provided a refuge for those seeking to follow the Buddha's example in leaving behind the pull of sexual activity and family life (which would so often have followed unprotected sex in ancient times). It is therefore hardly surprising that the monk–lay divide has characterized most traditional Buddhist societies, for it is the celibate, and therefore family-free, monks who can be assumed to be making the supreme effort as they study, meditate, and 'live the life' full-time. In those societies, the 'born Buddhist' laity are, minimally, expected to honour the Buddha, observe some core ethical precepts, and provide monks and nuns with material support. (Except in China, ordination lineages for women petered out in the East centuries ago. It is therefore from Chinese lineages that a women's monastic tradition is being brought back to life and imported back into some Theravādin and Tibetan sanghas.)

For Sangharakshita, the Buddhist life, at whatever level and under any conditions, is characterized by one's willingness to take radical steps and by an intensity of engagement. Immediately after the mass conversions in India, a radical step if ever there was one, he repeatedly reminded Dr Ambedkar's followers that there could be no such thing as a merely nominal Buddhist convert. To be a Buddhist, he'd say, is to be '100 per cent Buddhist'. The scriptures speak of the Buddhist path as being 'of the nature of a personal invitation'. It is something one *chooses* to take up, consciously and freely, with no sense of obligation or fear. You can't become a Buddhist, he once said, unless you feel free not to be one. So if you've made that choice, what would be the point of being anything less than committed to it and applying it to whatever circumstances you find yourself in?

The challenge Sangharakshita had set himself, his followers, and above all the members of his Order, was to forge a world of spiritual intensity in which everyone actively participated, irrespective of their living circumstances. But how would –

how could – his followers maintain a spirit of intensity usually associated with monks?

This wouldn't be easy. And bearing in mind that Sangharakshita had not only been a monk but had lived for twenty years in an Indian world of arranged marriages and extended families, it would have been obvious to him that our generation's way of doing sex, relationships, even family and child rearing, added layers of romantic idealism, insecurity, neurosis even, to the biological drives and the job of keeping our species going. Already critical of religious systems that enforced celibacy, it was also obvious that young Westerners were nothing like the people he'd been living among for years. He would have some catching up to do as conversations around sex, gender, sexual relationships, and the living of a Dharma life began to occupy his attention.

'The relationship'

Some time around 1970 Sangharakshita wrote a short story, 'The artist's dream', set in medieval times. Its hero was an artist creating a fresco for a new cathedral. The young men from the local town are curious and start showing up every day to watch him at work. Soon they're helping out, learning some of the skills and even collaborating. But then the womenfolk, worried that they might be losing their men, find ways to lure them back to the household life. As the story draws to its end, the artist is once again working on his own.

I don't remember Sangharakshita promoting the story with any great fanfare, but copies were lying around and most of us read it. This was one of the ways we began to get the message that he wanted us to think seriously about the time, attention, and emotional energy we were giving to our sexual relationships. In fact the very word 'relationship', which Sangharakshita would sometimes utter with a pronounced rolling of the 'r', seemed to carry an aura of danger and downfall. The sexual relationship, he suggested, was the 'group in microcosm', 'two people leaning against each other like broken reeds', 'a pair of ballet dancers tied together at the legs', or 'two paper bags trying to get inside each other'. It was the refuge of 'weak men' and 'needy women'.

The stark contrast between the partnerships he'd witnessed in India, arranged by caring parents and local elders, and the often impulsive, highly sexualized romantic idealizations he observed among his Western followers gave him pause. Finding himself being asked, maybe more often than he'd expected, to counsel his young friends as they wrestled with heartache and heartbreak, he couldn't help questioning the extent to which their lives were so preoccupied with thoughts of sex and relationships.

He'd make encouraging remarks about celibacy around the place from time to time, but never expected most of his followers to eliminate sexual relationships from their lives. Instead he asked them to question the way they arranged their 'personal mandala'. Might it be possible to shift that part of their lives from the centre of their mandala to the periphery? A range of books – *Men and Friendship*, *Ball-Breaking*, *Sex and Character*, *Sex is not Compulsory*, and *Beware of Pity* – became recommended reading, though not necessarily recommended by him. For sure he would discuss these issues, and maybe mention such books alongside Dharma texts and the works of Blake, Milton, Shelley, Goethe, and the classical Greek dramatists and philosophers, but his main concern was to keep the questions alive in people's minds.

Essentially he was trying to throw light on the way we spent our time and on our dreams. And as a consequence we did start to think and talk about our investment in these facets of life with a new level of openness and curiosity. But light can cast a shadow, and in our case this happened when something unhealthily prescriptive entered the scene, an outbreak of puritanical groupthink in some quarters, especially among the men. The results could be quite crude. Up in Glasgow one morning, an Order member who'd been spending the night with his girlfriend woke to find the other members of his community standing at the end of the bed, insisting he come home.

For a brief spell, as an approach to sorting out a sex life without falling into the pit of the scorned relationship, some people living around the main London centre informally collaborated in creating a field of friendly, no-strings sexual promiscuity. It seemed a relatively problem-free way of satisfying sexual urges between friends. One day I happened to be driving Sangharakshita through South London when the topic came up. We had hardly got started when he turned to face me from the passenger seat, wagging a warning finger, 'Well, for most people promiscuity is no more than a bridge to another relationship. And a very short bridge at that!'

And yet, on another occasion, when it was widely considered the failing of a 'weak man' to be involved in such a relationship, I went to see him. He smiled encouragingly but looked puzzled when I explained how I didn't feel ready to bring my own relationship to an end. 'But why should you end it?' he asked. 'Surely it's not a matter of deciding one way or the other, as if you just have to end the relationship for the sake of it. Just keep on with your practice, meditating, doing puja, enjoying your friendships and generally educating your emotional life. In time what you want to do will become clear, whatever that is.'

It was a general fact of our world in those days that Sangharakshita's views and opinions, or even mention over the dinner table of a book he'd read, could spark a run of half-baked rumours. True or false, though, they flowed through our collective bloodstream, triggering some strange ideas about his thinking, and creating at times a febrile atmosphere. He knew this was happening, and would challenge the more outrageous distortions. But he would also let some of them run. He liked to provoke, stir the cultural pot. But it didn't always work out so well.

What one would these days call a 'meme' got around that he was keen to promote *Greek Love*, a book by J.Z. Eglinton, which spoke positively about the kind of educative, sexual friendship between an older man and a youth in classical Greek times. Sangharakshita had certainly pointed people towards Plato's ideas on Beauty, as expressed in the *Symposium*, so it came to be assumed by some, perhaps given Sangharakshita's own sexual leanings, that he was promoting homosexuality as an approved, even *the* approved, catalyst for spiritual friendship between men.

A few people took up the notion with relish, and some took it on as an idea worth exploring. It was also around that time that Sangharakshita asked me, as editor of the *FWBO Newsletter*, to include an article by a male Order member entitled 'Leaving mother and initiation into manhood' in an issue of the magazine devoted to the theme of 'going forth'. Originally written for circulation among members of the Order, the 3,000-word essay explored a variety of issues related to male psychology and the theme of renunciation. Somewhere around the halfway point it included this short section:

> Finally many 'mummy's boys' have a fear of passivity in a homosexual relationship, even though that is what they may naturally want. To be sexually passive with another man is the ultimate insult to so-called masculinity as, in a sense, one becomes a woman; in any case, mummy wouldn't like it. [...] One could even go so far as to suggest that taking the passive role in a homosexual relationship would for some men constitute an initiation into manhood as (a) the man is surrendering his own pseudo-assertive side and therefore undergoing a sort of symbolic death and (b) is experiencing his sexuality in a situation that is free from women and all their associations (i.e. emotional dependency.)[191]

This section occupied a small place in the article, and by no means represented its central point. However, it caused a stir at the time, and decades later it was cited in *The Observer*, a British national newspaper, as our movement's 'Credo'.

It is true that Sangharakshita believed that a fear of homosexuality inhibited many men from forming intimate friendships. But the promotion of that book and of its theme had more to do with the workings of groupthink, and the wishful thinking of a few men, than anything Sangharakshita might have said. Talking about the issue with me one day, he was concerned and quite scornful of the motivation behind one prominent Order member's promotion of the idea. 'He's really gnawing on that bone. There must be some meat on it for him!'

One has to wonder what part homophobia might have played in the way the narrative around Sangharakshita and his movement has been shaped in some quarters. For sure, there was some active discussion around the theme of homosexuality for a while, but like many of our early phases and crazes it subsided into the background. This might be a good place to add, though, that Sangharakshita was without question pleased, even proud, that the FWBO/Triratna, coincidentally established in the year when 'sexual acts between consenting men in private' became legal, is a place where gay people will always feel welcome.

A woman's place

Cultivate an aphorism as you would cultivate a rose;
but be careful not to remove the thorns.[192]

The announcement in summer 1975 that the floors above our new London Centre should house only a men's community was followed come the next spring by a convention of the Order's fifty or so members. It took place in East London, just down the road from the Old Fire Station. At that time, it was still a grimy, dusty building site sporting few facilities (even windows in many of its rooms). All the same, most of the male Order members camped in it during the convention, while women Order members were lodged down the road in a set of rooms in the building we'd hired for our meetings. The spark-point for the discussions that followed wasn't to do with the disparity in living conditions so much as a feeling among some women that they were being sidelined. Albeit a building site, the Fire Station was to become the London Buddhist Centre, our headline project, the jewel in our crown.

The transformation of a lively, friendly, and mixed FWBO world into two increasingly demarcated gender-based wings took place over a short period of time, and was still a relatively new development. Although it was well established that the team working and teaching at the new Centre, once it opened its doors, would be composed of men and women, it was the men, give or take an occasional mixed-sex working weekend, who were organizing and working on the building project.

It upset some women to see most of the men staying together in the new building during the convention, and not even inviting them over for a morning meditation. Small though the Order still was, there was a much higher proportion of male Order members than female. For some of the women, it was hard not to feel as if the tide had suddenly gone out on the happy, busy world they'd known. Add to that the fact that a few men were enjoying a spell of male triumphalism, even making occasional misogynistic comments and creating an atmosphere that could feel hostile to women. One man who was working and living on-site complained when a local cat adopted the community, because of the murky 'female energy' it brought into the place. Nor did it help when a rumour got around that Sangharakshita was recommending Otto Weininger's *Sex and Character*,[193] or wondering aloud whether women really could live a committed Buddhist life.

The minutes of that convention record tensions emerging on each side of the gender divide, tensions that would dog our collective life for some years as we looked rather clumsily at the meaning and relevance of gender in our world.

◆

As a child, Sangharakshita had always got on well with his sister and aunts, and had a few close friends among the local girls. He was loving and loyal to his mother when she left her husband and their home for another man, even though this meant going against his father's wish. In India he'd enjoyed important friendships with many women, and years later promoted the publication of his correspondence with Dinoo Dubash, a woman he got to know during his stays with Dr Mehta and with whom he enjoyed a strong and enduring friendship. And as he worked among Dr Ambedkar's followers after the early mass conversions, it was often the women in Buddhist localities who arranged and organized his programmes.

When in 1960 Sirimavo Bandaranaike became prime minister of Ceylon, Sangharakshita wrote an editorial in the *Maha Bodhi Journal* containing this section:

> Our satisfaction is all the greater because the new government is headed by a woman. The great democracies, as well as the communist countries of the world, all pay lip service to the ideal of equality of opportunity for men and women; but we have yet to see, in any of them, a woman at the helm of affairs. [...] It was left to Ceylon, a Buddhist country, to distinguish itself by electing the first woman Prime Minister in history. Not that this was wholly unexpected, for unlike other religions Buddhism throughout its long history has stood for the spiritual and social equality of the sexes. That a Buddhist land should have taken the lead in such a matter was therefore right and natural.[194]

So far so good. However, in his first book of memoirs Sangharakshita recorded, without comment, that as a sixteen-year-old working at the London County Council he'd given a talk to the fellow members of a workplace social club on 'The inferiority of women'.[195] A backstory has it that he had a particularly difficult woman supervisor in mind, though it's possible that he included the story to illustrate his naive arrogance at that time in his life. More problematic was his decision to include in a collection of aphorisms, also published in the early years of the FWBO, a provocative adage: 'Angels are to men as men are to women – because they are more human and, therefore, more divine.'[196]

When in 1982 I joined his entourage on a speaking tour of Buddhist localities in western India, we'd sometimes drive past a set of roadworks where we'd see women wielding pickaxes and walking back and forth with hefty containers of wet cement or tar balanced on their heads. 'When we get back to England I hope you'll tell our women about this', he'd murmur from the front seat. A few hours later we'd arrive at a Buddhist locality where he'd be greeted by an elegant array of blue-sari'd women, gracefully waving trays of candles and flowers before him as he made his way to the stage. 'When we get back to England, you must tell our women about this', he'd say as his ceremonial procession through the vast crowd came within earshot.

If I could find his position confusing, then it was harder for the women. In 1982 he gave a talk, 'A wreath of blue lotuses', in which he discussed the issue of an over-wilful approach to the spiritual life. Sanghadevi remembers: 'This was a bit of a kōan for us. He gave the talk on a men's event, to an audience of men, and yet he talked about the emotionality of women. We just didn't know how to take it or what to do with it.' Another Dharmacharini remembers, 'When he saw men forming close friendships he rejoiced; when he saw women forming strong bonds he'd speak of pseudo-romantic attachment. We'd even get to hear that he was wondering whether women were capable of commitment as well as devotion. If there was a choice, we heard, a man rather than a woman should always run a mixed class, lead a retreat, or chair a public centre.'

When Vidyasri, a leading figure within the women's wing at the time, confronted Sangharakshita directly on a range of these matters during a specially organized women's event, he was shocked by what he heard, and warned people against believing all the rumours about what he did and didn't think: his view was that, whether it was the running of a retreat, a class, or a public centre, it should always be the best person, whether a man or a woman, who should take the job.

He obviously enjoyed and felt energized by the company of men, and there were more of them around, but did that mean he had no time for women? What did he really think about women? In those days of free love, feminism, and cultural revolution, was he, as some thought, a dinosaur, a man with the views of a pre-war generation? Had he picked up his ideas on gender from Schopenhauer, Otto Weininger, or the more misogynistic sayings of Dr Johnson? Did it have something to do with his being gay? Or did he simply not understand women?

Perhaps it's worth noting that, especially through the 1960s and 1970s, some time-worn assumptions about the position, role, and even potential of women were in creative and confusing flux within society at large. He was aware of this, and spoke about it in various contexts. But some women wondered whether he'd failed to notice the difference even between the women he'd met on his return to England in the early 1960s and those who were getting involved in the 1970s, so fast was society changing. A story has it that, when asked at the time whether he was a feminist, he replied, 'In India yes, in England I'm not sure, and in America, no.'

Or was he simply misrepresented, and, if so, to what extent? Opinions varied even at the time, even among women. Some women believed that the men were getting far more input from him than were the women, even when they took into account the higher proportion of men involved with the movement at the time. Whatever the case, Sanghadevi remembers thinking how generous, kind, and encouraging he was on the events he did run for women. Vidyasri remembers inviting him on several occasions to join a group of women for a meal or a study session. Her friends, she said, would invariably assure her that he wouldn't come. And yet her memory is that he always accepted her invitations, and, when asked straight questions about the issues the women were dealing with, he would always do his best to respond honestly and positively.

Seminar transcripts of the time show him making remarks about women in men's company that he'd surely not make when among women, as well as remarks about men he'd make in women's company. One theory has it that he was trying to jolt us all, men and women, out of our culturally conditioned idealizations of the opposite sex with a little therapeutic blasphemy. Maybe he was trying to save us from each other (and save himself from being abandoned like the artist in his story). But the fact that there were more men than women in the Order, with men occupying most of the prominent positions in our institutions, turned this into an inflammatory and often undermining strategy. It certainly wasn't helped when naive, cocksure men drew comfort rather than the intended challenge from his words.

Sanghadevi remembers joining the Order in 1977 and having to play catch-up as she discovered how painful the shift to a more gender-divided world had been for some of her sisters. She also discovered very quickly the responsibility she'd taken on as a woman Order member. Those new urban centres needed women Order members to cater for the women who were coming along, but there were very few of them to go round.

Whatever Sangharakshita did or didn't think about women in a general way, Dhammadinna is not alone as a senior Dharmacharini in remembering how supportive he was to her on the level of her personal life and practice at the time, and still keeps a stash of letters and postcards he sent her back in those days. She also remembers how consistently he urged the women to set up more of their own facilities. Far from harbouring questions as to whether women should join the Order, he was 'pushy, like a dog with a bone', she said, in asking the leading women to do whatever it might take to create not just residential communities but a retreat centre for women. This, he believed, would act as an intense focus of support for the women's wing, and would serve as an essential element in the development of an ordination process for women run by women.

In a kind of team-building exercise, most of the women Order members based in Britain took themselves off to the Scottish Isle of Muck for a month to strengthen their bonds, heal differences, and look for ways forward. Sanghadevi especially remembers the conversations around the theme of confidence. It was time to invest in confidence, to work together, support, and encourage each other. Before very long, there were more women's communities and businesses and a women's retreat centre. Nor was it many more years before there was a retreat centre specifically devoted to training women for ordination and in time another, in Spain, exclusively dedicated to running ordination retreats for women.

◆

In the mid-1990s, Subhuti, by then a prominent member of the Order, wrote an essay exploring the meaning of Sangharakshita's aphorism about 'women, men, and angels'. Having worked closely with him as his personal secretary for a number of years, he had a good sense of Sangharakshita's thinking. He wrote the essay while staying in a remote, pine-clad Spanish valley, and shared it with some friends, female and male. He had no plans to see it published widely, but Sangharakshita had read a copy and asked me, as director of Windhorse Publications in those days, to get it published, 'as a proper book, with a spine and a good cover design'. He wanted it to look like a 'real book' so it would be taken seriously. Finally, he promised to launch it himself at a fast-approaching Order convention.

The core proposition Subhuti set out to explore in *Women, Men and Angels: An Inquiry Concerning the Relative Spiritual Aptitudes of Men and Women* was Sangharakshita's contention that, 'at an early stage in the spiritual life', women have a more complex and deeply rooted set of biological, social, and emotional conditionings to deal with than men, and therefore find it hard to give themselves to the demands of such a life.

Published as it was in the early days of the movement, it is hard to know whether the aphorism was based on Sangharakshita's observations of women involved in the FWBO (even women in the Order), on his more general observations of women, or even just on his reading.

The effect of the book's publication was far-reaching. On retreats and in mitra[197] study groups, senior women Order members grappled honestly with the ideas contained in the book, and did their best to communicate their value as triggers for reflection rather than anger. But for some women it was the last straw. Some even walked away from the movement after merely hearing of the book's existence, and some must never have stepped through its doors. It was the first of our books ever to be reviewed in *Tricycle*, the international Buddhist magazine.

Sanghadevi remembers reflecting: 'I thought, "This is our wreath of blue lotus. This is our humiliation, and we have just got to bear it. If our ego buttons get pressed, then we've got to work with that." There were some points in the book worth reflecting on, but why did Bhante choose to do it that way? What was he saying to us?' Looking back now, she finds it hard to say anything positive about the episode.

It helped some women to discover, but unfortunately a fair time after the book's publication, that 'by an early stage in the spiritual life' Sangharakshita had meant a stage just beyond beginner's level. 'Oh, by the time a woman becomes a mitra,' he told me, 'she'll be well past that stage.' So it turned out that he was not thinking, as most people had believed, of long-term female practitioners – such as our own Dharmacharinis. He wasn't even thinking of mitras. This news, as it seemed, was beyond astonishing. Given the seriousness of the confusion, it was hard to understand why Sangharakshita hadn't made the point clearer at the time, not least when crude versions of his thinking were circulating through the grapevine. The number of talks and study groups, the thousands of difficult conversations that the book's publication had added to the workload of our Dharmacharinis, was so immense that few of them can believe even now that Sangharakshita didn't know about the effect it was having.

In time, Subhuti expressed wholehearted regret for the way the essay had been promulgated. 'I want to make it quite clear that I very much regret the publication of my book, *Women, Men and Angels,* which I think was a serious mistake. I am happy that the book was long ago withdrawn from distribution by the publisher, and that all remaining copies were pulped for recycling about ten years ago. Unfortunately, the book drew attention to a relatively peripheral aspect of Sangharakshita's thinking, giving it a status it did not warrant and having effects that I did not anticipate.'

Maybe Sangharakshita had needed convincing. Some people close to him would say that he found it easy neither to understand Western women, nor to be drawn to them in a general sense. And yet, none of this is to say that he didn't befriend or feel great respect for individual women. For all the confusion around these issues, many leading women of the time agree that he was unfailingly encouraging and supportive of them and the work they were doing. He always tried to meet and relate to people, male or female, simply as individual human beings, and tried to learn what made them tick. If one can speak of an inner circle of his closest friends, it is worth noting that it included a number of women.

As the gender balance in the Order has equalized, women have come to hold all and any of the highest positions of responsibility within the Order and wider movement. The current chair of the London Buddhist Centre, our largest public centre, that building site way back in 1976, is a woman, as is the chair of the College of Public Preceptors, the principal keystone of the Order's architecture. At the time of writing, there are about twice as many women as men training for ordination. Could that be in any way due to the challenge Sangharakshita presented in those early days, or despite it?

Sanghadevi is philosophical: 'He was working with a particular group of women at a certain time. Young women now, coming into contact with the movement, are probably already more empowered to think they can do pretty much anything men can do. For me and my own conditioning, this goes all the way back to Eve in the garden of Eden! I never

Vajrapushpa's ordination day, 1981

thought the women's wing of the Order would ever approach the size of the men's wing, as it now does, nor that the men's wing would accept women in significant leadership roles across the movement, other than in specifically women-only situations.

'I would have to say that, overall, Bhante *did* empower us women. He pushed us back on ourselves, and for some this was painful to deal with. Of course, we'll never know what might have happened if he'd done things differently. We'll just never know.'

The chair of Adhisthana, the movement's central base, and where Sangharakshita spent his final years, was for some years a woman, Saddhanandi. He'd barely known her before she became chair, but came to trust and appreciate her as a friend and colleague. For her part, she made her accommodation with that complex personality of his. Like many people, male and female, she'd learned to distinguish between the authority and quality of his Dharma teaching and the more provisional status of some of his actions and personal opinions. As she put it, she revered and worked closely with the teacher, and was willing to accept and help the 'grumpy old man'. She was certainly the only person ever heard to call him 'sweetheart'.

The nuclear family

Sometime around the year 2000, during a meeting of senior Order members at Madhyamaloka in Birmingham, Sangharakshita asked to see me. As I walked into his study, he asked what we'd been discussing that morning. 'Actually, Bhante, we've been talking about wedding ceremonies.' 'Ah, good,' he said, 'because one day we will be a people.'

Well, this was a new way of looking at things. In 1975, he'd attended the wedding ceremony of an Order member at one of our centres, and never did it again. Through the early decades, few members of the Order or core sangha were married, had families or conventional careers. And that seemed to be the way he liked it.

As the 'New Society' came to life through the 1980s and 1990s, its prevailing, even normative, culture was defined by young, single 'full-timers'. Inevitably people living in other circumstances could sometimes feel left out. Sangharakshita spent most of his time surrounded by single people and feeding many of his teachings and precepts into that segment of the community. There was the additional fact that his attitude to 'the relationship', and his frequent references to the family as 'the group par excellence', the very embodiment of a life lived in service to the 'Lower Evolution', made it difficult for people living in those circumstances to feel included or fully accepted.

In response to this prevailing atmosphere, some men who had been living with partners and children chose to move into men's communities, with varying degrees of fidelity to their commitments as fathers. Very few people chose even to think about having children, and even less of getting married.

Bearing in mind the narrow age range within our community, a time came when many of the Order's most committed women, who'd been involved since their early twenties, found themselves dealing with a conflict between the call of the spiritual life and an undeniable urge to bear children. Some chose to work, even struggle, with the urge, in some cases for years, feeling a strong desire to have children but prioritizing their counteractive desire to live the kind of Dharma life they'd envisaged. Some women living around the London Buddhist Centre did become mothers, and continued living in their women's communities while the fathers remained in their men's communities.

Two Order members, Vajrapushpa and Hridaya, did take those steps. It didn't go down well. Vajrapushpa received a cool letter from Sangharakshita, warning her that she would probably gain a reputation for being an 'individualist'. It is true that Sangharakshita felt let down that neither of the pair had discussed their plans with him beforehand, but there was more to it than that. At a meeting of male Order members, Sangharakshita expressed his disappointment, speaking of his choice as representing 'the loss of a good Order member'. Hridaya still remembers the group discussion that followed as a 'ritual humiliation'. Another Dharmacharini remembers her shock when Sangharakshita phoned to let her know that he'd advised her partner, who had asked for his advice, against fathering a child, given how much he had to offer the Order. When she asked what advice he had specifically for her, he asserted his strongly held view that, once someone – male or female – joined the Order, he would expect them to avoid taking on fresh worldly responsibilities such as becoming a parent.

Those now feel like ancient times, almost hard to believe, but they did happen, and they had a powerful and painful effect on some people. It was decades before Vajrapushpa allowed herself to re-read Sangharakshita's letter. It still hurt. It bewildered her too. Surely, with so much focus on the contemplation of death in the Buddhist world, how could there be so little interest in birth, the beginning of life – which is just as mysterious? She felt very angry with Sangharakshita and with those who promoted his views and ideas – with which she strongly disagreed. What shocks her now is the unease, even guilt, she allowed herself to feel, as if she really had done something wrong.

Perhaps more than many others, this issue highlights the fact that there were no old hands, no elders in our new community, women and men who'd been through it all before and could act as mentors for people encountering these dilemmas once the spiritual life started biting. For a long time, Sangharakshita was our only mentor, yet he'd not grown up in the same world as us. He'd had to deal with his own difficulties and tensions, of course, but they were not the same.

As the years went by, his view softened as he saw a number of Order members making a success of integrating the duties of parenthood with a spiritual life. The Dharmacharini whose partner had been advised away from fathering a child with her even came to hear that Sangharakshita questioned, even regretted, the stance he'd taken in her case. In 1994 he gave a talk, 'Fifteen points for Buddhist parents', and led a question-and-answer session on the theme. His treatment of the points ranged from the commonplace to the challenging. Albeit a brief overview, it demonstrated that he not only had things to say about families and children but had, by then, a fair understanding of the issues and concerns parents deal with every day. The session was well attended and gratefully received as a good start. But it had certainly been a long time coming.

It might come as a surprise to learn that very few people living as parents or in couples in those days left the Order or movement. Vajrapushpa and Hridaya moved to another part of London, away from the 'Buddhist village' around the London Buddhist Centre. But they maintained strong friendships within the Order and visited the Centre regularly, several times a week in Vajrapushpa's case, to participate and teach at classes and study groups.

So, yes, there were those bonds of friendship and duty to the community that kept us together. But there was too that respect for Sangharakshita as a Dharma teacher, which few people lost, no matter how much they struggled with some of the things he said or attitudes he encouraged. To begin with, there was the sheer effect of his presence, which had always contained an element of challenge, as if he embodied an existential question: 'What are you doing with your life? Do you really mean it?' There was too the simple fact that he was the person who'd introduced us to the ideals and values that were now at the heart of our lives. And there was, for all its faults and tensions, this lively and tightly bonded community he'd helped us to shape, not least by the challenges he kept alive. It was a community in which we felt more like siblings than friends.

◆

Although regarding the modern phenomenon of the nuclear family as a historical and biological aberration, Sangharakshita was willing to stress the psychological, even spiritual, value of staying on good terms with one's parents, the source of one's life. One couldn't expect the relationship to be a total one; there would be no-go areas, aspects of one's choices they might find hard, even impossible, to understand. But one's parents deserved gratitude, respect, and love.

In his own life, he honoured his relationship with his parents. His father died soon after he returned to England, but until she died, well into her nineties, he paid regular visits to his mother, often taking a friend or two with him to help her to feel involved in his life. (After all, she'd gone about twenty years without so much as a letter from him when he was in India.) In his own nineties, he took an interest in seeking out his family roots, visiting the towns and regions where they'd lived, perusing church records, and unearthing ancient family memorabilia.

Despite the discouraging letter she'd received from him when she was pregnant with her first daughter, Vajrapushpa decided to visit him some time later to let him know she was pregnant again. His response was as unencouraging as before. And yet, the pregnancy led to the birth of a second daughter who now, decades later, is preparing to join the Order. As her mother wryly put it as our conversation came to an end, 'Things are not always so simple.'

◆

So, irrespective of the stresses and strains through those tough years, many of us stayed with Sangharakshita. Neither straying off distracted, nor walking away in confusion or anger, we helped him to paint his fresco and lay down the first draft of a Western Buddhist world, even if it hurt at times. This was a brief historical moment when social and economic conditions allowed him to do what he did, and us to do what we did. Despite how little we knew about the Dharma when we started, or how much Sangharakshita had to learn about guiding us, we got something going, and he was there for fifty-five years to guide it. Now, the Triratna world is almost unrecognizable. The age range alone represents a complete transformation, and of course many people have started coming along to our centres long after starting families and establishing careers. Meanwhile, those of us who were there in the early days have turned into the elders our community once lacked.

Asked during the convention in 1975, 'What would be the worst thing that could happen to our movement?', he replied: 'If it were to become conventional and staid.' While we were young and adaptable, he pushed us hard. The Buddhist vision is of a life that goes against the grain of worldly, even biological, conditioning. No one, least of all Sangharakshita, least of all the Buddha, ever said it would be easy. As our movement spreads, geographically and demographically, as the conditions change and as we grow older, the pull of worldly conditioning can seem to get stronger, not weaker.

As he moved into the last phase of his life, the 'New Society', the 'three C's' near-monoculture in which so many of his disciples had lived through the early decades, was being nibbled at by a range of forces. Harsher economic conditions played a part, but above all the growth, the geographical and demographic spread, of the movement's population meant that an ever-smaller proportion of the sangha was living and working within a 'total' Triratna world. It was not over by any means, and the influence of those living that way was and is considerable, an essential backbone to the rest, as Sangharakshita would say. But it has been a while since it was the dominant Triratna lifestyle.

Because Sangharakshita fed so much of his formal teaching into that youthful 'three C's' world, and identified so many key principles in collaboration with the relatively young British people living that way, he left us with questions that only time will answer. If the 'New Society' was one particular generation's partial answer to the 'neither monastic nor lay' question, was it an experiment that petered out? Will it resurrect? Or has it left, at least, a legacy of proof that there are many ways of living an intense Buddhist life waiting to be discovered by future generations?

Some aspects of our experience make it easy to see why the traditional Buddhist world has been characterized by a divide between the 'full-timers' and the lay folk. But Sangharakshita was determined to assert the priority of going for refuge, one's commitment to the Buddhist path as the crux of the spiritual life, rather than details of lifestyle – no matter how relevant they might be as supports to and expressions of one's practice of that path. So he challenged us with the vision of an Order that is neither monastic nor lay, and dared us to find out what that might mean, individually and collectively. Can we, will we, continue to build a movement that is guided and mentored by Order members living the Buddhist life with real passion and intensity under a wide range of circumstances? Only time will tell.

Taking the Platform

Formerly one needed courage to attack institutions. Now
one needs courage to defend them – and still more to create
them.[198]

In 1986 we launched a revamped version of the FWBO's
quarterly journal. Called *Golden Drum*, it featured a double-
page spread headed 'Outlook'. Here, the reader was treated
to an array of short pieces in which we'd comment on
significant developments, mainly in the Buddhist world. I
say 'we', but, with his range of contacts, views, and ability to
absorb the Buddhist journals that dropped into his mailbox,
Sangharakshita would feed me with suggestions, usually
spelling out in detail what needed to be said.

When he came across an article in the journal of a significant
English Buddhist sangha that touched on the Christian funeral
given to an *anagārika* in the Vihara's grounds, he asked me to
write something. Had it been wise to advertise the fact, without
explanation, that a committed member of their sangha had
been given a Christian funeral? Over the years, he had been
disappointed to see a number of prominent Buddhists, even
the Dalai Lama (if possibly for diplomatic reasons), speaking

in ways that blurred the distinction between Buddhism and Christianity. Christmas Humphreys had even stated on a BBC radio programme that one could be a Buddhist *and* a Christian. With some trepidation I wrote the article, probably not as well as I could have, and wasn't surprised to receive within days of publication an avalanche of angry letters and postcards, most of them from within the FWBO.

'But do these people think Buddhists should have Christian funerals?' asked Sangharakshita when I reported back to him.

'I'm sure they don't, but I don't think they're happy to see us taking what looks like a high-handed stance over such a sensitive matter. It seemed cruel.'

'But do they think Buddhists should have Christian funerals?' he repeated.

'No, Bhante, I'm sure they'd agree with you. But they're not happy to be associated with the article. It seems mean-spirited. They point out that the funeral was probably a kind gesture towards the woman's relatives.'

'Yes, but do they think Buddhists should have Christian funerals?' By now he'd levered himself from his commodious armchair and was pacing the room's tartan carpet at speed. Colouring, he spoke with obvious frustration. 'I thought I'd established a movement in which I could say the things I need to say. I thought I had a platform so that I wouldn't have to compromise.'

It's worth pausing to wonder: did he ever *not* want a platform? His first article for *The Middle Way* on 'The unity of Buddhism' was already a declaration of intent, a clarion call.

There he stood at the age of eighteen, addressing the Western Buddhist world and beyond, declaring with precocious confidence how limited was its grasp of Buddhism. Through lectures, books, and booklets as well as the magazines he edited or contributed to, he had seen it as his duty to speak out and share his views on the Dharma, on the state – and shortcomings – of the Buddhist world, about the spiritual life and about life in general. It was as if, for him, the experience of an insightful reflection wasn't complete until he'd shared it in a poem, an aphorism, an essay, or a book. Now, the Buddhist movement emerging under his stewardship was not only a living embodiment of his position on a number of issues, but a platform from which he could address the wider Buddhist world.

Back in the late 1970s, when we were setting up urban centres and building the first retreat centres, he had asked me to stop including so many photographs of building sites in our magazine. I explained my thinking, that people would be inspired to see how much was going on, the spread of our movement, the growth of the Order, the new facilities... But with an eye to the magazine's mailing list, which included many of his Eastern friends and connections, he wasn't happy. 'When they see pictures of young people in overalls working on building sites, they'll think we're poor and *lacking* in facilities. They won't take us seriously.'

The fact that we *were* young, poor, and lacking in facilities wasn't the point. He had things he needed to say, and not much time to say them. He wasn't getting any younger, and the Buddhist world in the East was, as one writer put it, just a few revolutions away from being overwhelmed by totalitarian secular governments. The very future of Buddhism might depend on how it would be taken up in the West.

From the age of sixteen, Sangharakshita had related to Buddhism as a whole, in its heights, depths, and breadth. He'd studied it and tried to communicate its literary and practice traditions from the standpoint of a knowledgeable devotee. His books, essays, and talks bore witness to his knowledge of the various schools, but he wrote as a practitioner who had encountered and observed the followers of those schools, and not as an academic. This didn't always go down well. Along with praise, *A Survey of Buddhism* attracted criticism for what was considered a partisan, anti-Theravāda bias. Of this he'd write:

> Though I have tended, in my writings, to criticize only Theravādin formalism, it should not be thought that other forms of Buddhism are free from this canker. The reason for my criticizing Theravādin formalism, specifically, was that it was Theravādin formalism which, in my early days in India, I came across, not to say came up against. Subsequently I became aware that formalism, whether monastic or non-monastic, was a feature of much traditional Buddhism, almost regardless of school.[199]

When he wrote the *Survey*, he was young, passionate, and living in the thick of things. The views he expressed were always based on his observations. Kalimpong's Buddhists were plagued by predatory Christian missionaries, while representatives of Tibetan schools took it in turns to assert their ownership of the highest teachings, or could sometimes suspiciously discover the incarnations of great teachers in the richest, most influential, families. He was never interested in voicing criticisms for the sake of it or to gain notoriety. As he composed his survey of the Buddhist tradition, it had mattered to him that he should speak honestly. For the rest of his life, he believed in speaking out, and, as he established a new Buddhist community in this new territory, not just of England but of the modern, post-industrial world, he felt the need to speak out more, not less.

He was a rare and perhaps unique figure at the time. He had been ordained according to the Theravāda Vinaya, taken the Mahāyāna Bodhisattva vow with Dhardo Rimpoche, and received a range of Vajrayāna initiations. He had established 'the monastery of the three ways' in Kalimpong. He was a Triyana Buddhist, though it is worth mentioning that he would sometimes assert that he and his followers were 'Ekayāna' Buddhists, meaning, '*just* Buddhist' or 'radically Buddhist' in the sense of referring back to the foundations, to the unified intention at the heart of the tradition.

The issue of 'orthodoxy' had been on his mind for years. What did it mean in the Buddhist context? He knew that, in the eyes of most if not all Eastern Buddhist schools, our Order members weren't the real thing. At conferences they'd invariably be redirected to the 'lay' section of the dining room if they were seen approaching the area reserved for 'the Sangha'. Yet in Sangharakshita's eyes it was the Eastern schools that had departed from orthodoxy, while his Order was manifesting it in the only way that mattered. Speaking in 1990 about the Order's relation to the rest of the Buddhist world, he said:

> paradox or no paradox, we have to take into account the fact
> that the followers of the four schools [...] are not orthodox
> Buddhists because, for them, something other than Going
> for Refuge is of primary importance in the Buddhist life,
> at least in practice, and the fact that such is the case affects
> the nature of our relation to them as, indeed, it affects the
> nature of their relation to us.

As Kulananda wrote in his introduction to the talk when it was first published:

> So long as Buddhists relate to each other chiefly in terms of
> what is secondary – the number and type of precepts that
> they follow – or in terms of what is tertiary – their chosen
> life-style – rather than in terms of what is primary – the fact
> that we all, to whatever extent, go for Refuge to the Three
> Jewels – then we will inevitably fail to communicate with
> each other.[200]

He had no wish to offend others or to isolate his Order and movement from the rest of the Buddhist world. But with the future of Buddhism at stake, he felt it his duty over the years to share his views with extended papers such as 'The meaning of orthodoxy in Buddhism', 'The history of my going for refuge',

'Forty-three years ago', 'Was the Buddha a bhikkhu?', and 'The ten pillars of Buddhism'. In the days before the internet, our publishing wing and our collection of his recorded talks were his platform; they amplified his voice, preserved and published his thoughts. But as we collaborated with his ideas to create a 'world within the world', the movement became at least to some extent a living expression of those ideas. This meant, among other things, that we, his followers, were on the receiving end of his views and opinions more than anyone else.

The scope of his commentary was not restricted to the Buddhist world or ostensibly Buddhist issues. When the publishers of the magazine *Gay News* were convicted under Britain's blasphemy laws for publishing a poem that gave a homoerotic twist to Christ's crucifixion, Sangharakshita wrote an essay in response. 'Buddhism and blasphemy: Buddhist reflections on the 1977 blasphemy trial' was published as a booklet and even quoted in the course of a parliamentary debate. That his views made a contribution to the public debate would have satisfied him, no doubt, but he'd written the essay mainly with Buddhist readers in mind. His theme was not homosexuality but the effect of Judaeo-Christian cultural conditioning and the value of 'therapeutic blasphemy':

> The ex-Christian may be an atheist or an agnostic, a humanist or a rationalist, a secularist or a Marxist – or a spiritualist or a Satanist. He may even be a Buddhist, i.e. a Western Buddhist. Whatever it is he may be, it can be safely asserted that despite the completely genuine nature

of his conversion to the new philosophy and the new way of life, in the vast majority of cases he has *not* succeeded in abandoning the religion in which he was born and brought up as completely as he would like to do and that, to some extent, he is at heart still a Christian. The fact need not astonish us. Christianity is not just a matter of abstract ideas but also of emotional attitudes, and easy as it may be to relinquish the one it is often extremely difficult to emancipate oneself from the other.[201]

The essay, and especially what he had to say about 'therapeutic blasphemy', had a strong effect on his young community. It brought new energy and freedom to conversations about the place of devotional practice in Buddhism, about approaches to an ethical life that did not depend on divine sanction, conversations about the very nature of a 'spiritual' life.

It was an exciting and challenging aspect of being around him as he communicated his thoughts, about religion, the family, sexual relationships, the myth of progress, the pitfalls of some meditation practices when insensitively or prematurely taught, the false view that one 'has to go through things' before taking up a spiritual life, to recall just a few examples.

In relation to social commentary, which emerged in fragments as he mentored his followers' efforts to create a 'world within a world', some of us would try to work out whether he was coming from the so-called left or the right. It shocked a few people to discover that he received the *Daily*

Telegraph (for its better news coverage, he said), as did rumours that he held a certain admiration for Margaret Thatcher, though for her forthrightness, her lack of 'pseudo-liberal' compromise, and her determination, and not necessarily her policies. As a friend put it, 'He would always surprise you, there was always something fresh and unexpected about the perspective he'd bring to the discussion.'

But you would have found it impossible to fit him into any kind of party-political box.

During one of his study seminars, he shared some thoughts on the matter:

> When I was working among Dr Ambedkar's followers, some
> of their political leaders tried to get me on their side against
> other leaders, but I always avoided that and confined myself
> to strictly religious activities. Since my return to England,
> I have sometimes wondered whether it might be a good
> or necessary thing to get involved in politics, because it
> does seem that one needs to operate on that front too, but
> in Britain politics is party politics, and I couldn't see any
> party with which I could sympathize. I could occasionally
> agree with some of the things that some of them did, but I
> couldn't say more than that.[202]

There were a few hobby horses, themes he'd return to, explicitly or implicitly, again and again. The laws of a society, he believed, should reflect the laws of karma: actions should be seen to have appropriate consequences. He lamented the way the language of rights was prioritized over the language of duties. This was a theme he'd first written about in India but would return to regularly throughout his life:

> Social and political discourse is dominated by the concept
> of rights. Rights are of many kinds and the number seems
> to be constantly on the increase. [...] The confusion that
> has been generated by the one-sided emphasis on rights
> can be resolved by a greater emphasis on duties. The
> Buddha spoke of duties, not of rights. According to him
> duties are complementary: parents have duties towards
> their children, and children have duties towards their
> parents, and so on through the whole gamut of human
> relationships.[203]

Another frequently revisited issue was the decline in fidelity to the notion of objective truth in the public domain:

> Actual lies may not be told, but those facts which are not
> in accordance with the feelings and interests of this or that
> individual or group are increasingly ignored, misrepresented,
> distorted, and suppressed. In extreme cases such facts are
> not allowed ever to have existed at all. From the stage where
> loyalty to the notion of objective truth becomes selective
> – that is to say, becomes that which is in accordance with
> certain personal or sectional interests – it is not a very big
> step to the stage where that which is in accordance with
> those interests becomes the truth. At this stage, therefore,
> there is a breakdown of the notion of objective truth. [...]
> Words no longer have the same meaning for everybody, and

what one group regards as facts another regards as non-facts. There is a failure of communication.[204]

When laying down general principles for the kind of society he hoped his followers would develop, he would speak of the 'love mode' as distinct from the 'power mode'. In a letter to a friend, he wrote: 'More and more I see the spiritual life in terms of learning to switch from the power mode to the love mode. If one can do that, everything else will follow.'[205] With great conviction, he shared his feelings on the subject with a vast crowd of listeners in the Worli district of Mumbai:

> I believe that humanity is basically one. I believe that it is possible for any human being to communicate with any other human being, to feel for any other human being, to be friends with any other human being. This is what I truly and deeply believe. This belief is part of my own experience. It is part of my own life. It is part of me. I cannot live without this belief, and I would rather die than give it up. For me, to live means to practise this belief. Therefore, this belief is part of my religion. It has nothing to do with the way in which I dress, nothing to do with what I call myself. It is a matter of the way I am, the way I exist. It is the way I naturally function in the world. This is what religion really is. It is what you most truly and deeply believe. It is what you are, what you are prepared to die for. It is your life. It is what you are, what makes you behave in the way that you do. Religion is therefore a very important thing. In fact, it is the *most* important thing.[206]

Inevitably this overriding view carried through to his thoughts on racism:

> We can't just look the other way and content ourselves
> with the fact that we ourselves don't personally practise
> that discrimination or indulge in that prejudice. I'm not
> suggesting we take a militant attitude – that is often counter-
> productive – but in a gentle and kindly and non-violent
> way we must do everything in our power to counteract this
> menace, which is obviously quite opposed to the whole spirit
> of the Dharma.[207]

To live in the love mode did not, he'd say, preclude the occasional need to deploy the 'power mode', just as a parent might rather sharply pull their child's hand away from a fire. But it should be considered always and only in the service of the love mode. As we've seen, though, in the sometimes crudely prescriptive world of a young spiritual movement, that qualifying comment could be used to rationalize immature zealotry. When he came to hear that some people at one of our centres were being shamed and even bullied, supposedly for their own good, his pain was almost too much to witness. For once he allowed himself to reveal the intensity of his care and concern. During a meeting he was attending with a few FWBO chairs, he received a letter from a mitra that contained a disturbing account of his treatment by the local Order members. He decided to share it.

We had just finished dinner and were sitting with him in a half-circle round the fireplace, talking about this and that.

During a short pause he produced the letter from his jacket pocket and started to read. When he came to the descriptive passages, he could hardly speak. Tears filled his eyes and the words came from his depths, almost one at a time, almost strangled by the intensity of his emotion: 'I... did... not... establish... a movement... so that people... could turn it... into a dictatorship!' It was a heart-stopping glimpse into the intensity of his care for the people, the individuals our movement was meant to be serving.

Pick up a transcript of any study seminar, and you'll get a taste of how he taught, mentored, and illuminated Dharma issues seamlessly alongside shafts of personal observation and opinion. Even if some of those opinions could unnerve some of his more liberal followers, the pay-off was that we were getting the whole man, a man who cared for people, for truth, and for living within the truth. He was willing to think outside the tramlines, and communicate as a human being, a passionate Buddhist, and not just 'the teacher'. But, in that he *was* the teacher, we would listen and try to absorb it all. There was of course the handicap many of us suffered from, of not being nearly as thoughtful, fluent, or spiritually experienced as him. He worked hard to make his thoughts accessible to us, as the seminar transcripts demonstrate, but it is still tempting to wonder what difference it might have made had more of us been capable of engaging with him more energetically and in more detail.

And yet, no matter how much or how little we were able to absorb, we'd come away feeling somehow initiated into something worth striving for – which might have little to do with the exact content of the discussion. We'd got to spend some time around someone altogether different, broader, deeper, unique, even though it wasn't always comfortable. It's not surprising that most of us would find him turning up in our dreams, shaking things up, and pointing the way.

He had considerable knowledge and deep appreciation for aspects of other religions, but was, without question, an undiluted, unapologetic advocate for Buddhism. Buddhism, he stated, was not just a religion, but *'the religion* par excellence', the Ur religion. In his view it was the only universal religion that spoke directly from and to the truth of things without introducing a splinter of the reification or historicity that, he believed, had corrupted other religions. Further, Buddhism, he said, is the only religion that applies what he called 'the transcendental critique of religion' to itself:

> The purpose of the transcendental critique of religion is not to destroy religion, its purpose rather is to restore religion; to restore it to its true function – its function of being a means to an end. That means being of course always the spiritual development of the individual. [...] We should apply this critique, even this criticism, to everything that presents itself to us as religion, should apply it to Christianity, should apply it to Buddhism, apply it to the Hīnayāna, apply it to the Mahāyāna, apply it to the Vajrayāna, should apply it to our own practice of the Dharma. If we practice meditation we should ask ourselves 'is it really helping me to develop?'[208]

When an academic sociologist wrote a thesis[209] containing a number of inaccuracies and misunderstandings in relation to the FWBO, Sangharakshita was inspired to respond with a substantial essay, which was published in book form. Sangharakshita considered *The FWBO and Protestant Buddhism: A Protest*[210] one of his most important publications. In his view, the author's account of the FWBO in his thesis required nothing less than a forensically detailed examination and rebuttal. In this way, Sangharakshita was able to clarify a number of important points about Buddhism and the *raison d'être* of the FWBO. Once the book was published, he let it be known that he wanted every Order member to read it – for its important content and in part as a demonstration of his critical method.

Some readers found themselves uncomfortable with the uncompromising energy behind the response. For his part, Sangharakshita was surprised that his disciples couldn't appreciate what he simply regarded as a 'robust exchange of views'. Here, it's perhaps helpful to remember that his childhood reading had permanently moored a part of him in the eighteenth and nineteenth centuries. He would happily have been at home crossing swords and exchanging insults as well as ideas in the hurly-burly of the coffee house so beloved of Dr Johnson. Add to that his sharp nose for 'pseudo-liberalism', a term he invented to cover what would later be referred to as 'illiberal liberalism', a kind of over-prescriptive deployment of liberalism, and it is hardly surprising that he was more interested in speaking the truth than in catering for our oversensitive times. 'These days,' he would say, 'one should not waste time helping the weak. Nowadays it is the strong who need help.'[211] On those occasions when I showed some hesitation around publishing something likely to win us more critics than friends, he'd come straight back: 'Well, even if some people don't like what I have to say, there will be others who'll be relieved to know that someone is prepared to say it.'

Taken superficially, for a man committed to bringing the Dharma into the modern world for the sake of all beings, some of his more robust stances might seem paradoxical. Shouldn't he have been in the business of making friends and influencing people at every opportunity? But as a true individual, and in line with his concern for the 'true individual' as a vanishing species, he never saw himself as a popularizer, nor did he see it as his job to be one. Time was short. His priority was to lay down a clear line of approach to the Three Jewels, and to light a beacon for the 'true individuals' out there, alerting them to the riches of Buddhism. It would be up to his followers to write the popular books should they wish.

I was once commissioned to write a short article about him, a brief character sketch. I opened one paragraph with the words, 'He likes to be liked, but...' The next time we met, he seemed concerned. Why, he wondered, had I suggested in print that he liked to be liked?

It's not that he didn't like to be liked. He regularly voiced his delight when people expressed gratitude and appreciation for what he and the movement had given them. But he didn't want anyone to think, even for a moment, that he'd prefer to be liked than to speak the truth.

24

Guru, Teacher...

The guru's business is not to teach the disciple anything,
but simply to be himself in relation to the disciple.[212]

He was in the USA, spending time with the men's community adjacent to our public centre in New Hampshire. Following routine, he'd been up since 5am, meditating, reflecting, and juggling words into what might become a poem. The others were still upstairs meditating when he made his way to the dining area. He sat down by the window and mused while taking in the view. That's when he noticed a broad-winged hawk perched on the bird table a little way off. Sitting dead-still it watched and waited. Sangharakshita watched too. As the residents came downstairs he met them with urgent hand gestures, signalling silence, beckoning them cautiously forward so they'd get a chance to see the bird.

But while he looked through the window, the others were looking at each other. Who was going to tell him he was looking at a farmer's decoy that had been there for years? Maybe they felt awkward, embarrassed because of his age and worsening eyesight. Or maybe they were in awe, too caught up in their projections onto him as a teacher, founder, even guru, to know how to act? At least their hesitation gave him more time to swoop and soar in the clear blue sky with his imaginary bird.

Why did so many people find it difficult to relax in his presence? It hurts to recall the painful dinner parties he had to sit through during his centre visits. Even though I worked and lived with him for years, I could be equally affected. Chatting over lunch one day, I noticed he was ready for tea. Without breaking off the conversation I mindfully poured tea into his bone-china cup and ever so consciously added a dash of milk, and then just in time saw his eyes flash down to the table and back – as I was about to plunge the teaspoon not into the sugar but in the margarine.

He wasn't our headmaster, our boss, or a visiting rock star. So what was it about him that had that effect? Not on everyone I should add. There were some who could be around him easily without feeling overwhelmed, and who'd find it funny to watch the rest of us tripping over ourselves like gangly adolescents.

Maybe there was a desire to impress or win his approval, even though he was studiously careful not to give it, so strong was his wish to avoid getting caught up in that kind of relationship.

But because he was so contained and mindful, you couldn't help making an extra effort to be contained and mindful in his presence. And unless you were as habitually mindful as he was, having being told at the age of eight to stay in bed and avoid any careless movement, it was hard not to feel clumsy around him.

He was a man who could sit still for hours on end, turning over in his mind a single Dharma point, a poem, or an issue that had arisen in the movement. Consequently, the quality of his reflection and the breadth of his perspective on most issues would cut much deeper than your own, so it could be tempting to keep your thoughts to yourself. Those who self-consciously tried to approach him as an ordinary person, luring him into casual exchanges, could find their efforts having the opposite effect. As someone desperately put it during an awkward first meeting, 'You just don't play social games do you?' 'No,' he replied, smiling but not really helping, 'no, I don't.'

For many years, he lived at Padmaloka, a retreat centre devoted to helping men prepare for ordination. Each afternoon, a short line would form in the hallway as two or three retreatants waited for their twenty-minute meeting. This first contact, and perhaps a chance to discuss ordination, was a big moment heaped with significance. But for his part the sessions felt contrived, too unnatural to give him a meaningful idea of the person he was meeting. 'To be honest,' he once told me, 'I get a better sense of who they are and whether or not they're ready for ordination when I look out the window and see them walking across the lawn.'

He knew the effect he could have. It saddened him, he told me, to hear the shift of atmosphere in the community dining room as he headed back to his study after a meal. But he couldn't be other than he was. He enjoyed and was energized by younger people but he was never just one of the lads. He liked to eat his meals in silence before sparking a meaningful

Sangharakshita at Padmaloka, 1986

conversation about art, literature, or recent developments in the movement. It's not that conversation was never light; he enjoyed sharing anecdotes and teasing his friends. But, whatever side of his personality you met at any time, you could sense the poised energy, the hum of an internal gyroscope pinning him to his sense of purpose.

Living around him, as Bhikkhu Khantipalo had discovered even back in the Kalimpong days, it would take a while to get used to a way he had of engaging with you deeply over lunch, yet affording you a quizzical glance if your paths crossed a couple of hours later, as if he was wondering who you were and why you were there. Well, he was a writer after all; there was hardly a day in his life when he wouldn't have a tricky sentence or the possibility of an especially felicitous phrase on his mind. And as the movement took off there was always a lot to think about, so much, he once told me, that he kept a diary to note down a time when he would *think* about something.

So, yes, it could be uncomfortable, embarrassing, even implicitly humiliating to be around him sometimes. But that was because he had a way of reminding us, just by being himself, that there was more growing up to do. And maybe that's what a guru is.

What was he in relation to us, and we to him? There's no single answer. By the time he died, some of us had known him for fifty years or more, others for just a handful. Over time, he became an increasingly distant, iconic figure. With age came less energy and failing eyesight. Then, when the internet gave access to talks by hundreds of Order members, as well as by teachers from all points of the Buddhist compass, his lectures and writings could be seen by some as one set of options among many. Coming forward in time, his aura was affected by in-house controversies stemming from his past sexual activity or some troubling accounts of the FWBO's early days.

In a 2009 interview, 'What is the Western Buddhist Order?', he referred to his followers as 'disciples'. This came as a shock to some. Even though he'd been using the term freely and unchallenged since the earliest days, a vociferous cohort declared it to be something new, an unprecedented assertion of authority. They weren't happy. Was he comparing himself to Christ and the rest of us to the apostles? Was he placing himself on a level with the Buddha? Was he claiming to be a *guru*?

'Guru' was not a word he used about himself. To begin with, most of us were not in a close and regular relationship with him, a qualification he saw as essential to the traditional guru–disciple relationship. Then, he was founder, teacher, preceptor, and head of a new Buddhist order and movement. How could he act as a guru in the traditional sense as well? 'I would say', he once wrote, 'from my own observation and experience this very rarely happens indeed, because, one might say, the qualities that make one a guru are not necessarily those that make for promotion within the ecclesiastical system.'[213] In his case, it wasn't a matter of promotion within an existing school or lineage. He had been duty-bound to act as a jack-of-all-trades as he brought a new lineage into existence.

The word 'disciple' comes from the Latin *discipulus*, which means 'student', 'learner', or 'follower'. 'Student' never felt right to him. The Dharma should be caught, not taught, he'd say. A Buddhist teacher must do more than teach; he or she should communicate their commitment, their going for refuge, and not just their knowledge. 'Follower' was maybe okay, if a bit vague and weak. To his mind, being a stickler for appropriate etymological usage, the word 'disciple' suited the situation better than the alternatives. We were engaging with the Dharma-discipline in the light of his distillation, his presentation, and following a particular system of practice under his guidance.

A sociologist commentator broached the issue head-on by describing the FWBO as a model of charismatic authority 'because Sangharakshita is understood to have the personal authority to be able to distinguish between what is, and what is not, essential Buddhism'.[214] In response, Sangharakshita wrote:

> But what is this 'personal authority'? In what does it consist? Whence is it derived? I would say [...] that it is not a question of first having the personal (i.e. charismatic) authority and then, because one has that authority, being somehow able to distinguish between what is, and what is not, essential Buddhism. [...] First one becomes able, by virtue of study and meditation, to distinguish between what is essential Buddhism, and what is not, and then one is understood as having personal authority because, appealing to their reason and experience, one enables people to see the difference for themselves.[215]

It's a fact that he knew more about Buddhism, its history, its development, and its philosophy, than any of his followers, and he'd been practising it for longer and more assiduously than any of us. He'd been giving thought to ways of communicating the Dharma to Westerners for longer than us, and probably longer than anyone else. And he was sufficiently further along the path than us to be an effective and compelling guide. He had not only the vision to establish a spiritual community, a living environment of friendship, support, teaching, and challenge, but also the commitment to stay around and guide it for fifty-five years.

But there *was* more. Whether or not it comes across in his writings or recorded talks is hard to say. But when you were around him, listening to him talk about Dharma principles or about the fruits of practice, you knew he knew, and had experienced, what he was talking about. This doesn't mean he was the kind of teacher who referred to his own practice, his own struggles, defeats, and breakthroughs, as many modern teachers do. Actually he did very little of that, preferring to keep the Dharma, not himself, centre stage.

And then, beyond the knowledge, his ability to identify principles, and his clarity, there was a certain magic touch. Sometimes you'd come away from a meeting with him able to recall an atmosphere of mutual transparency, or of the warmth that had spread between the two of you as you talked, more than anything in particular he'd said. Someone who visited him during his sabbatical in Cornwall described his presence as being so refined that 'It was as if he was almost transparent.' There were similar stories doing the rounds, but it feels inappropriate to put them into words. How do you put these things into words? But they were there, part of the mix. And, in some ways, they were rather peripheral in terms of the total effect he had on us.

For my part, a couple of relevant memories go back to the early days of a public centre where I was working. He came to visit us one evening, and talked informally with our regulars about their meditation practice. As he explained the relationship between the dhyānas (states of meditative absorption) and the arising of insight, I watched my new friends leaning progressively further forward in their chairs, utterly rapt. Somehow he'd made this aspect of Buddhist experience feel so real, so attainable, that you could have reached out and touched it. I watched him do this sort of thing again and again, and it certainly wasn't because he'd read a lot.

After the class, he stayed overnight. The next day was to be a public open day for our little centre. After our community morning meditation, I found him in the dining room waiting for breakfast.

'What meditation practice did you lead today?' he asked.

'*Mettā bhāvanā*,' I said. 'I thought it best we should meet the public with *mettā*.'

A pause, then, 'Hmm. Not with mindfulness?'

He was never what you expected, and always brought that sense of challenge.

Addressing a gathering of Order members with a paper in 1990, he said:

> I would [...] preferably not apply the word 'guru' to myself
> nor have it applied to me by others. We have in Buddhism
> the wonderful term 'spiritual friend' and this I am more than
> content to apply to myself and to have applied to me by others.
> Indeed, there are times when I think that 'spiritual friend' is
> almost too much and that just 'friend' would be enough.[216]

◆

Whether or not he was a guru, he certainly was a teacher. He couldn't help himself. He loved to share his knowledge, his references, his enthusiasms, for Buddhism of course, but also and especially for literature and art. In the course of just five minutes of a recorded conversation on 'The artist as rebel', he referred to Blake, Dickens, Rembrandt, Gainsborough, Damien Hirst, Andy Warhol, Mozart, Bach, Handel, Sir Walter Scott, the Brontës, and Haydn. The references suggested he was familiar not just with their works but with their lives by way of the biographies he loved to read. It saddens me to recall how few of us could meet him on his level. But that didn't stop him from talking, sharing, encouraging.

Perhaps reflecting on what he had gained from his friendship with Dhardo Rimpoche, he once said: 'One cannot, in fact, be a teacher without being a friend – cannot be a spiritual teacher without being a spiritual friend.'[217] In his case, the opposite applied as well: he could not be a friend without being a teacher. When he and Paramartha began what would become a close, thirty-year friendship, Sangharakshita handed him a reading list of sixty essential books, and set him his first essay, on 'Buddhism and Stoicism'.

When he returned to the West, he was a Dharma teacher at a particular time in his life, under particular social and historical conditions. On the ground, day to day in London, he was addressing a small but growing community of men and women in their mid-twenties, at the height of the 1960s revolution, with their particular conditioning, concerns, and preoccupations. However, with tape recorders and printing presses running, and with his confidence in the movement's future, he knew he was broadcasting his teachings to the wider Buddhist world as well as into the future.

For sure, some details in the way he talked and taught would have been influenced by circumstance and the people he was talking to. But there is that quality to the Dharma, which when faithfully expressed by a good teacher has a way of revealing its depth to the listener in accordance with their readiness to receive it. That is why we can return to Sangharakshita's early talks and books and discover more in them each time. But it is highly unlikely that his youthful audience of the time had anything to do with the choices he made in terms of general content and direction. When he emphasized the language of evolution, of positive emotion, of benevolent action, growth, and development, he simply believed he was coming closer to the way the Buddha would have taught as he befriended and talked to people, as evidenced by the Pali suttas.

His relationship with the Tathāgatagarbha doctrine provides a useful example. It's not that he didn't understand or respect the poetic Mahāyāna teaching that a human being is blessed with a kind of innate 'seed' of Buddhahood waiting to be discovered and revealed. His 1970 lecture series on *The White Lotus Sūtra* took his listeners into that territory richly and inspiringly. And yet, almost at the same time, he would warn us away from that language. His 1974 seminar on D.T. Suzuki's *Outlines of Mahāyāna Buddhism* saw him lamenting day by day how easily the metaphor could be grasped the wrong way, as a

Buddhist version of the soul, or, thanks to the legacy of hippy Zen, as an invitation to do nothing but wait for Enlightenment simply to arise. 'All that these teachings are saying', he once declared with considerable feeling, bringing his hands down onto the arms of his chair with a slap, 'is that Enlightenment is possible – *if you make the effort.*'

◆

Another time, another world. It is January 1982 and we're in Pune. Sangharakshita has given the first few of thirty talks he'll be giving on this, his second extended visit to India since Lokamitra started running Dharma classes in Maharashtra, the heartland of Dr Ambedkar's 'movement of mass conversion'. Since he got started with a handful of Western companions and a number of Sangharakshita's old friends, including his regular translator Dharmarakshita, things have been moving fast. There's a lot of interest and an appetite for more branches of our movement in India.

I've been watching Sangharakshita in action here, and it's obvious that he is well remembered, well loved, and able to draw a crowd of thousands. People come from all around, maybe travelling for days, often on foot. Many of them are poor, many are illiterate. They've come because they know Sangharakshita provides a living link with 'Babasaheb', as they call Dr Ambedkar, their saviour, their father. They come too because they know Sangharakshita can bring to life the vision Ambedkar handed them when he urged them to leave the Hindu fold and convert to Buddhism.

It has been fascinating to see and hear him speaking so fluently the language of the 'Dhamma Revolution', explaining the principles of Buddhism in social, rather than psychological, terms, and creating instant rapport with his audience who laugh, clap, and burst into cheers and spontaneous Ambedkarite chants along the way. He talks about the evils of dowry marriage and of alcohol, of how important it is to work together in harmony. But he also teaches meditation practices and explains a range of foundational Buddhist teachings, always finding ways and stories to make them immediate and relevant to the conditions of his listeners' lives. He is clear and direct, but never simple – he never talks down to his audience.

Over lunch one day, I ask whether those continual references to the social dimension of life are just a 'skilful means'.

'What do you mean?' He seems perplexed.

'Well, in the West, you explain Buddhism much more in terms of individual, even psychological, development. Isn't that where all this must lead in the end, to individual Buddhists working on themselves to develop enlightened qualities?'

He laughs. 'Well, in the West, people are far more individualistic and psychologically oriented, so I talk in more psychological terms. Here, people experience themselves as members of a community, members of a family. So I talk in more social terms. But, actually, I'm using a skilful means in both situations. You mustn't assume that either approach is any closer to the fundamental Dharma than the other. The Dharma is whatever helps people to grow. They may choose to work on themselves first, or they may choose to work on society. Either way they will be growing, and setting up the conditions for their own further development – and for the society in which they live.'

◆

He started teaching in the West at a time when very few people knew much about Buddhism as a path – as opposed to a collection of ideas and proverbs. He set out to train a community of disciples drawn from a particular era who, as Swami (not Baba)[218] Ramdas might have put it, needed a strong sense of the goal and a clear idea of how they could reach it. When writing or speaking in public on a Dharma theme, he would often take the oldest canonical teachings as his baseline. When talking one to one, or in small groups, he'd allow himself to explore the issue, informed by the breadth of his Dharma knowledge along with his own reflections and insights as he spoke friend-to-friend. The result would be something more empathic, more invitational and immediate.

That doesn't mean he was making up his own Dharma, much less that he didn't revere the Dharma tradition; how else could he have written *The Eternal Legacy* and the *Survey*? But he never overlooked the Buddha's reminder that the recorded Dharma is a raft, a finger pointing to the moon, not the truth itself nor an end in itself – and especially not the orthodoxies of any one school. As he put it to me that night in Ahmedabad, he never lost the confidence that came with his own glimpse into the heart of things at the age of sixteen. His intuitive link with that experience, and through that with the Buddha's

Enlightenment, was the ultimate reference point in relation to which he allowed himself to work creatively.

'I'm not trying to "adapt" the Dharma', he once wrote,

I'm just trying to make it understandable. If one can talk of a Western Buddhism [at all] it is only in the sense of a form in which the Dharma can be understood and practised in modern Western society. [So far as I am concerned] it is not an 'interpretation' of the Dharma. In other words I [...] envisage a form of Buddhism that is traditional yet sensitive to its local context.[219]

Sometimes, comparing himself to St Jerome, translator of the Vulgate Bible, he'd put it more grandly, acknowledging the epochal nature of the project:

One who is literally a translator brings a word, sentence, speech, book, poem, etc. from the obscurity and darkness of an unknown tongue into the light of one that is known and understood. One who is a translator metaphorically brings a discipline, or a set of ideas, or a culture, from the obscurity and darkness of unfamiliar terms into the light of terms that are familiar [...] I was thus a translator, with all that that implies in the way of seeking to fathom the uttermost depths of what one is trying to translate so that one may translate it faithfully, i.e. bring its meaning to the surface, or from darkness into the light.[220]

His talks, given in the West and the East, his books and essays, and the recordings of his study seminars stand ready to be explored and mined. He took us to the heart of Buddhism and did everything he could to ensure that we understood what the Buddha had achieved and what he had communicated. Then, on a day-to-day basis, he guided our efforts to 'live the life', individually and collectively. Can one expect more of a Buddhist teacher? He died feeling confident that, whatever evolutions awaited his followers, he was leaving sufficient guidance, enough of a start, to support them as they carried the Dharma into a new era.

25

... Lover, Friend

You are important to me by virtue of the fact that you are human beings who live and must die, who experience pleasure and experience pain. You are important to me by virtue of the fact that you have gone for Refuge to the Buddha, Dharma, and Sangha.[221]

By the time he died, there were about 2,000 members of the Order, thousands more men and women training for ordination, and thousands more at greater and lesser levels of involvement with the Triratna community. Even if he couldn't know everyone, not even all the Order members, he claimed to feel a strong sense of connection with us all, especially when he meditated. He was always happy to meet visitors from all corners of the world. Meanwhile, in his dreams, he maintained a vivid and constant connection with his spiritual teachers, initiators, and guides.

On the level of day-to-day life, he enjoyed a range of connections. There were intimate friends, colleagues, and a pool of men and women whom he considered close friends. Many were involved with our community in the West, naturally enough, but there were many in India and elsewhere with whom he maintained a lively correspondence when he became too frail to travel.

For about seventeen years there were his sexual partners too. For those of us around at the time, being neither homophobic nor particularly concerned with that aspect of his life, there didn't seem to be anything worth noticing or worrying about. Whatever he was doing didn't impact on the way he conducted himself in other circumstances, or how he came across as a teacher and friend. At the time, his sexual partners appeared content with the arrangement – even though one could tell that, for some at least, the end of the relationship could be painful and confusing. In later years, stories emerged suggesting there were some men left very unhappy with their experience and its long-term effects. As the stories surfaced, the disparity between his memory and that of others could puzzle and upset him, especially in the case of two long-term monogamous relationships. It could puzzle some of us too, those who'd been around and observed them from the sidelines. But clearly something was amiss.

Before going further down this track, it is important, not least as an insight into Sangharakshita, to note his disappointment with the nature of the discourse around his sexual activity. For him, the way it was discussed, even among his friends, showed that we had missed what was for him an essential point. In a letter he wrote to Subhuti, in the course of their ongoing conversation about this aspect of his life and its effect, he expressed disappointment:

The whole discussion about my sexual activities back in the 60s and 70s started off on the wrong foot, so to speak, and has been following a false trail ever since. In reality we are not discussing sex at all, we are discussing energy. I remember that some years ago someone recalling my lectures at Theosophy Hall, Bombay, back in the 50s and 60s, told me that my energy had been demoniacal. This rather surprised me, as although I was aware that I had plenty of energy in those days, and still had in the early days of the FWBO, I would not have described it as demoniacal. But evidently other people seem to have experienced it differently, at least sometimes. This probably means that, not realising just how much energy I had, I did not always appreciate its effect on other people, whether within a sexual relationship or in other ways. I may also say that in recent years, and looking back over the history of FWBO/Triratna, I have been amazed at what has been accomplished. At the same time I have felt, or rather seen very clearly, that it had not been accomplished just by me. It was as if there was a supra-personal energy or force working through me.[222]

So, even though some of his partners thought or felt otherwise, sex had a place in his life that was not just about sex. As we've seen, this does not mean he denied the involvement of appetite or his drives. But as an aspect of his life's journey he looked back on those days as an experiment, an exploration – with himself, with life, with communication, with energy. And, given the way sex was being revisioned in the 1960s, he entered that arena, albeit as a virtual beginner, seeking to find out whether it really did offer a path to deeper communication with another human being. That, he often said, had been his primary concern.

To know Sangharakshita was to know that his take on things usually came from a highly individual perspective, and often from a deeper or broader one than you'd meet elsewhere. So it's hard to imagine he wrote those words in order to rationalize his actions. That just wasn't his style. The fact remains, though, that some men were hurt, and many people remain confused and unhappy with that aspect of Sangharakshita's legacy.

During an interview we conducted in 2003, I asked him whether he thought he could have made mistakes. Admitting that he could have done he said, 'Of course one can make mistakes; it isn't always possible to know what the other person is thinking.' Returning to the theme during a series of 'Conversations with Bhante', recorded in 2009, he said that, rightly or wrongly, he'd always thought there had been a mutual openness, a 'sexual frisson', as he put it, that led to his sexual encounters.

Asked whether he'd realized how his position as the older man and teacher might have put some people in an awkward position, his response was revealing:

> I did not regard myself as a teacher with a capital 'T'. I related to people on the level [...] [I believe] one should approach another person without any assumption that you are

either more or less developed than them – you just approach them directly, individual to individual. I generally approached all people on the level, all the more so in the sexual context. I did not see myself as sort of coming down from on high in my sexual relationships with those younger than myself or who were part of the Movement. It was just me.[223]

Subhuti, who probably discussed these matters with Sangharakshita more than anyone else, put it to me: 'I honestly do think he thought like that. His experience really was more in the way of a certain humility based on insight than people give him credit for.... I remember giving a talk at Padmaloka during which I referred to my first meeting with him and the powerful impact it had on me. Later, he told me he was surprised to hear that, because he didn't really experience himself that way.'

No matter how confident and teacherly he might have been in public situations, he was still relatively young, still relatively new to modern Western culture, and, no matter how he came across to his followers, he was experiencing himself as a vigorous 'work in progress', surrounded by an adventurous, non-conventional group of friends (inside and outside the movement), and experiencing a freedom, institutionally and sexually, such as he'd never known before.

In October 1997, *The Guardian* newspaper carried an extended article containing detailed allegations by a former partner of sexual abuse. Over the following years, more stories emerged online. Less sensational, but affecting in its honesty, an Order member published a short account of an unwanted approach in the Order's internal newsletter, *Shabda*.

Sangharakshita was silent. This phase of our collective life began in his late seventies, when he'd been dealing with protracted periods of insomnia. Even so, many of us hoped he would say something, talk about what really happened, or just explain himself. I can certainly remember feeling frustrated by his silence – though even now I'm not sure what I or anyone else was wanting from him.

For him, though, there were several factors in the mix, along with the stance represented in his letter to Subhuti quoted above. In his conversation with Mahamati and Subhuti, he told them:

> From an early age I realized that my serious interests were not shared by anyone else I knew, so I just did not talk about them. As time went on, that included my interest in the Dharma: there was no one in my immediate circle I could talk to about that – although after a while I did contact the Buddhist Society and make a few friends there with whom I could discuss the Dharma. However, I think my general tendency has been not to disclose my deeper feelings or real thoughts. That has of course spilled over and reinforced my reluctance to talk about my sexuality. It's not that it's the one issue I don't talk about, it's one of several more intimate or profound interests that I haven't talked about.[224]

Maybe it's worth reminding ourselves that he discovered his homosexual feelings at a time when homosexuality was punishable by prison and never talked about in polite company. He once wondered aloud whether the people living around him, even members of the Order who'd known him for years, had really tried to imagine the effect that would have had on him.

Even when he did feel ready, and saw the need to discuss these things, he struggled with the ethical implications of talking about his sexual encounters and relationships as if they were just about *him*. There were other people involved, he'd point out. He did try to make contact with the people he'd hurt, if not always successfully, and he did eventually publish an apology:

> I being its founder, Triratna sometimes bears the mark not
> of the Dharma but of my own particular personality. That
> personality is a complex one and in certain respects I did not
> act in accordance with what my position in the movement
> demanded or even as a true Buddhist. I am thinking in
> particular of the times when I have hurt, harmed or upset
> fellow Buddhists, whether within Triratna or out of it [...]
> I would therefore like to express my deep regret for all the
> occasions on which I have hurt, harmed or upset fellow
> Buddhists, and ask for their forgiveness.[225]

These are personal, complicated, and painful matters. Recent years have seen us reaching out as a community, encouraging people to come forward with their stories, stories about Sangharakshita as well as about the negative ripple effects of his actions on the ethos of our early community. Safeguarding systems and training in restorative work are increasingly well established features of the Triratna world. It has been painful and disorienting at times to hear the stories. The numbers in Sangharakshita's case are actually rather small, but that's not the point – except to say that newspaper headlines that have branded him as a 'sexual predator' seem grossly unfair. But that is the way of the world, and this is something we've had to learn from and deal with. As a friend once put it in a talk, 'We are and always will be *that* movement founded by *that* man.'

◆

Although unlikely to court interest from the press, by far the most significant relationships in his life were his intimate, non-sexual friendships with just a very few people, notably Terry Delamere and Paramartha, Nityabandhu and perhaps just a few others. The vision of an ideal friendship as a gateway to beauty and truth, as evoked in Plato's *Symposium*, affected him very deeply when he was young, and he returned to the text often throughout his life. It was in those friendships rather than in any of his sexual relationships that he touched his ideal:

> The primary meaning of *kalyāṇa* in *kalyāṇa mitratā* (spiritual friendship) is 'beautiful'. In spiritual friendship we take delight in the spiritual beauty of our dear friend. This aspect of 'taking delight' means that we not only see a person as a person, but also like what we see, enjoy and take delight in what we see, just as we do with a beautiful painting or poem – except that here the painting or poem is alive: the painting

can speak to you, and the beautiful poem can answer back. This makes it very exciting and stimulating indeed.[226]

Yes, if Sangharakshita ever truly found the kind of love that really mattered to him, I'd suggest it was in the context of his enduring non-sexual friendships. There were several levels and gradations of his friendships, and a fuller picture would extend to include quite a few more men and women. These friendships were essential sustaining forces in his life. Whether he ever looked for or expected to experience anything like such friendship in his sexual relationships is another matter. Even if he started out with such a hope, he certainly concluded that they were the wrong place to look.

Paramartha met Sangharakshita for the first time during his ordination retreat at Guhyaloka, our men's retreat centre in Spain. Paramartha describes how their friendship began: 'We'd dine alfresco there, and it seemed to me that people were terrified of sitting at the end of the table next to him. Maybe there was some projection going on, maybe people were afraid to ask him difficult questions about the Dharma. But I was a naive New Zealander, fresh off the boat, who didn't really know much about anything, and I was straight in there. I'd sit next to him all the time and we quickly established a good rapport. God knows what was coming out of my mouth, of course, but at least it got us building a relationship in an informal way, just chattting.'

This was the start of a thirty-year friendship, one of enormous loyalty, respect, and mutual affection. Soon after his ordination, Paramartha moved to Padmaloka to live in the community with Sangharakshita: 'At that time, there was a heap of stuff going on in the movement, some of it very demanding, and Bhante had a strong need to communicate himself. We would sit sometimes for hours and just talk. He would tell me about his life, his childhood, his relationships with people, about his friendship with Terry Delamere. He was just communicating himself, even sometimes with tears.

'It was very full-on, very intense. It was as if someone was leaving the lights on all the time; at times a part of me would want to switch off, sort of pull the metaphorical duvet over my head. But I'd signed up for this.... I was learning a lot about him as a human being. I hadn't known him before, and I suppose I had related to him as a teacher – and of course he *is* a teacher. But now he was opening up the entire human dimension of his experience with no holds barred.

'I'm sure he was responding to the fact that I was a young guy, good-looking, idealistic. And I guess I was aware of that. But I chose not to take it personally; in some ways I took it quite seriously; it was not as if he was 'in love', it was more as if there was something Platonic in the relationship that had an effect on him, that set a match to something in him. I got that. I was respectful of that, but didn't need to take it as something to do with me in a personal way.'

Beyond these very close friendships lay, and had always lain, a substantial hinterland of strong friendships with men and women whose company he enjoyed, and with whom he could be himself. Lama Govinda, Dhardo Rimpoche, Dinoo

With Paramartha, 1989

Dubash, Ayya Khema, Dharmarakshita, Ananda, Abhaya, Suvajra, Mahamati, Saddhanandi, Dhammadinna, Subhuti, Vidyadevi, Kalyanaprabha, Lilavati, and many more. Some of these were people he worked with closely, others were people he had simply taken to along the way, irrespective of their involvement in the life of our Order or movement. Even if he experienced a psychic reach towards an ideal of perfect communion, he was able to enjoy friendships of all kinds, and rejoiced to see friendship thrive as a defining feature of the world he had initiated.

This is not to say that he constantly presented a jolly or outwardly friendly manner. He was a serious man. One day, when I was working with him quite closely, I sensed an atmosphere of disapproval, and so asked whether I'd done something to upset him. He was taken aback and assured me

I hadn't. There was a reflective pause before he continued: 'You know, I seem to be cursed with a personality that is completely ill-equipped to communicate the extent of the positivity I feel. I'm sometimes woken out of my sleep by a flood of mettā. It's so powerful that I can feel it surging through me like a golden river. But I know this is not at all obvious on the outside.'

From the early days, and in retrospect almost ridiculously soon after our ordination, he made a point of meeting regularly with those of us he considered 'senior and responsible Order members'. In time the meeting transformed into a meeting of chair persons, and then a Preceptors' College Council, and so on. But in whatever shape or under whatever title we met, Sangharakshita kept in regular, friendly, and close contact with those of us holding major responsibilities. The vision of a community bound by links of spiritual friendship began at the top.

This was an important support and a privilege. I consider myself lucky to have spent so much time around him. Not that it was always easy. He openly confessed that he was a 'worrier' by nature; this was something he'd inherited from his mother. But, more to the point, he was driven by a profound sense of urgency. His drive, his attention to detail, and his ambition for the movement's development could make him a demanding taskmaster. There would be times when this could take you beyond your comfort zone. If that happened, then the question you had to ask yourself was, 'Is this a teaching? Is he pushing me towards some higher level he knows me to be capable of? Or is he just unaware of the pressure he's putting me under?' This was a real and, for some of us, frequent kōan, for he wasn't omniscient and didn't always get things right.

If you did let him know you were feeling overburdened or too busy, he could be sympathetic, but he might also respond with a challenge: 'Maybe you aren't doing *enough*, enough to balance the work you're doing' – by which he would have meant not enough meditation, not enough time on retreat, not enough time with friends, with nature, or with culture. No matter how much was going on in his life, he always made a point of spending part of his day writing, reading, listening to music, and above all enjoying the company of friends. As a teacher, this was no small part of his skill: exemplifying a life fully lived and purposefully nourished by all the inspiration, beauty, and support the world and his friendships could offer.

Jarā-maraṇa[227]

Hour after hour, day
After day we try
To grasp the Ungraspable, pinpoint
The Unpredictable. Flowers
Wither when touched, ice
Suddenly cracks beneath our feet. Vainly
We try to track birdflight through the sky trace
Dumb fish through deep water, try
To anticipate the earned smile the soft
Reward, even
Try to grasp our own lives. But Life
Slips through our fingers
Like snow. Life
Cannot belong to us. We
Belong to Life.
Life is King[228]

'You know, I'm afraid I'm reluctantly coming to the conclusion that I must face up to the fact that I'm not as young as I used to be.'

I caught this rococo snatch of conversation through an open window just as Sangharakshita was about to give a talk in Panchgani, a hill town halfway between Bombay and Pune. It was January 1982. He'd been back in India for a couple of weeks, resting from the journey, catching up with old friends, preparing and giving the first talks. He was also dealing with the signs of an incipient sore throat. Over the next two months there would be miles of travel, late nights, dusty air, and, occasionally, basic accommodation. At fifty-six he was beginning to feel his age.

The overheard remark gave me pause. There had always been something ageless about him, as if the way he lived and the level of attention he devoted to his work came from an inexhaustible source. Sometimes he'd wondered where it came from himself. 'There are times', he wrote, 'when, far from feeling that it was I who took on the responsibility, I feel that it was the responsibility that took on me. There are times when I am dimly aware of a vast, overshadowing Consciousness that has, through me, founded the Order and set in motion our whole Movement.'[229]

On his sixtieth birthday, a number of us gathered for a dinner party with gifts and speeches. Happy and healthy though he was, when he rose to respond he used the opportunity to remind us that we should 'hear time's winged chariot drawing near'. He wouldn't be around for too much longer. It was time to prepare for the future.

Unlike any other pioneering Buddhist teacher, he was clear from the start that he wouldn't be nominating a sole successor. In line with his views on spiritual friendship and spiritual community, he hoped to hand his responsibilities on to a team, a close-knit community of experienced male and female Order members. Its membership would serve as the focal point for what he'd come to term a 'lineage of institutions'.

Life being uncertain, and because, as he once wrote, 'ordination is the crux of our whole system of spiritual life and practice',[230] the conducting of ordinations, the witnessing of a person's 'effective going for refuge' at the point of ordination, was the most urgent item on his agenda. He had personally ordained 350 people, more than enough for any one person, he said. So, around the time of that dinner party, he asked three men to visit India on his behalf and conduct ordinations for some men there. A year later he asked three women to conduct ordinations for some women, also in India.

By the time he died, there was a growing circle of men and women actively engaged in training people for ordination, and sufficiently rooted in their own practice to carry the necessary weight when conducting the ceremonies. As new generations of Order members appeared, Sangharakshita would express delight, referring lightly to his 'spiritual grandchildren'. More seriously, he knew he could relax, knowing that a core element in his vision of a living spiritual community was in place and would survive him.

Just a couple of years after his sixtieth birthday, life's uncertainty began to make itself known when prostate trouble landed him in hospital. In his late seventies, he'd suffer the first of two extended periods of acute insomnia, between which he began to lose his eyesight through age-related macular degeneration. This latter came as a shock to those of us who knew the vital part reading and writing had played in his life. But he spoke with remarkable equanimity when I tried to commiserate: 'Well, I've read so much, perhaps quite enough for one lifetime.' He took the shift remarkably well, making good use of spoken-word libraries, and finding willing readers among his secretaries and friends who helped him to keep up with correspondence and Buddhist publications.

He also continued to write, albeit more slowly. He'd dictate a sentence, hear it back, make changes, hear it back again, and so on... and so on. Paying him a visit one day, I took a turn as his scribe. In two hours we completed a paragraph about as long as this one. Even so, his output through those darkening decades would match many a lifelong writer's entire oeuvre.

More general questions about the future continued to occupy his mind for much of the time. Before going into hospital for the prostate operation, he composed a document outlining his key thoughts on the future leadership of the Order. The document was handed to a small number of Order members in sealed envelopes, which were 'to be opened in the event of my death'. Living as he did for almost thirty more years, the envelopes were never opened, and he was able to oversee the developments cited in the document himself.

For as long as health allowed, he travelled far and wide, visiting Triratna centres around the world. Right up to his last days, he kept a close eye on developments and in good contact with the people holding responsibilities in the movement. Along the way, he continued to refine and communicate the defining features of his presentation, its emphases, and its four 'lineages' – of teaching, practice, institutions, and inspiration. Inevitably, as his energy diminished, he became a more distant figure, but he stayed in touch, was sharp as a tack and willing to intervene, or to ask a trusted emissary to intervene on his behalf if he felt the need.

A notable example of such an intervention was the movement's name change. Given its global spread, and especially bearing India in mind, the 'Friends of the Western Buddhist Order' had long been a misleading name for the movement. He therefore asked the relevant consultative teams to come up with something new and fitting. In 2010, after a year or two, and even an inconclusive referendum within the Order, he felt it necessary to step in. Before he died, he wanted to make absolutely sure that there would be no sense of separation between the Indian branch of our movement (or any future Eastern developments) and the rest. From now on, we would be known as the 'Triratna Buddhist Order and Community': the Order and Community of the Three Jewels.

His last years saw a few signs of tension. In any religious community it will happen that some people will come to feel that their true spiritual home lies elsewhere. This can be a complex and painful process for someone who's made a commitment in good faith and developed strong bonds of friendship within the initial community. Actually, in the case of Triratna, and particularly in the Order, this has been remarkably rare. But when anything gets to a certain size, the law of averages will take an interest.

When a fairly senior Order member sat down with Sangharakshita to discuss the undeniable pull he felt towards Zen, the outcome was an amicable recognition that he'd found the style and approach that truly suited him. There was no fault, no blame, but it was time to move on. When someone else, having become drawn to a Tibetan teacher in his area, started introducing elements of the teacher's approach into the way he taught at his local Triratna centre, however, there was confusion and even some conflict. 'But why do things have to be so *narrow*?' the Order member lamented when we met. He spoke with real feeling, real regret. And yet how strange it seemed that Triratna, possibly the most ecumenical Order and practice community in the current Buddhist world, should seem 'narrow' to someone choosing to focus on the teachings of a sub-branch of one traditional school.

That there might be people, even members of the Order, who might decide to move on did not surprise Sangharakshita. He counselled patience and tolerance when tensions emerged. In Triratna, where people find nourishment in teachings and practices from the broad Buddhist tradition, it is probably inevitable that a few people will wish to specialize elsewhere. But that does not make of Triratna an umbrella organization offering only a 'taster experience'. Sangharakshita was assertively confident that the sum of his work, the movement he'd established, added up to a comprehensive path to Enlightenment. When interviewed in 2009, he addressed the matter directly:

Anyone who has practised within the FWBO and who finds
the FWBO unsatisfactory is, of course, free to start teaching
their own disciples and found their own organisation as
I have done. But they would be leaving the Order. They
cannot try to gather a group of disciples around themselves
within the Order or movement to whom they are imparting
something that is basically different from what has been
taught by me. Because, to put it in a slightly different way,
every Sangha presupposes a Dharma: a particular Sangha
presupposes a particular presentation of the Dharma.
The Order and the FWBO presuppose the particular
presentation of the Dharma which I have given over the
years.

The interview was circulated as a document: 'What is the
Western Buddhist Order?' It became generally known that
Sangharakshita was informally referring to it as a sort of 'last
will and testament'. In the course of the interview, he gave
this short but comprehensive summary of what Triratna has
to offer:

My particular presentation consists of those teachings and
practices I have stressed during my teaching life, through
speaking and writing, and I hope by example. What I have
taught pertains both to doctrinal understanding and to
practice and it is what I have said about these that is the
basis for the Dharma as practised by my disciples in the
Order and as taught by them – the basis of our 'particular
presentation of the Dharma'.

At the doctrinal level, I see the teaching of pratītya-samutpāda [conditionality, dependent origination] as most basic and from it follow the teachings of the Four Noble Truths, the Twelve and Twenty-Four Nidānas, and also the teachings concerning Nirvana, anātman, and śūnyatā. My teaching of Dharma as doctrine is essentially based upon and derived from, directly or indirectly, these teachings that, of course, go back to the Buddha himself. And I explicitly exclude whatever ideas are incompatible with them.

My teachings pertaining to method, and therefore those of my disciples, all centre, directly or indirectly, on the act of going for refuge to the Buddha, the Dharma, and the Sangha. These comprise all the practices that I have myself taught: for instance, the observance of the Five or Ten Precepts; the performance of the Sevenfold and Threefold Pujas; the practice of meditation, in the framework of the System of Meditation; the group study of the Buddhist scriptures; the cultivation of spiritual friendship, and the enjoyment of poetry, music, and the visual arts as aids to the spiritual life. These teachings pertaining to method are connected, directly or indirectly, with the Buddha's teaching of pratītya-samutpāda through the sequence of positive, spiral nidānas, for all these teachings contribute, in one way or another, to my disciples' progress to ever higher levels of being and consciousness, even from the mundane at its most refined to the transcendental. Looked at from another point of view, they contribute to the deepening of my disciples' going for refuge, so that from being provisional it becomes effective, and from being effective it becomes real in the sense of being irreversible.

One could also explore my particular presentation of the Dharma in terms of the Six Distinctive Emphases of the FWBO; to give their headings: critical ecumenicalism, unity, Going for Refuge, Spiritual Friendship, the New Society, and culture and the arts. Of these, my emphasis on Going for Refuge is the most essential and probably the most distinctive. The others too are distinctive, for instance, the emphasis on the importance of spiritual friendship is certainly not explicitly taught by any other Buddhist school.

These teachings and emphases, together with the range of institutions I have established, between them create something not really definable: a certain atmosphere or attitude that is found within the FWBO and nowhere else. All of them are contained in a network of spiritual friendship and they are to be handed on faithfully from generation to generation in a chain of discipleship.[231]

He would be granted another ten years of life beyond that interview, long enough to collaborate with Subhuti in devising a series of papers that added colour, depth, and detail as they visited some core elements of his presentation. It was in this context too that the outline of an all-round synthetic model of spiritual life emerged, a 'system of practice'. This laid out the path as a set of five progressive but interconnected phases, of integration, positive emotion, spiritual death, spiritual rebirth, and spiritual receptivity.[232]

◆

Having completed four volumes of memoirs, he continued to write, composing subsidiary books based on themes from his life. In 'From Genesis to the *Diamond Sūtra*' he shared his appreciation of the language and mythology of the Bible – as well as mentioning for the first time in print his recognition as a young man that he was homosexual (he never took to the word 'gay'). In *My Precious Teachers* he offered pen portraits of the teachers who had made significant contributions to his spiritual life and his unfolding appreciation of the living Buddhist tradition.

For years he wrote lengthy, detailed letters to his fellow Order members from his travels, or simply from his everyday life, keeping us in touch with his prolific reading, his observations and reflections, or even the sublime perfection of an omelette prepared by a chef with the appearance of a Renaissance angel in the cafeteria of a Norwich department store.

He loved to write; he enjoyed sharing himself with his disciples, he appreciated the quality of reflection that writing demanded. He even relished the feeling of contact between nib and paper. Bumping into each other one day outside the Cherry Orchard, a women's right-livelihood project neighbouring the London Buddhist Centre, we popped in for lunch. We'd each spent our morning writing, and he was talking enthusiastically about the pleasures of the craft. Suddenly he leaned across the table, one hand raised to shield his mouth from the rest of the room, and declared in a gleeful stage-whisper, 'It's better than sex, isn't it?'

For many years, his place in our world was assured given his position as founder and teacher, and given his personal connection as preceptor to so many members of the Order. But as numbers grew, as the movement spread geographically and demographically, and when the ground-up influence of social media began to challenge the top-down hierarchical culture we'd grown up with, things were less straightforward.

As time and distance make Sangharakshita a less prominent presence in our world, then whatever mistakes and misjudgements he made forty or fifty years ago will probably seem by stages less relevant to the life of the movement he established. But for some people, at least at the time of writing, stories about his sex life have challenged their confidence in him as a teacher whose presentation and guidance was born of insight. What can one say?

Around the time I first came upon the FWBO, Sangharakshita would sometimes invite a Japanese Sōtō Zen monk to join our retreats. He would lead optional sessions of meditation in the afternoons. Back home in South London, he ran his own evening sessions and occasionally organized intense sesshins. In his dark blue robes, he'd sit with such commanding stillness that even the air in the room seemed to stop moving, and peace would roll off him to lap at your knees as you sat around him meditating. He looked the part too, the real deal, with his perfect posture and shaven head.

One afternoon, during one of those sesshins, as we sat in the shrine room sipping tea, he announced his decision to start a sangha, a practice community of his own, and invited anyone interested to consider joining him. Years later, in a letter to Sangharakshita, I explained why I'd decided not to take up his invitation: 'What he was offering seemed like a direct path towards the sun. But what you were offering was a path to the sun, the moon, the stars and all the dark places in between.'

Without wishing to make light of the shadow side of our history, I've never regretted the choice I made. It was always obvious that Sangharakshita was a complex man who didn't play by the usual rules. One evening in 1978, just after we'd opened the London Buddhist Centre, he shared a reflection with a few of us: 'The forces at work in my personality when I was young were so powerful, so complex, so self-contradictory, that, had I not discovered something as worthy of my commitment and devotion as the Three Jewels, I honestly believe they would have ripped me apart. I would have gone mad.' So yes, he had a complex personality, but it was a complexity he never hid from us, and which somehow matched the mood of the time. It somehow made the existential challenge he represented less easy to dismiss.

His prose writings chronicle his thoughts, his knowledge, and his outer life; his poems chronicle his inner life. But, as a baffled Allen Ginsberg exclaimed after one of their meetings, 'How can someone so radical write such square poetry?' The radical and the square, the monk and the poet, Sangharakshitas I and II, and perhaps we should add the sinner and the saint. He was all those things, and for many of us he was enough. 'I am much worse than people think I am, and also much better', he once wrote in a letter to a friend.[233]

He lived for seventy-six years after his experience with *The Diamond Sūtra*, and never let its significance slip from the centre of his life's purpose for a moment. I lived in two communities with him, altogether for about six years, and never saw him waste a minute.

In his last years, and as *Shabda* kept him in touch with, among other things, some criticisms being voiced about him, he was remarkably equanimous, even praising the literary merit of one especially scathing contribution. It's not that he didn't care about the tensions. But they didn't surprise or worry him. In fact he often let people know that these were the happiest years of his life. He couldn't know what the future held, but he knew he had been true to his vision, true to himself, and true to the Dharma. And he was confident that he'd made a meaningful contribution to an arc of history in which nothing gets lost.

He had always experienced himself, and our project, not just in space but in time. I once asked him whether he thought Western Buddhists will ever take advantage of the inspirational energy latent in the Christian symbols and archetypes embedded in our cultures. He answered immediately, 'Oh, I'm sure we will.' After a pause he added, 'Yes, probably in about 500 years' time.'

That was the dimension he lived in. The forces of conditionality would do with his work and his reputation as they pleased. What more could he do? And, having done what he could, he was content. So, as the old Zen master said, 'You spit, I bow.'

During his extended periods of insomnia, when he did manage to fall asleep, even for short snatches, he would have wonderfully vivid, colourful dreams. He would dream of his teachers in India, and again and again of 'a secret temple tucked behind a much larger public monastery high on a snowy mountain ridge'.

Circumstances had handed him the opportunity to play a significant role in bringing the Buddha's teachings into the modern world. He had embraced the project without hesitation and without stint. But, even as he absorbed himself in the demanding life of that 'public monastery', an important part of him remained in the secret temple where he could maintain his connection with the Buddha, the Bodhisattvas, and great teachers through the ages who kept the flame of his inspiration alive:

> I find it very easy to venerate, to look up: I enjoy looking up to those who are better or more advanced than me in this or that respect. I found it easy to look up to my own Buddhist teachers and I find it easy to look up to the great religious figures, philosophers, poets, and artists of the past. I am very glad that there are people who have been much greater than me: I would hate to think I was the summit of human evolution – that would be a terrible thought.[234]

Traditional schools of Tibetan Buddhism each have their own 'refuge tree', a stylized pictorial representation of their school's lineage. On the petals of a huge lotus tree are arrayed their historical and legendary forebears, with a dominant figure at the centre: the historical Buddha or maybe Padmasambhava or Milarepa. The devotee will visualize this symbol as he or she prostrates in an embodied act of 'going for refuge', normally 108,000 times, during a period of foundational training.

It is now several decades since Sangharakshita devised a refuge-tree visualization practice for our Order. Our lineage being entirely new, the figures who populated it could not be approached as an assembly of our teachers; instead, Sangharakshita offered it as 'a tree of refuge and respect'. At its centre, seated on the primary lotus flower, we see the Buddha Sakyamuni. Behind him, set on its own lotus flower, we see an arrangement of texts representing the scriptural tradition. Then, to each side of him, we see assemblies of arhants and Bodhisattvas. In this way, the Three Jewels of Buddha, Dharma, and Sangha are present and prominent. Above and beyond the central figures, we see great teachers, historical and archetypal, spiritual heroes who inspire our respect and devotion. Finally, in the foreground, arrayed on a lotus flower that reaches out towards us, we see Sangharakshita flanked by his own teachers and major influences: Jagdish Kashyap, U Chandramani, Dhardo Rimpoche, Mr Chen, Dilgo Khyentse, Jamyang Khyentse, Dudjom Rimpoche, Chatrul Sangye Dorje, and Kachu Rimpoche, as well as Dr Ambedkar and Anagarika Dharmapala.

Some people have admitted to feelings of discomfort. Given the controversies around Sangharakshita, they wonder whether he should hold a place among those figures as an equal object of reverence. What is he doing there? Are we expected to feel the same devotion towards him as we do to the others?

In a letter to a friend, he once wrote, 'I do not see myself as being an object of refuge to anyone. So far as I am concerned, there are only three Refuges, namely, the Buddha, the Dharma and the Sangha. [...] If I am put on the shrine, I am there only as one of the Teachers of the Present.'[235]

So we're left with a choice. We can look away. We can even walk away. Or we can prostrate before the tree, deepening the strength of our faith and devotion towards the Three Refuges and as many of the figures on the tree as have meaning for us. For many people, it will come quite naturally to revere Sangharakshita as their preceptor and root teacher, and even as something more, quite at home alongside all the other figures.

For those who do not, or cannot, relate to Sangharakshita in such a way, then surely it will be no small matter to reflect on the gifts he has handed us. He found ways to communicate the Buddha's vision and teachings in ways that made them immediate and 'of the nature of a personal invitation' in this new age. He demonstrated the organic coherence at the heart of the Buddhist tradition, and offered the modern Buddhist a considered, non-sectarian approach to accessing its riches. He educated, inspired, and challenged into life a dynamic, warmly interconnected, worldwide community of fellow Buddhists who share a defined approach to the Triple Gem, an evolving body of practices, and a language in which to discuss the spiritual life.

I believe that in the secret temple of his inner world he sat, like us, *facing* the tree: a complex human being, a Buddhist, meditating, revering, drawing energy, inspiration, and insight from those great figures as he brought something miraculous into our world.

Approaching it that way, surely anyone can respect, even feel a degree of awe for, a boy who was stranded in bed with only his books, a sixteen-year-old who accidentally saw for a moment into the very heart of things, the twenty-year-old who wandered barefoot from swami to saint to monk to teacher to ordination and onwards to snow-clad mountains and a magical world of incarnate lamas. And then we meet the forty-, fifty-, sixty-, seventy-, eighty- and ninety-year-old man who lived his life with us, working to the best of his ability, not just for us, but for the sake of all beings.

And then it becomes clear why he belongs on that tree, and why he is looking outwards, towards us. Far from being suspended, mute, in some mythic dimension, he is alive, smiling, his expression is welcoming. He is inviting us to contemplate those wonderful beings around and above him on the tree, and the universe of potential they represent. 'Why not let them inspire and enrich *your* life?' he is saying, 'just as they've inspired and enriched mine? Why not let the Buddha and these benign teachers accompany and support your attempts to be free and happy, to find meaning, and to be of help to others as we all make this mysterious, fragile journey together, from birth to death?'

I'll leave you with Sangharakshita, speaking in 1990:

It is partly because I am a rather complex person that I am a mystery to myself, even if not to others. But though I am a mystery to myself I am not, I think, so much of a mystery to myself as to cherish many illusions about myself. One of the illusions about myself that I do not cherish is that I was the most suitable person to be the founder of a new Buddhist movement in Britain – in the world, as it turned out. I possessed so few of the necessary qualifications; I laboured under so many disadvantages. When I look back on those early days, and think of the difficulties I had to experience (not that I always thought of them as difficulties), I cannot but feel that the coming into existence of the Western Buddhist Order was little short of a miracle. Not only did the lotus bloom from the mud; it had to bloom from the mud contained within a small and inadequate pot. Perhaps it had to bloom just then or not at all, and perhaps this particular pot was the only one available.

Now, hundreds of lotuses are blooming, some of the bigger and more resplendent flowers being surrounded by clusters of half-opened buds. During the last twenty-two years a whole lotus-lake has come into existence, or rather, a whole series of lotus-lakes. Alternatively, during the last twenty-two years the original lotus plant has grown into an enormous lotus-tree not unlike the great four-branched Refuge Tree – has in fact grown into a whole forest of lotus-trees. Contemplating the series of lotus-lakes, contemplating the forest of lotus-trees, and rejoicing in the strength and beauty of the lotus-flowers, I find it difficult to believe that

they really did all originate from that small and inadequate
pot, which some people wanted to smash to bits, or cast into
the dustbin, or bury as deep as possible in the ground.

In brief, dropping the metaphor and speaking quite
plainly, when I see what a great and glorious achievement
the Order represents, despite its manifest imperfections,
I find it difficult to believe that I could have been its
founder.[236]

Endnotes

Chapter 1

1 Located in the English Herefordshire countryside, Adhisthana is a Triratna facility that combines two residential communities as well as Urgyen House, Sangharakshita's final home (now an exhibition space) and the Sangharakshita Library. It is extensive enough to accommodate several retreats and conferences at the same time, and thus serves as a sort of headquarters for the Order and movement.

2 Sangharakshita, 'My relation to the Order', in *The Complete Works of Sangharakshita*, vol.2: *The Three Jewels I*, Windhorse Publications, Cambridge 2019, p.530.

3 Bhikkhu: the general term for a monk in the Theravāda world. The Mahāyāna/Sanskrit equivalent is 'bhikṣu'.

4 For that see Vajragupta, *The Triratna Story*, Windhorse Publications, Cambridge 2010.

5 Bhante: a title of respect, literally meaning 'Venerable Sir'.

6 Terry Pilchick (Nagabodhi), *Jai Bhim! Dispatches from a Peaceful Revolution*, Windhorse Publications, Glasgow 1988.

7 Subhuti (Alex Kennedy), *Sangharakshita: A New Voice in the Buddhist Tradition*, Windhorse Publications, Birmingham 1994; *Bringing Buddhism to the West: A Life of Sangharakshita*, Windhorse Publications, Birmingham 1995; *The Buddhist Vision: An Introduction to Theory and Practice of Buddhism*, Rider, London 1985; *Buddhism for Today: A Portrait of a New Buddhist Movement*, Windhorse Publications, Glasgow 1983.

8 See especially *The Essential Sangharakshita*, Wisdom Publications, Boston, MA 2009 (also to be published by Windhorse Publications as vol.6 of *The Complete Works of Sangharakshita*).

9 The Three Jewels, or Three Refuges: the Buddha, the Dharma (his teaching), and the Sangha (the community of his followers).

Chapter 2

10 Sangharakshita with Saddhanandi, *The Complete Works of Sangharakshita*, vol.25: *Poems and Short Stories*, Windhorse Publications, Cambridge 2020, p.69.

11 Sangharakshita wrote and spoke in terms of a two-year period. Towards the end of his life he wondered whether it might have been considerably less, something more like eight months.

12 Sangharakshita, *The Complete Works of Sangharakshita*, vol.20: *The Rainbow Road from Tooting Broadway to Kalimpong*, Windhorse Publications, Cambridge 2017, pp.22–3.

13 Sangharakshita, *The Rainbow Road*, p.36.

14 Sangharakshita, *The Rainbow Road*, p.37.

15 Sangharakshita, *The Rainbow Road*, p.40.

16 Sangharakshita, *The Rainbow Road*, p.41.

17 Sangharakshita, 'From Genesis to the *Diamond Sūtra*', in *The Complete Works of Sangharakshita*, vol.13: *Eastern and Western Traditions*, Windhorse Publications, Cambridge 2019, p.610.

18 Sangharakshita, 'From Genesis to the *Diamond Sūtra*', p.530.

19 Sangharakshita, *The Rainbow Road*, p.49.

20 Sangharakshita, *The Rainbow Road*, p.52.

21 Sangharakshita, *The Rainbow Road*, pp.60–1.

22 Sangharakshita, *The Rainbow Road*, p.78.

23 Sangharakshita, *The Rainbow Road*, pp.87–8.

Chapter 3

24 Shantideva, *Guide to the Bodhisattva's Way of Life*, trans. Kelsang Gyatso, Tharpa Publications, Ulverston 2002, p.6.

25 Sangharakshita, *The Rainbow Road*, p.482.

26 Sangharakshita, *The Rainbow Road*, p.73.

27 Sangharakshita, *The Rainbow Road*, pp.73–4.

28 Sangharakshita, *The Rainbow Road*, pp.63–4.

29 Sangharakshita, 'I believe...', in *The Complete Works of Sangharakshita*, vol.7: *Crossing the Stream: India Writings I*, Windhorse Publications, Cambridge 2021, p.38.

30 Sangharakshita, *The Rainbow Road*, p.85.

31 *Buddhist Wisdom Books: The Diamond and the Heart Sūtra*, trans. Edward Conze, Allen & Unwin, London 1975, p.68.

32 Sangharakshita, '*Attavāda* and *Anattāvāda*', in *Crossing the Stream*, pp.132–3, 134.

33 Sangharakshita, *The Rainbow Road*, p.86.

34 Sangharakshita, 'I believe...', p.38.

35 Sangharakshita, 'The unity of Buddhism', in *Crossing the Stream*, p.32.

Chapter 4

36 Sangharakshita, 'Alternative lives', in *The Complete Works of Sangharakshita*, vol.26: *Aphorisms, the Arts, and Late Writings*, Windhorse Publications, Cambridge 2022, p.583.

37 Sangharakshita, *The Rainbow Road*, pp.109–10.

38 Sangharakshita, *The Rainbow Road*, p.112.

39 Sangharakshita, 'An Occidental ear listens to Indian music', in *Crossing the Stream*, p.81.

40 Sangharakshita, *The Rainbow Road*, p.113.

41 Sangharakshita, *The Rainbow Road*, p.117.

42 Sangharakshita, 'The practice of the presence of God', in *Crossing the Stream*, p.91.

43 Sangharakshita, 'The practice of the presence of God', pp.88–9.

44 Sangharakshita, 'The practice of the presence of God', pp.86–7.

45 Sangharakshita, *The Rainbow Road*, p.164.

46 Sangharakshita, *The Rainbow Road*, p.128.

47 Sangharakshita, *The Rainbow Road*, pp.113–14.

48 Sangharakshita, *The Rainbow Road*, p.125.

49 Sangharakshita, *The Rainbow Road*, p.133.

Chapter 5

50 Sangharakshita, *The Rainbow Road*, p.157.

51 Sangharakshita, *The Rainbow Road*, p.115.

52 Apparently the cement magnate who sponsored the building of the temple insisted that it should include the Buddhist temple.

53 Sangharakshita, *The Rainbow Road*, p.115.

54 Sangharakshita, *The Rainbow Road*, p.122.

55 Sangharakshita, *The Rainbow Road*, p.126.

56 Sangharakshita, *The Rainbow Road*, p.252.

57 Sangharakshita, *The Rainbow Road*, p.143.

58 Sangharakshita, *The Rainbow Road*, p.145.

59 Sangharakshita, *The Rainbow Road*, pp.142–3.

60 Sangharakshita, *The Rainbow Road*, p.147.

61 Sangharakshita, *The Rainbow Road*, p.149.

62 Sangharakshita, *The Rainbow Road*, p.151.

63 Sangharakshita, *The Rainbow Road*, p.157.

64 Sangharakshita, *The Rainbow Road*, p.136.

65 Sangharakshita, *The Rainbow Road*, p.170.

66 Sangharakshita, *The Rainbow Road*, p.165.

Chapter 6

67 Sangharakshita, 'Above me broods...', in *Poems and Short Stories*, p.175.

68 *Mother, as Seen by Her Devotees*, Benares, Anandamayee Ashram 1995, p.61.

69 Sangharakshita, *The Rainbow Road*, p.183.

70 Sangharakshita, *The Rainbow Road*, p.198.

71 Sangharakshita, *The Rainbow Road*, pp.187–8.

72 Sangharakshita, *The Rainbow Road*, p.206.

73 Sangharakshita, *The Rainbow Road*, p.222.

74 Sangharakshita, *The Rainbow Road*,
   p.225.

Chapter 7

75 Sangharakshita, from 'Village
   India', in *Poems and Short Stories*,
   pp.212–13.
76 Sangharakshita, *The Rainbow Road*,
   p.230.
77 Sangharakshita, *The Rainbow Road*,
   pp.240–1.
78 Sangharakshita, *f*rom 'Meditation',
   in *Poems and Short Stories*, p.41.
79 Sangharakshita, *The Rainbow Road*,
   p.257.
80 Sangharakshita, *The Rainbow Road*,
   p.302.

81 Sangharakshita, *The Rainbow Road*,
   p.302.
82 Sangharakshita, 'Advent', *in Poems
   and Short Stories*, p.79.
83 Sangharakshita, *The Rainbow Road*,
   p.301.
84 Sangharakshita, *The Rainbow Road*,
   p.256, plus a detail from p.284.
85 Sangharakshita, *The Rainbow Road*,
   p.306.
86 Sangharakshita, *The Rainbow Road*,
   p.316.

Chapter 8

87 Sangharakshita, *The Rainbow Road*,
   p.345.
88 Sangharakshita, *The Rainbow Road*,
   p.329.
89 Sangharakshita, *The Rainbow Road*,
   p.322.
90 Sangharakshita, *The Rainbow Road*,
   pp.340–1.

91 Sangharakshita, *The Rainbow Road*,
   p.345.
92 Sangharakshita, *The Rainbow Road*,
   p.379.
93 Sangharakshita, *The Rainbow Road*,
   p.394.

Chapter 9

94 Sangharakshita, from 'To the
   recumbent Buddha', in *Poems and
   Short Stories*, p.196.
95 Sangharakshita, *The Rainbow Road*,
   pp.410–11. In fact U Chandramani
   gave the two men their names in
   the Pali form: Buddharakkhita

and Sangharakkhita, as per
Theravāda custom. I have not
been able to discover exactly when
Sangharakshita changed over
to the Sanskrit form – certainly
at some point during his time in
Kalimpong.

Chapter 10

96 Sangharakshita, *The Rainbow Road*,
   p.444.
97 Sangharakshita, *The Rainbow Road*,
   p.443.
98 Sangharakshita, *The Rainbow Road*,
   p.395.

99 Sangharakshita, *The Rainbow Road*,
   p.448.
100 Sangharakshita, *The Rainbow Road*,
    p.451.
101 Sangharakshita, 'Getting beyond
    the ego', in *Crossing the Stream*, p.407.

102 Sangharakshita, *The Rainbow Road*, p.463.

103 Sangharakshita, *The Rainbow Road*, p.464.

104 Sangharakshita, *The Rainbow Road*, pp.465–6.

105 Sangharakshita, *The Rainbow Road*, p.470.

Chapter 11

106 Sangharakshita, 'Animist', in *Poems and Short Stories*, p.233.

107 Sangharakshita, *The Rainbow Road*, p.469.

108 Sangharakshita, *The Complete Works of Sangharakshita*, vol.21: *Facing Mount Kanchenjunga*, Windhorse Publications, Cambridge 2018, pp.14–15.

109 Sangharakshita, *The Complete Works of Sangharakshita*, vol.22: *In the Sign of the Golden Wheel*, Windhorse Publications, Cambridge 2019, pp.464–5.

110 Sangharakshita, 'Lines' (1951), in *Poems and Short Stories*, p.231.

111 Sangharakshita and J.O. Mallander, 'In the realm of the lotus', in *Aphorisms, the Arts, and Late Writings*, p.244.

112 Sangharakshita, 'The religion of art', in *Aphorisms, the Arts, and Late Writings*, p.167.

113 Sangharakshita, 'Peace is a fire', in *Aphorisms, the Arts, and Late Writings*, p.23. The poem quoted is Shelley's 'Skylark'.

114 Sangharakshita, 'Dear Dinoo', in *Facing Mount Kanchenjunga*, pp.455–598.

115 Sangharakshita, *In the Sign of the Golden Wheel*, pp.299–300.

116 Sangharakshita, *In the Sign of the Golden Wheel*, pp.300–2.

117 Although technically ordained in a Theravada context, Sangharakshita always said he had experienced himself as being ordained quite simply, and significantly, 'as a *Buddhist*', as someone committed to living the Buddhist life.

118 Sangharakshita and J.O. Mallander, 'In the realm of the lotus', p.220.

119 Sangharakshita and J.O. Mallander, 'In the realm of the lotus', pp.248–9.

120 Sangharakshita, from 'Himalayan sages', in *Poems and Short Stories*, p.183.

121 Sangharakshita, *Facing Mount Kanchenjunga*, p.93.

122 See Khantipalo, *Noble Friendship: Travels of a Buddhist Monk*, Windhorse Publications, Birmingham 2002.

Chapter 12

123 Sangharakshita, 'A case of dysentery', lecture available at https://www.freebuddhistaudio. com/texts/lecturetexts/152_A_ Case_of_Dysentery.pdf, accessed on 19 July 2022.

124 Sangharakshita, 'My precious teachers', in *In the Sign of the Golden Wheel*, p.424.

125 Sangharakshita, *The Endlessly Fascinating Cry*, in *The Complete Works of Sangharakshita*, vol.4:

The Bodhisattva Ideal, Windhorse Publications, Cambridge 2019, p.221.

126 Suvajra, *The Wheel and the Diamond: The Life of Dhardo Tulku,* Windhorse Publications, Glasgow 1991, p.124.

127 Sangharakshita, from 'The Bodhisattva's reply', in *Poems and Short Stories,* p.260.

Chapter 13

133 Sangharakshita, from 'The ballad of the return journey', in *Poems and Short Stories,* p.382.

134 Sangharakshita, *The Taste of Freedom,* Windhorse Publications, Glasgow 1990, p.73.

135 Sangharakshita, 'Moving against the stream', in *The Complete Works*

Chapter 14

137 Sangharakshita, 'Was the Buddha a bhikkhu?', in *The Three Jewels I,* pp.649–50.

Chapter 15

140 Sangharakshita, 'The time has come... (for Lama Trungpa Rimpoche)', in *Poems and Short Stories,* p.323.

141 Sangharakshita, 'Moving against the stream', p.103.

142 Sangharakshita, 'Moving against the stream', pp.93–4.

143 Sangharakshita, 'Moving against the stream', p.94.

Chapter 16

149 Sangharakshita, 'A stream of stars', in *Aphorisms, the Arts, and Late Writings,* p.56.

128 Dr B.R. Ambedkar, speech at Yeola, October 1935.

129 From an address by Dr B.R. Ambedkar to All India Radio, 1954.

130 Nagabodhi, *Jai Bhim!,* p.122.

131 Sangharakshita, 'Dear Dinoo', p.523.

132 Nagabodhi, *Jai Bhim!,* p.122.

of *Sangharakshita,* vol.23: *Moving against the Stream,* Windhorse Publications, Cambridge 2020, pp.6–7.

136 Sangharakshita, 'Buddhism in England', *The Buddhist* (June 1965) (to be published in vol.11 of *The Complete Works of Sangharakshita*).

138 Sangharakshita, 'The history of my going for refuge', in *The Three Jewels I,* p.428.

139 Sangharakshita, 'Forty-three years ago', in *The Three Jewels I,* p.580.

144 Interview: 'Sex and spiritual life', *Golden Drum* 6 (October 1987).

145 Sangharakshita, 'Alternative lives', pp.577–8.

146 Sangharakshita, 'Moving against the stream', p.273.

147 Sangharakshita, 'Moving against the stream', p.268.

148 Sangharakshita, 'Moving against the stream', p.376.

150 Sangharakshita, 'The history of my going for refuge', pp.471–2.

151 Subhuti and Sangharakshita, 'What is the Western Buddhist

Order?', *Seven Papers* (revised December 2018), available at https://thebuddhistcentre. com/system/files/groups/files/ seven_papers_by_subhuti_with_ sangharakshita_-_version_2_with_ index.pdf, accessed on 19 July 2022, p.10.

Chapter 17

153 Sangharakshita with Subhuti and Mahamati, 'Conversations with Bhante' (2009), available at https://www.sangharakshita.org/ articles/conversations-with-bhante, accessed on 19 July 2022.

154 Sangharakshita, 'Love's austerity', in *Poems and Short Stories*, p.223.

155 Sangharakshita, 'I want to break out...', in *Poems and Short Stories*, p.309.

Chapter 18

161 Sangharakshita, 'The Wind', in *Poems and Short Stories*, p.450.

162 Sangharakshita with Subhuti and Mahamati, 'Conversations with Bhante'.

163 Confucius, *Analects*, translated by James Legge, in *The Chinese Classics*, vol.1, Trübner & Co., London 1861, book 13, chapter 3, verses 5–7, p.128.

164 Subhuti, *Buddhism for Today*, p.108, quoted in Sangharakshita, 'The FWBO and "Protestant Buddhism"', in *Eastern and Western Traditions*, p.433.

165 Sangharakshita, 'The essence of Zen', in *Eastern and Western Traditions*, pp.319–64.

152 Sangharakshita, 'Wisdom beyond words', in *The Complete Works of Sangharakshita*, vol.14: *The Eternal Legacy/Wisdom beyond Words*, Windhorse Publications, Cambridge 2020, p.183.

156 Sangharakshita with Subhuti and Mahamati, 'Conversations with Bhante'.

157 Sangharakshita, '1970 – a retrospect', in *Moving against the Stream*, pp.449–73.

158 Sangharakshita, from 'Homage to William Blake', in *Poems and Short Stories*, p.340.

159 Sangharakshita, 'Moving against the stream', p.444.

160 Sangharakshita, 'Moving against the stream', p.446.

166 'Mind – reactive and creative' (to be published in vol.11 of *The Complete Works of Sangharakshita*).

167 Sangharakshita, 'The FWBO and "Protestant Buddhism"', p.431.

168 Sangharakshita, 'The history of my going for refuge', pp.475–6.

169 From a study-group leaders' Q&A on 'The Higher Evolution of man', available at https://www. freebuddhistaudio.com/texts/ seminartexts/SEM137_Higher_ Evolution_of_Man_-_Unchecked. pdf, accessed on 22 July 2022.

170 Sangharakshita, '1970 – a retrospect', p.463.

171 Geshe Wangyal, *The Door of Liberation: Essential Teachings of the Tibetan Buddhist Tradition*, Wisdom Publications, Boston, MA 1995.

172 Sangharakshita, '1970 – a retrospect', pp.462–3.

173 Sangharakshita, '1970 – a retrospect', p.463.

Chapter 19

174 Sangharakshita, from 'Easter retreat', in *Poems and Short Stories*, p.333.

175 Sangharakshita, *The Rainbow Road*.

Chapter 20

176 Sangharakshita, from 'Song of the windhorse' (1976), in *Poems and Short Stories*, p.338.

177 Sangharakshita, 'The history of my going for refuge', p.461–2.

178 Sangharakshita, 'Forty-three years ago', p.584.

179 Transcript of 1975 Western Buddhist Order convention minutes.

Chapter 21

180 Sangharakshita, 'Four gifts', in *Poems and Short Stories*, p.335.

181 Sangharakshita, 'Enlightenment as experience and as non-experience', lecture available at https://www.freebuddhistaudio.com/texts/lecturetexts/119_Enlightenment_as_Experience_and_as_Non-experience.pdf, accessed on 20 July 2022.

182 Sangharakshita, 'Evolution or extinction: a Buddhist view of current world problems', lecture available at https://www.freebuddhistaudio.com/texts/lecturetexts/094_Evolution_or_Extinction_-_a_Buddhist_View_of_World_Problems.pdf, accessed on 20 July 2022.

183 Dr B.R. Ambedkar, speech to the World Fellowship of Buddhists, Kathmandhu, November 1956.

184 Sangharakshita, 'Building the Buddha land', lecture available at https://www.freebuddhistaudio.com/texts/read?num=144&at=text, accessed on 20 July 2022.

185 Sangharakshita, 'The ten pillars of Buddhism', in *The Three Jewels I*, p.362.

186 Sangharakshita, 'Authority and the individual in the New Society' (1987), seminar transcript available at https://thebuddhistcentre.com/system/files/groups/files/bhante_-_seminar_25-authority_and_the_individual_in_the_new_society.pdf, accessed on 20 July 2022.

187 The Vinaya: the portion of canonical Pali literature dealing with monastic rules and procedures.

188 Sangharakshita, 'The history of my going for refuge', pp.405–6.

189 Sangharakshita, 'Art and the spiritual life' (1969), lecture available at https://www.freebuddhistaudio.com/texts/lecturetexts/077_Art_and_the_Spiritual_Life.pdf, accessed on 20 July 2022.

Chapter 22

190 Sangharakshita, from 'Homage to William Blake', p.340.

191 Chintamani, 'Leaving mother and initiation into manhood', *FWBO Newsletter* 35 (summer 1977), available at https://adhisthana.org/wp-content/uploads/2022/03/FWBO-NEWSLETTER-ISSUE-35-SUMMER-1977.pdf, accessed on 20 July 2022.

192 Sangharakshita, 'A stream of stars', p.70.

193 *Sex and Character* (1903) by Otto Weininger. Part of his thesis describes the male aspect of character as active, productive, conscious, and moral, while the female aspect is passive, unproductive, unconscious, and amoral.

194 See Sangharakshita, *Beating the Drum: Maha Bodhi Editorials*, Ibis Publications, Ledbury 2012 (also to be published in vol.8 of *The Complete Works of Sangharakshita*).

195 Sangharakshita, *The Rainbow Road*, p.83.

196 Sangharakshita, 'Peace is a fire', p.27.

197 A mitra is someone who has made a formal declaration that they intend to deepen their connection with Buddhism in the context of Triratna. It may or may not indicate that they are hoping to join the Order.

Chapter 23

198 Sangharakshita, 'A stream of stars', p.73.

199 Sangharakshita, 'Extending the hand of fellowship', in *The Three Jewels I*, p.559.

200 Sangharakshita, *Extending the Hand of Fellowship*, Windhorse Publications, Birmingham 1996, p.25, and pp.8–9 for Kulananda's introduction. For the talk, see also *The Three Jewels I*, p.558.

201 Sangharakshita, 'Buddhism and blasphemy', published in *The Priceless Jewel*, Windhorse Publications, Glasgow 1993, pp.106–7. See also *The Complete Works of Sangharakshita*, vol.11.

202 Sangharakshita, 'Buddha and the future of his religion', in *The Complete Works of Sangharakshita*, vol.10: *Dr Ambedkar and the Revival of Buddhism II*, Windhorse Publications, Cambridge 2021, p.77.

203 Sangharakshita, 'What might have been', in *Aphorisms, the Arts, and Late Writings*, p.588.

204 Sangharakshita, 'Buddhism, world peace, and nuclear war', in *The Complete Works of Sangharakshita*, vol.12: *A New Buddhist Movement II*, Windhorse Publications, Cambridge 2022, p.351.

205 Sangharakshita, 'A stream of stars', p.56.

206 Sangharakshita, 'A new Buddhist movement: talks in India and England 1979–1992', in *Dr Ambedkar and the Revival of Buddhism II*, p.342.

207 Sangharakshita, 'The next twenty years', in *A New Buddhist Movement II,* p.409.

208 This is from the transcript of a talk, 'The transcendental critique of religion', available at https://www.freebuddhistaudio.com/texts/lecturetexts/146_The_Transcendental_Critique_of_Religion.pdf, accessed on 21 July 2022. A slightly edited version appears in *The Inconceivable Emancipation,* in *The Complete Works*

of Sangharakshita, vol.16: *Mahāyāna Myths and Stories,* Windhorse Publications, Cambridge 2017, pp.505, 515.

209 Philip A. Mellor, 'Protestant Buddhism? The cultural translation of Buddhism in England', *Religion* 21:1 (1991), pp.73–92.

210 Sangharakshita, 'The FWBO and "Protestant Buddhism"', pp.365–512.

211 Sangharakshita, 'Peace is a fire', p.35.

Chapter 24

212 Sangharakshita, *What Is the Sangha?,* in *The Complete Works of Sangharakshita,* vol.3: *The Three Jewels II,* Windhorse Publications, Cambridge 2017, p.554.

213 From the transcript of Sangharakshita's 1970 lecture 'Is a guru necessary?', available at https://www.freebuddhistaudio.com/texts/lecturetexts/090_Is_a_Guru_Necessary.pdf, accessed on 21 July 2022; a slightly edited version appears in *What Is the Sangha?,* p.553.

214 Mellor, 'Protestant Buddhism?', p.84.

215 Sangharakshita, 'The FWBO and "Protestant Buddhism"', pp.472–3.

216 Sangharakshita, 'My relation to the Order', p.529.

217 Sangharakshita, 'My relation to the Order', p.528.

218 Baba Ram Dass (Richard Alpert), author of *Be Here Now,* Crown Publications, San Cristobal, NM 1971, among other books.

219 Sangharakshita, 'The FWBO and "Protestant Buddhism"', p.423.

220 Sangharakshita, 'My relation to the Order', p.526 (up to ellipsis); Sangharakshita, 'Saint Jerome revisited', in *Aphorisms, the Arts, and Late Writings,* p.268 (after ellipsis).

Chapter 25

221 Sangharakshita, 'My relation to the Order', pp.520–1.

222 Sangharakshita, personal correspondence.

223 Sangharakshita with Subhuti and Mahamati, 'Conversations with Bhante'.

224 Sangharakshita with Subhuti and Mahamati, 'Conversations with Bhante'.

225 Sangharaskita, 'A personal statement', available at https://www.sangharakshita.org/articles/a-personal-statement, accessed on 22 July 2022.

226 Sangharakshita, 'A stream of stars', p.79.

Chapter 26

227 Meaning 'Old age, decay, and death'.

228 Sangharakshita, 'Life is king', in *Poems and Short Stories*, p.324.

229 Sangharakshita, 'My relation to the Order', p.531.

230 Sangharakshita, message introducing 'Initiation into a new life', in *Seven Papers*, p.127.

231 Subhuti and Sangharakshita, 'What is the Western Buddhist Order?', pp.12–13.

232 Subhuti and Sangharakshita, 'Initiation into a new life', pp.132–4.

233 Sangharakshita, 'Peace is a fire', p.34.

234 Sangharakshita with Subhuti and Mahamati, 'Conversations with Bhante'.

235 Sangharakshita, private correspondence.

236 Sangharakshita, 'My relation to the Order', p.531.

Photograph Credits

PAGE x Nagabodhi and Sangharakshita, summer 1976
TPA02213. © Copyright Urgyen Sangharakshita Trust.
Photographer: Vajradipa.

PAGE 95 Monks at last: Sangharakshita (L) and
Buddharakshita at Kusinārā, May 1949
TPA00287. © Copyright Urgyen Sangharakshita Trust.

PAGE 111 At the microphone in Nepal, 1951
TPA00261. © Copyright Urgyen Sangharakshita Trust.

PAGE 131 With Dhardo Rimpoche, Kalimpong, 1967
TPA01463. © Copyright Urgyen Sangharakshita Trust.
Photographer: Terry Delamere.

PAGE 171 The farewell tour to India, 1967
TPA01681. © Copyright Urgyen Sangharakshita Trust.
Photographer: Terry Delamere.

PAGE 195 With Terry Delamere at Keffolds, 1968
TPA02076. © Copyright Urgyen Sangharakshita Trust.

PAGE 209 Interviewed for BBC Radio, London 1968/1969
TPA3860. © Copyright Urgyen Sangharakshita Trust.

PAGE 228 The writer at his desk, Padmaloka, late 1970s
TPA4146. © Copyright Urgyen Sangharakshita Trust.

PAGE 276 Vajrapushpa's ordination day, 1981
TPA02302. © Copyright Urgyen Sangharakshita Trust.

PAGE 304 Sangharakshita at Padmaloka, 1986
TPA7069. © Copyright Urgyen Sangharakshita Trust.
Photographer: Vimalachitta.

PAGE 327 With Paramartha, 1989
TPA7366. © Copyright Urgyen Sangharakshita Trust.
Photographer: Gunavati.

Index

Introductory Note

References such as '178–9' indicate (not necessarily continuous) discussion of a topic across a range of pages. Wherever possible in the case of topics with many references, these have either been divided into sub-topics or only the most significant discussions of the topic are listed. Because the entire work is about 'Sangharakshita', the use of this name (and certain other names or terms which occur constantly throughout the book) as an entry point has been restricted. Information will be found under the corresponding detailed topics.

Index

Index

Index

Index

Index

Index

Index

Index

WINDHORSE PUBLICATIONS

Windhorse Publications is a Buddhist charitable company based in the United Kingdom. We place great emphasis on producing books of high quality that are accessible and relevant to those interested in Buddhism at whatever level. We are the main publisher of the works of Sangharakshita, the founder of the Triratna Buddhist Order and Community. Our books draw on the whole range of the Buddhist tradition, including translations of traditional texts, commentaries, books that make links with contemporary culture and ways of life, biographies of Buddhists, and works on meditation.

As a not-for-profit enterprise, we ensure that all surplus income is invested in new books and improved production methods, to better communicate Buddhism in the twenty-first century. We welcome donations to help us continue our work – to find out more, go to windhorsepublications.com.

The Windhorse is a mythical animal that flies over the earth carrying on its back three precious jewels, bringing these invaluable gifts to all humanity: the Buddha (the 'Awakened One'), his teaching, and the community of all his followers.

Windhorse Publications	Consortium Book Sales	Windhorse Books
38 Newmarket Road	& Distribution	PO Box 574
Cambridge	210 American Drive	Newtown
CB5 8DT	Jackson	NSW 2042
info@windhorsepublications.com	TN 38301	Australia
	USA	

THE TRIRATNA BUDDHIST COMMUNITY

Windhorse Publications is a part of the Triratna Buddhist Community, an international movement with centres in Europe, India, North and South America, and Australasia. At these centres, members of the Triratna Buddhist Order offer classes in meditation and Buddhism. Activities of the Triratna Community also include retreat centres, residential spiritual communities, ethical Right Livelihood businesses, and the Karuna Trust, a United Kingdom fundraising charity that supports social-welfare projects in the slums and villages of India.

Through these and other activities, Triratna is developing a unique approach to Buddhism, not simply as a philosophy and a set of techniques, but as a creatively directed way of life for all people living in the conditions of the modern world.

If you would like more information about Triratna please visit thebuddhistcentre.com or write to:

London Buddhist Centre	Aryaloka	Sydney Buddhist Centre
51 Roman Road	14 Heartwood Circle	24 Enmore Road
London	Newmarket	Sydney
E2 0HU	NH 03857	NSW 2042
United Kingdom	USA	Australia

CPSIA information can be obtained
at www.ICGtesting.com
Printed in the USA
JSHW031448050223
37295JS00005B/6